PARIS
POINTS OF INTEREST

JARDIN
LUXEMBE

VI
Av. De L'Observatoire

Boulevard Raspail

St. Germain
Boulevard
Rue De Rennes

Boulevard Raspail

Boulevard Du Montparnasse

CIMITIÈRE DU
MONTPARNASSE

Raspail

Leclerc Ave. Renan

XIV

Avenue
Du M

VII
B. Des Invalides

Av. De Breteuil

Picquel
La Motte

Avenue Des Bourdonnais
Avenue De Suffren

Boulevard Garibaldi

Rue De Vaugirard

Rue De Vaugirard

LA RUCHE

Rue De Vouillé

Boulevard

Lefebvre

Boulevard Brune

Boulevard

XV

Convention

La

De

Rue

TOUR EIFFEL

SEINE

De Versailles

Avenue

Boulevard Exelmans

Boulevard Murat

Boulevard

VANVES

Avenue Gambetta

Boulevard Aug

TE UN

Jourdan

Hôtel Royal
"   Venise
"   Friedlander (?)

Other Books by Kate Simon

New York Places & Pleasures

Mexico Places & Pleasures

New York (with Andreas Feininger)

KATE SIMON'S

PARIS

Places & Pleasures

An Uncommon Guidebook

G. P. Putnam's Sons NEW YORK

To the memory of
Fernande Yvon
and Roger Bernard

Foreword

In fairness to the reader of a travel-guidebook, the hypothetical questioner who asks, "Is this the sort of information I want? Do our tastes and interests match?" he should be offered a verbal sketch of inclinations, a weather map of the mental climate he will encounter: "Tends to favor the sudden alleys north of the Porte St. Denis to the empty stateliness of the Boulevard Raspail. Prefers the poetic patch of park behind the Carnavalet Museum to the contemptuous gardens of the Tuileries. Enjoys the wandering-gawking that the French call *badauder*, hoping for the un-expected gift to the eye or ear. Does not believe that Paris is the most expensive city in the world, nor that there every prospect pleases and only man is vile in Paris; nor that Parisians especially hate Americans. Considers that being the richest member of the family is rarely a lovable or comfortable position and, in any case, Parisians irritate each other, too. Likes the modest, specialized museums and finds the great omnivores asphyxiating rather than alluring. Finds splashing through heaps of unconsidered trifles more stimulating than orderly rows of shopping."

The book-monologue that follows the sketch is the result of an earlier dialogue, an exchange of photos, as it were, a questioning of an imaginary reader—"What have you seen, what would you like to see? What do you know? What do you not especially care to know?"—and a few hypothetical answers, and questions returned as answers. "What is behind the high, long galleries of the Louvre through which a guide swept me and my undigested lumps of too much seen too fast? I know the Jeu de Paume collection and shall probably return to them and to the Musée de l'Art Moderne if there is an important show. I shall go again to see the stained glass in Sainte Chapelle and probably the Rodin Museum and Notre Dame. I've eaten in a couple of starred restaurants and been to the flea market on Sunday afternoon and to Les Halles at 4 A.M. and

7

Versailles. I've shopped (or don't care to shop) the golden alleys. I already know the Seine bookstalls to be unrewarding and irresistible. What's north of the department stores on Boulevard Haussmann? South of the Luxembourg Gardens? East of Les Halles? West of the Etoile? What else is there?" The "what else" determined to a considerable degree the pattern of the book. Its division into ten overcrowded, if not impossible, days on a second or third visit is designed to display variations on Paris themes grouped, wherever it could be done, for proximity and to accommodate to museum hours, to the ebb and flood of street and market life. There is no reason why you cannot mix or match your own days or for that matter, blindfolded, put a pin into a map of Paris, to stroll and sit and stroll again wherever it might lead you. "The city is inexhaustible. And to master it, one must be a vagabond-poet or a poet-vagabond" says Jean-Paul Clébert, in his book about the *clochards'* city, *Paris Insolite*. Few visitors hope to conquer Paris, nor need they qualify as poet-vagabonds, but the Circe that Paris can be (even though her underwear may be dirty under the cloth-of-gold dress and her manners the high bleat of a tart at times, rather than the honeyed tones of the siren) easily turns a purposeful, well-planned schedule into shapeless, dreamy, *flâneur* days. Let it, if you have the temperament. Culture and shopping are ubiquitous and timeless; having waited, they can wait, as the time for being a poet-vagabond rarely can.

It isn't necessary to say that Paris is superbly beautiful. What you may not yet know is that it is not all beautiful, nor beautiful in the same way from place to place, nor beautiful in the same place, always, in the same way. When the summer night's illuminations make luminous green clouds of trees on the river banks, the leprous alleys beyond the trees disappear. The lights on the Place de la Concorde, lanterns over a smoky lake on a rainy night, erase the maniacal daytime furies of its traffic. The Seine can look like silk or sewer, depending on weather and place. The Place des Vosges is confused and marred in the summertime; of a stately, triste perfection when its trees are bare.

The tourists' *Ville Lumière* is a rather small jewel made brighter by the surrounding dark or, to change the metaphor, a velvet-petaled camellia growing out of assorted (some of it quite colorful) trash. The city one normally sees sits in an irregular lozenge, open at one end. It starts, to make an arbitrary beginning, at the Etoile, moves east and a bit south toward the Opéra, loops around Les Halles, encloses the Ile de la Cité and the Ile St. Louis, curves back westward and south to the Panthéon and the southern edge of the Luxembourg Gardens. Northwestward, it goes along the Avenue de Suffren to include Les Invalides, the Eiffel Tower, the Champ de Mars, the Trocadéro complex. The open area between the Trocadéro and the Etoile is the escape hatch for the westward flow of prosperity, forming the famous 16th arrondissement which takes its long shape, as the map will show, from flattening against the eastern limits of the Bois de Boulogne. Quite detached from the ellipse is the northern suburb of tourist Paris, Pigalle leading to Montmartre and, beyond that, the famous flea market of the Porte de Clignancourt.

The wobbling loop sketched above does not mean that the enclosed streets all glow, that all have the bright cheeks of successful, wholesome living. For instance, the stretch from Les Halles northward to Boulevard St. Denis is a busy area of inexpensive prostitution sold in the cells of hotels lost in sunless alleys (page 99). Directly to the east of that, palaces eaten by time and decay stare out of the ghetto slums of the Marais (page 110). To the south it includes the old, tough market quarters of the Place Maubert, the ageless smells and glorious tones of the M̄etard-Monge area (page 80). The expanse leading to Les ...les is a large, flat gravel desert, a singularly ugly place ...ting in the ponderous building that houses Napoleon's ...d souvenirs of the arts of war. There is little of the frothy ...at one's imagination makes around the word "Paris" in ...s, but they are indispensable parts of the composition; it ...: depth and contrast without them.

...is darker, frayed edges, usually splashed with a sudden ...color. Fifteen minutes southeastward by car or Métro ...date, retiring poise of Faubourg St. Germain (for *its* ...y look into the courts of the embassies and govern-...s on Rue de Grenelle, Rue de Varenne, the courts ...ard St. Germain, west of St. Germain des Prés, ...e of the "don't touch me" mood on the small street and square of Luynes) lands one in the bare avenues and bitter courts of Kremlin-Bicêtre (page 157). A similarly short trip southwestward leads into the new, flat, colorless working-class respectability of the Porte de Vanves, backed by a broad highway which separates it from alleys of desperate shacks. One can go from gray to darker gray, along the parched dreariness of the Boulevard de Ménilmontant, the western edge of Père Lachaise Cemetery; in the threatening restlessness around the Goutte d'Or in the 18th arrondissement and the Place du Maroc near the Stalingrad station in the 19th; among the blind crippled houses surrounded by warehouses, railroad sidings and *bidonvilles* along the network of canals that spreads northward and eastward from the Seine (page 62). But Paris has been so beautiful for so long that, with few exceptions, every neighborhood has some treasure or other to show. It might be a well-designed antique water pump in a forbidding alley in the Glacière section of the 13th, a handsome fountain and a street of curiously designed apartment houses not far from the nondescript Rue Monge, an old court, wrinkled and molten and still a grande dame, in the fur district—and everywhere, the rhythms of old streets meeting, proliferating, branching like the veins of a leaf.

To reveal some of the variety of these beauties and beasts in their sullen and amiable moods is the attempt of the explorations that follow.

Contents

1 The First Sunday

Early Sunday Afternoon

(After any abundant cornucopia market nearby—Buci, Maubert, Neuilly, Montorgueil, etc. At your hotel desk.)

Ideally, a stay in Paris should consist of a long row of Saturdays and Sundays. Unlike London which doesn't come to visible life —except on Petticoat Lane and Hyde Park Corner—until late Sunday afternoon, Paris takes the string bag off the hook and starts looking and shopping early in the day, first for food, later for clothing, plastic dish drains, motorcycle helmets, old copper pans and denuded chairs in the ubiquitous markets; then to eating and the movies.

Sunday afternoon is, also, a time for buying birds, plants, fish, the things they need and the things that enhance them. For this one goes, first, to the Quai de Louvre (station Pont Neuf or one of a number of buses, depending on your route) and down along the Quai de la Mégisserie (the place for the curing and tanning of skins and leather in ancient times) whose present sidewalk is an aviary of exotic chickens, pheasants, tawny pigeons and black pigeons with ruby underskirts. A world of goldfish, sleek and fringed, fat and slender, pale and the deep gold of a Roman sunset. Occasionally a frog shows up or a few white mice or a coil of harmless snake among the small straw cages that form a miniature tropical village. In the big garden shops, effigies of fat stone babies and ugly ceramic boars surrounded by garden instruments and furniture, books on the care of pets and plants and, in one large shop, seasonal displays of vegetables and fruits, artfully arranged and a relief from the dull sheen of trowels and tractors.

Find a seat, if you can, at one of the cafés that flow into each other. Watch the bugs of new *bateaux-mouches* skitter by, people leafing through the repetitious prints on the bookstalls, the nervous

13

metallic whip of cars lashing the sides of the river. Directly across
the river, the Conciergerie (page 97), the bloody brother of
London's Tower; on your side of the river citizens strolling by, one
arm embracing a bowl of goldfish, the other dragging a string bag
heavy with seeds and fish food. Anyone with a free hand—usually
the children—nibbles at *gaufres* (waffles) grilled at a local stand,
leaning forward as he eats, to keep the powdered sugar from
falling to the chest of his Sunday sweater. To the left, the squares
of Notre Dame's towers and almost behind you, toward the left,
the superb flamboyant Gothic Tour St. Jacques, all that remains
of a church that was an important stopping point on the pilgrimages to the church of St. James of Compostela in Spain.

In slow, good time, start across the Pont Neuf, the oldest bridge
in Paris (late 16th–early 17th century). Below, at the tip of the Île
de la Cité, a woman is washing her dog; a few painters have set up
their easels on the 17th century Place Dauphine, an early example
of neighborhood planning. The indispensable fisherman stands
and thinks (no fish ever disturbs him), while his silent friend sits
and thinks on a patch of sparse grass. A pair of lovers lose the
world in each other's faces, a small motorboat cuts arcs in the
placid water, a slender yacht tries to moor among the stolid barges.
Behind you the magnificent courts of the Louvre, heavy with history and poorly lit art. Immediately in front, facsimiles of that
art done in pastels on the walk of the bridge, usually accompanied
by a sign that says the painter is an art student and would appre-
ciate your appreciation of his skill, in francs. (The pitch in early
summer is that now, with school closed, he needs the money for
train fare home.) His girl friend in her skinny totem dress guards
her impromptu stand of inept, thin dangles of "modern" jewelry
which she sincerely thinks is good, or at least good enough for
tourist bait. ("I bought it from the art student who made it, right
on that old bridge; you know, the one near Boul' Mich'.")

Resist the sullen girl (life is hard and it's all your fault) and
walk on, past more bookstalls, more cafés, to the Pont St. Michel,
the living room of the American beats and the friends they picked
up in Korçula and Istanbul, all recoiling from the conformities
that imprison their parents by establishing strict counter-conformi-
ties: Buster Brown haircuts for the boys, Greek-woven shoulder
bags for the girls; aggressively unkempt, all to the same degree;
aggressively bi- and tri-racial whether they like each other or not,

defying a world that insults them by not being much impressed. They stay out of most local cafés because those are expensive and, in any case, ease them out to make room for the Good-time Charlie tourists. One of the cafés hangs conspicuous signs advising that for each sitting hour there must be one order per person. It doesn't matter—little does. There are the bridges and the banks of the river for their reluctant, monosyllabic "communications," and if the *flics* are busy elsewhere that night, the Rue de la Huchette and the shelter of the bridges for sleeping.

Stop for a drink on the Place St. André des Arts and survey the scene, in both classic and hip senses. There goes the young blond messiah who doubles as a fire-eater on a fair, lucrative evening. Examining him for other skills is the man with the fatty back, the glowing suntan makeup and the glistening black wig. Across the square marches a tall young ascetic in a homemade cloak of a church order yet unknown to the Vatican, exclusively his own. Past this latter-day Baron Corvo strides a gentleman equipped with hip boots, good fishing jacket, a hat brim bristling with flies, his fishing pole sheathed in canvas and leather bought on the Avenue Victor Hugo in the 16th; he'll show the neighbors the proper dress in which to meet the spirited fish leaping out of the turbulent Seine. A few old houses peer dully from under their wooden bandages; they've seen it all before.

On the Boulevard du Palais at the corner of the Quai de l'Horloge (the residence of kings in the late Middle Ages) hangs the first public clock of Paris, originally placed here in 1353 and restored in 1574, the loveliest thing in the neighborhood except, possibly, for the long flaxen hair of a few of the local boys. Gold fleur-de-lis on a vibrant blue background, surrounded with fruits, flowers, royal shields, angels and ram's heads, and held in a deep ornamented arch which is supported (inevitably) by two caryatids; and it still works as well as charms. The bell high above it has, however, fallen from use; the old version (demolished in 1793) was kept busy sounding special royal occasions like the births and deaths of kings, when it rang for seventy-two hours at a stretch.

The Quai de Corse supplants bookstalls with a minor jungle of small lemon trees, short firs and tall chrysanthemums visible at this time only through slats and the glass of greenhouses. The Sunday P.M. on Place Louis Lépine belongs to little birds—to buy, to barter, to exclaim over, to supply with seeds, berries, bells, mirrors and cages. They huddle, boxesful of unset gems, in pointillist compositions of yellow, coral, peach, stained-glass reds, pinks the color of cream dissolved in borscht; emeralds, sapphires; minute dusty burrs spattered with varicolored paint, dark bundles with red collars and sharp cones of red bill. The middle of the market is the place for discussions, technical and financial. One Papageno holds one pole, one cage; another dangles a few cages from a music stand; a younger man carries a strip of cages looped to a horizontal bamboo pole balanced on his shoulder, not aware that he comes out of a Chinese painting. It is a market, the vendors are French and so are the customers; everyone talks lightly, animatedly, chirping (unlike the frightened birds) until one adventuresome bird escapes a hand and every head turns skyward to watch the nervous fluttering in the branches of an overhanging tree.

NOTE: Never tested, but often told: The birds of the most extraordinary colors are clearly the most expensive and it is these loveliest that often turn to pale canaries after their first bath. If you're thinking of buying one for the child of your French hostess, caveat.

Later on Sunday Afternoon, in the 14th & 15th

(Bus 48 or 89 to Morillons or Métro to Porte de Vanves)

Bordered by Rue des Morillons, Rue Brancion, Rue de Dantzig and a waste of demolition and reconstruction to the south is the set of elementary, low buildings and yards which constitute the Left Bank abattoirs. The official entrance is on Rue de Dantzig, announced by two figures of bulls, life-size and furious, more suitable for the entrance to a bullfight arena than as a door to pedestrian, practical death. On the Brancion side the identity of the slaughterhouses is echoed in the large number of butcher shops, one of them a big place bristling with hooks and fresh paint. It is on this side, near the southern end of the abattoirs, that the Sunday afternoon dog market takes place. Like all markets, this one is also affected by the weather: the rain ripens the odor of horse manure and makes the walking both slippery and sticky, the number of dogs diminishes, the customers are fewer, but in any case it makes a lively half hour in an unusual Paris mixture. On the silent street the sleek cars of Passy, the small work-trucks of Ménilmontant, the animated cans called cars by the intellectual young. Under the shed of the yard, an unsteady lady whose matted hair and strayed makeup suggest one of the mangy hotels in the St. Denis area (page 55) offers a shivering little something of a dog, a confusion of bits of lineage and all terror. A man who might be a gypsy from one of the encampments northeast of the city brushes down the coat of a handsome young police dog tied to a post by a very short rein; the dog resents both grooming and rein. Young men and women in neat slacks and bulky sweaters supervise frothing masses of puppies in fruit crates and laundry baskets. And looking seriously, studiously at all of them, the children in little white gloves and exquisitely starched dresses, the children in hand-me-down sweaters, the lean little darting boys, traveling in a pack to see what they can see on a dull Sunday afternoon.

Before you plunge into the market just south of the Porte de Vanves station, follow Dantzig past the bulls rampant, into a showcase of different kinds and periods of housing. On Dantzig itself there is a set of apartment houses of a time when the approved style was an echo of prison blocks: the discouraged graying yellowing of aged concrete with hard rectangles cut out as ornaments and repeated in the shape of the windows. But there is space and grass (not to be walked on) and trees to relieve the bitter mood of the buildings. Much of the Rue de la Saïda, around the corner, is taken up by a housing project built in 1906, a series of yellow and brick-red squarish towers laced together by stairways and the pleasant rhythm of the bands of structure which hold and shelter them, studded with a bit of tile here and there to give it the definite stamp of its time (a more imaginative time, at least for public housing, than ours). At the end of the street, across the road, is a set of buildings whose tops are elaborately carved in a later style, about twenty years later, and coming up again on the Rue de la Saïda, across from the 1906 buildings, a scattering of very functional, inexpensive new buildings with big patches of optimistic yellow, aseptic white and wholesome blue. One of them is a school which, in addition to serving the young of the neighborhood, offers adult classes, not yet an ordinary fact in Paris and an indication of the ambitious quality of this neighborhood: large stretches of emptiness, cages of girders riding the skyline and the new flat-faced housing projects.

The Passage de Dantzig, which leads from the Rue de la Saïda back to the Rue de Dantzig, clings to its furtive, picturesque decrepitude, hiding from the rebuilding furies around it. Much of its short extent is taken up by old ateliers or studios, whose sections of long window are broken or obscured not by curtains so much as by lengths of assorted cloth to hang as they may. Romantically appealing buildings like these were pictured in *Moulin Rouge* and other films, but without the art of set designers and the kindly haze of colored camera lenses, they look poverty-stricken, disorderly and above all, very cold. Down toward the end of the passage, a space and a brush of greenery. Inside a set of gates gnawed by rust one sees dimly an entrance arch held up, again, by the same two Paris ladies with the strong, ample shoulders. Beyond the ladies there is a small round building, cut like a pie, in sections of doorways, the famous "Ruche" (bee-hive) which once housed a gelid hungry colony of painters, including Soutine, Modigliani, Léger, Lipchitz, and—less hungry than the others—Chagall.

According to a contemporary, La Ruche was built of materials discarded in the destruction of pavilons following the great 1900 Exposition and opened as a "Villa Médicis," with considerable official fanfare in 1902. It was splendid, a "city of culture" which exhibited local paintings and established a theater in which young actors and playwrights were to be given scope for their work. Writers came to stay and art critics and, once in a while, foreign savants. For one period, the nephew of an Indian maharajah fed and wined his impecunious neighbors in his sybarite's apartment. When they had to, Léger and Archipenko earned their bread by singing and playing in the streets; Archipenko sang sad Russian songs and Léger played a harp. Some of the others ate the bread and herrings brought by an old bearded gentleman from the Marais whose credit terms were boundlessly generous. In the winter when the pipes froze, there was little water to drink, much less to wash in. The summer brought long evenings in the simple cafés on the Boulevard Montparnasse. Life was productive, tough and colorful in La Ruche and it all began to stream away with the dispersals of World War I. The house is still several layers of studios, children in the scrappy vegetation and a black irascible dog for guardian but the luster is gone; it looks peculiar, listless and forgotten.

Housing projects, one notices, can't spare the space or humaneness for cafés and the few that exist in this neighborhood are closed on Sunday, suggesting that decent housing, television sets, cars and money for the movies may expunge, in time, the allure and the need for café sitting. But cafés usually abound near the stations, welcoming arms to soothe away the bruises of the Métro. The logical shelters and refreshers here would be at the Porte de Vanves, at the mouth of the Sunday afternoon market, and a good place for sensing who and what goes on in the *quartier*: neat young women waddling in maternity dresses, holding carefully groomed children by the hand; the dark and darker tints of African skin color of the people who enter and leave the local movie house; the clutter of cheap housewares in the window of a corner shop hideously jazzed up by do-it-yourself bands and squares of primary colors. On the edge of the sidewalk near the café sits the black-dressed, gray-aproned, felt-slippered flower lady, nodding sleepily on the chair next to her cart. From time to time she shakes herself awake to arrange one bouquet, nods off again, awakens to have her lunch of a chunk of bread out of a brown paper and falls asleep again, undisturbed by the crowds from the cinema, the people who brush by as they leave the station, the clatter of cups and conversation from the café, the nervous charges and braked halts of cars. What finally brings her to animation in her customless afternoon is a visit from a neighbor, wearing a similar shapeless dress and gray patched apron, who displays her varicose veins and etches with her finger the purple crescents under her eyes, complaining vigorously, not in the frail querulous voice of the tired and sick, but in the French manner, strongly indignant. The same mood and tone then move without change into a discussion of the new apron she has just bought and its unjust cost.

Like its surroundings, the market is working class pushing into the best of its possibilities and dragging along a residue of its worst. Going southeastward from the Place, along the Avenue de la Porte de Vanves, brings one to the area of house-pride, gleaming refrigerators and stoves, kitchen appliances, fresh impossible paintings, showy overdesigned vases and, unexpectedly, a vast array of wooden napkin rings with girls names burnt into them (seemingly an article too effete for boys).

Directly east of the Place, more things for the self-respecting house including fish tanks and bird cages, wicker seats, a cemetery's worth of gaudy, hard wax flowers, and all the colors, shapes, sizes and uses that plastic can be. The concentration is mainly on clothing, though, as work pants and Sunday pants, cotton house dresses and rayon knit suits, stockings, sweaters, suits and coats. The whole range, in other words; cheaper than they are on the Grands Boulevards but not as cheap as you might expect—or as chic, except in dresses for little girls, and the curiously attractive shoes (tried on over a spread of cardboard on the sidewalk) with slightly turned up points—a melding of Italian and Arabic style— preferred by the young bloods of the North African quarters.

Where the market turns the corner, it loses the noise of its sturdy shouters and the gleam of starch on new shirts, and slips quickly down to flea market—sometimes literally, if it is a warm day and you susceptible to fleas or the suggestion thereof. A minute replica of the outer edges of the famous Marché aux Puces at St. Ouen-Clignancourt in the northern limits of the city, it deals in the discards of some hoping to become the valuables of others: glasses with lenses, without lenses, with smashed lenses; false upper teeth or lowers, one lucky vendor with a matched pair joined in a square grin; mounts of wrinkled (though washed) dungarees, shirts, tired underclothes and faded sweaters; battered paper valises full of used radio tubes; bits of lace and enough rusty bolts, nails, keyless locks and homeless keys to make a galleryful of new sculpture. Books not old enough or new enough sprawl on the gravel, partnered by a torn section of once-beautiful Mandarin coat, one epaulet and one upper of a boot. A trio of dented fenders curves around a copper table of Persian design bearing a worn velvet-lined spectacle case and a small, dog-eared notebook. The walk is heaped with shoeless rubber heels, battered coach lamps, wild vines of beads, the entrails of dead machines, the severed limbs of once-precise instruments. In spite of the charnel-house objects, it can be a rather gay little market, the customers alert for the hidden treasure about to appear, the vendors adroit in several languages, well-dressed Parisians looking for one antique dish or a long-handled copper bed warmer, poorly dressed Algerians examining secondhand work shirts. A Berber woman with tattoo marks on her forehead rummages through the scuffed children's shoes, and, having found nothing, turns to a careful examination of a naked, broken doll, its head sweetly, obscenely smiling from between its legs. A few yards beyond her, a skinny pale young man sings in a thin, true voice, his eyes cast down, never looking at the people who surround him, never proffering his begging bowl; he places it to find its own luck on a table behind him.

The flea market of *this* flea market has its independent being across the highway where a half-dozen male and female *clochards* recline on heaps of rubble, bleary but still talkative, sucking at their bottles of cheap red wine, feeling around in their bundles of rags for the crust of bread they picked up or cadged, and vaguely waiting for customers to buy the empty bottles, the scraps of cloth and string and the old newspapers they trundle around in their improvised baby carriages. Not the most edifying of sights but then, not the least, because these winos have—except when they have passed out or are huddled, shivering, over steam vents—an expansiveness, a teetering joie de vivre, considerably less depressing than the sodden inertness of the whiskey bum Americans are accustomed to.

Sunday Night: Café Flore—Lipp's— Le Drugstore

Extending the ordinary light voyeurism of the tourist (what, au fond, makes a traveler?) to include the concentrated stare of the café sitter, critic, commentator and battener on human frailties as he observes them passing before his cool eye, is a simple, natural step, and there is no reason why you shouldn't take it. If it is any comfort, you, too, will be impaled and turned on an invisible spit.

Having viewed and been viewed at the Raspail-Montparnasse complex of cafés (page 270) and sat out the permission of a cup of coffee along the Boulevard St. Michel, go, at about midnight, to the Café Flore just off St. Germain des Prés. Outside or in, depending on the weather (although the viewing inside, like a theater in the round, offers fuller scope on the rest of the clientele who, sheltered from a too-large public, sometimes give a better performance), you will find the bony, short-haired woman talking urgently to a delicate Modigliani girl whose hand she clasps tightly. At another table, two young men with puffy faces, both wearing overfitted pants and big, hairy sweaters feed each other, giggling winsomely. A tall, thin man with a scored, though still handsome, face weaves his way in, carefully tossing the romantic front lock of his nut-brown wig. He sits down, gives his order, then continues to toss, to stare burningly from table to table and having found no one new or old to attract, rattles papers, his cup, the ashtray; anything that will rescue him from being disregarded. Through the door comes a proper, respectable ménage—husband, wife and regal poodle wearing a chic, showy collar. The husband is sturdy and broad-shouldered, of the same general physique and coarse features as the men who carry sides of beef in Les Halles. This one, however, wears a skirt with her severely tailored jacket, shirt and tie, and her paunch is about a foot higher than theirs. A frequent variation on the couple theme is the charming boy with a shock of blondined hair and a girl in bizarre white, death-mask makeup, friendly, lightly affectionate with each other, yet keeping a sharp, flirtatious eye out—he on the men, she on the women. Upstairs (look as if you were looking for a friend) courtiers cluster around reigning favorites, all mobile gestures and alert charm.

The man search continues on the sidewalk, into the darker quiet of the Boulevard toward Rue des Sts. Pères, near where there is a pissoir, one of the few left in the neighborhood. It is one of the markets for boy prostitutes, in boisterous, playful groups of three of four, or silent, starved solitaries, all of them especially eager and hopeful early in September, after the long August drought of the annual closing. Their ambitions are singularly female and bourgeois; they will take the one-night stand (it's a living) but like their female counterparts, they want to be set up in a clever gallery or antique shop or among the pink and gold clouds of a chic hairdressing salon—in London, in Berlin, in New York, preferably. Some of them make it.

Lipp's, across the Boulevard, is—whether its habitués like the word or not—infinitely more respectable. Confined to banquettes behind continuous rows of tables in a coziness of close space and shared conversations, absorbing the atmosphere—or the actuality —of beer and Alsatian choucroute, one settles in among better-padded, better (if less colorfully), dressed bodies, particularly on Sunday evenings. That is the time for families back from a country weekend, or escaping the endless rows of plump houses bristling with chimneys, mansard windows and balconies on the Avenue

Malakoff or Boissière in the 16th, to visit the zoo of St. Germain. On other days the fauna is somewhat leaner and more vivacious: three long-faced high-strung editors from local publishing houses, a few shaggy bearded writers, a pair of pale actresses starved into looking significant.

The adjoining Drugstore is the playground and arena of a curious variety. The *jeunesse dorée*, traveling in packs to anything new, jam the upstairs booths. (From the street they look like oversized puppets on a tiny stage.) A few not quite so young hang around, waiting, for what? It's hard to know; but one remembers that Ben Barka was kidnapped here, an event tamped down, hidden for a while, then erupting as a police-gangster-government scandal. The *jeunesse* not quite so *dorée* are part of the busyness but not central to it; like the young who hang around the entrances to amusement parks or small-town railroad stations because there is nothing else to do or no money to do it with.

❧ How Come the Angry Parisian?

In the Middle Ages the image of a Parisian was often that of a scholar, an inhabitant of the European center of lay and ecclesiastical learning. In the time of Louis XIV, the Sun King, he was a man in silks and lace, embedded in an enormous wig of curls, a connoisseur of tapestries and women, a practicer of exquisite manners and mannerisms. Later the world saw him wearing the face of enlightenment, of the Encyclopedists and the Revolution, and a century after that as the militantly liberal writer, a Lamartine, a Hugo, a Zola. The present-day portrait an American tends to see is that of a man who wears a snarl and a knife for slashing his pockets and ego. All the images are, of course, shorthand and consequently distortions, but Parisian rudeness is a real and present thing, and as oppressive to Parisians who taking an occasional fresh look at the city and their fellow citizens find both *deraciné*, as if the graceful city had lost its indigenes whose places were filled by new barbarians. The tourism authorities also clearly find the rudeness a depressant. Otherwise, why the witless system of "smile certificates" devised in 1965 to lure waiters, chamber-

maids and taxi drivers out of their lowering clouds and in 1966 the
rarely seen "friendship buttons"?

Much of the fault is ours. We go frightened, inviting disdain. Armed
only with our big grins and money, crippled by our reputation,
partially self-imposed, of being untutored and incomplete, we timidly
gird, defeated before we begin by the dazzling Goliath of French
Culture: the language that expresses emotion and thought more precisely and elegantly than any other, the mastery of all the secrets of
cuisine, sex and joie de vivre, the womb and cradle for the arts, the
temple of good taste served by alluring women and men of quick
charm and superb intelligence. Goliath has become a shadow giant in
recent years, however, and there is little reason for feeling awed by
the faded legend even though some Parisians cling to it, the more
desperately as they begin to doubt its present validity.

The language? There is reason for opera as an Italian invention,
the language sings itself felicitously. Although the Russian upper
classes spoke only French with their peers, Dostoevski and Chekhov
wrote their demonically astute works in the native tongue. Shakespeare
and Keats managed with English, the German philosophers and
scientists expressed themselves well, if turgidly, in German. Then
what about taste? It is no more ubiquitous or egalitarian in Paris
than anywhere else; taste is everywhere a minority property and
ephemeral. To see how it can lapse and sink in Paris one need only
glance at the tinny decor of the new cafés and the furnishing displays
for middle-class purchase, at the tortured caves and excrescences that
are the new "fun" shops, the "pubs" that are slavishly "Edwardian"
and miss entirely, the dour houses of brick and stone, pimpled with
stucco, on the outskirts of the city.

The most stimulating element of the Opéra is the incredible building
itself. The rest, other than good costuming is, to use the kindest word,
haphazard. The Opéra Comique is usually just that. Painting is shored
up and consequently stifled by The Grand Old Men; its dissidents
follow the modes of New York and London. Literature tends to re-
linquish matter for manner, and postures—at times brilliantly, too often
lengthily—in autobiographical displays of how wonderful and wounded
am I. The joie de vivre, the esprit are patchy, certainly not the ebullient crackle that once was the sound and air of Paris, according to
many writers. (One present-day French writer, appalled by the dis-
pirited, uncurious lassitude, defines it as the effect of a national
lobotomy.) Skilled cuisine is still available, but being supplanted by
quick and easy grillades. The former zesty give-and-take of street
soliciting hides in corners, but the vigorous public necking still goes
on and nudity is as easy to find as bread. Nudity straight, nudity

covered with spots of twinkle or bits of fur, nudity in boots and helmet, carrying a whip; nudity female, nudity male and in mixtures, is the métier of several neighborhoods. The friendliness rarely found in ordinary circumstances is expressed in the camaraderie of group sex, almost as easily arranged as a bridge game.

The legend diminished, one is left with people who like to eat well and therefore treat food with respect, who like sex to see and show, who look as hangdog in the Métro as New York subway riders, who are harried by traffic and the rising cost of living, who are as neurotic and more irritable than other 20th century city dwellers. The irritability seems to cause two supposedly core "truths" of our time to totter perilously. In Marxist logic a well-fed people should be a fairly contented people. In Freudian logic a well and busily bedded people should be a fairly contented people. Since the Parisian is well and pleasantly fed and so loved and loving—if there is any verity in the myths, literature and public displays—so fulfilled sexually in the famous game of musical beds, why is he so taut and ready to break at the lightest touch? The truths might be suspect or the fault may lie in aspects of Paris life not directly related to the eating and the bedding. In addition to the usual yokes and thorns, Jean has to cope with the urgencies of modern life while stumbling over anachronisms, the restraints of his early training warring with his volatility, and the burden of pumping life into moribund legends.

As soon as he is old enough and weather permits, Baby Jean is taken in his pram for a shopping tour of his *quartier*, the area of the Ecole des Beaux Arts, let us say. Maman, pram and baby emerge from a low, crowded *entresol* apartment which lacks a bath and shares a hall toilet with the neighbors. They try to make their way down the Rue Visconti, a slit of street with a few inches of token sidewalk, wide enough for the foot and cart traffic of the Huguenot colony that settled there in the 16th century, inhospitable now to the cars and people who try to squeeze past parked delivery wagons and other pedestrians. Little Jean, cradled in hand-knit woolens and ready for sleep, is bumped awake by the scraping and pulling of the pram wheels against the side of a building as his mother averts collision with another pram flanked by a child and a dog. On the Rue Bonaparte there is a Sèvres bowl Maman has been watching for a possible drop in price. Crossing the street to the shop is a dark journey of jerks, darts, stops for Jean and tense alertness for Maman. Three bus lines, not all sharing the same stops, lumber their way to the river and so do thousands of cars on this absurdly narrow artery that serves the quais and the bridges to the Right Bank. Traffic lights exist but who has the time to pause, and there is, in some statute book, a speed limit but who cares? Maman, long practiced, negotiates the crossing adroitly only to find her progress on the narrow sidewalk blocked by a gaggle of German tourists marching on her from one direction and a swift phalanx of art students from the other.

Having checked the unchanged price of the bowl she makes her wary way to the market around the Carrefour de Buci. Jean, still yearning to sleep, is bumped, lifted and dropped on and off the jammed strips of sidewalk around the fruit stalls, jarred by bulging shopping baskets, dashed across the path of an oncoming meat truck and pounded by the market shouting. Home again, pale and tired, little Jean has absorbed his first lesson in being a Parisian: in the anarchy of foot and car traffic, in the clash of wills and uneven powers, the rule is *sauve qui peut*. It is a nerve-wracking way to live and he learns to live it, nerve-wracked.

When Jean can toddle it is time to loosen him, stringently, in a local park. The patch at the side of the church of St. Germain des Prés is too full of tourists come to sit with the Picasso head, disputatious students and sprawled *clochards* blinking and dozing away a few hours. Nor does Maman like the triangle near the Bon Marché department store because the traffic on three large avenues pours its noise and fumes into the park. She prefers a small, secluded park off the Rue du Bac. The park is fenced and its gate an act of exclusion rather than welcome. Near the gate, and itself protected by close iron meshing, is a sign instructing invaders of the rigid little close in a list of *prohibé* and *interdit*. The child does not have to read the sign; he soon learns what it means. Should his ball roll onto the grass, he has created quite a problem. Neither he nor Maman (whose temper isn't improved by her stiff bench) may step on the grass to retrieve it. Because the park is so neatly kept, there is no twig or stick to reach for it and they must look for the elderly wearer of a cane or umbrella who may or may not lend it. When Jean is still a stumbler, he must be guided and held by reins from touching the flowers in the correct, classic borders. When he is a runner, he must learn to fall on gravel. He may not bat a ball—again, there are the grass and flowers to worry about; he cannot skate because there is no cement; there is no sandbox, no jungle gym, no bicycle path. He no longer wears the white gloves that so charmed tourists, but he might as well for all the athleticism the park affords him. He has, however, learned to be *sage* and *propre*, to suppress lively impulses, a possible base for the pot-au-feu of anger which simmers throughout his life and so easily brims over later.

The French school day is a long one. True, it encompasses a generous lunch break, but the young moles must leave home in the

morning dark and return in the afternoon dark through half the
school year, catching a few bleary rays of pale winter daylight on
their way to and from the midday meal. Immediately after school
they buckle down to substantial loads of homework and study, a
boxed-in existence symbolized by the tiny boxes ruled into the pages of
their notebooks, cramping strictures which, like the boxes of park, force
them into neat constraint.

Jean's university life is famously lacking in space, calm, study halls,
laboratories (being remedied, slowly) and if he is poor enough,
lacking in food and adequate warmth in the grim hotels that wear
their age like dank mosses around the Rue Mouffetard. In these Lower
Depths rooms he must prepare to meet merciless examinations and
exigent competition.

Finally, he has come through. Thin, pale and jumpy (the Francophile calls it "mercurial") he settles into man's estate with a job and
a flat. He may have a wife and/or a mistress and/or be playing the
field; he may, in addition, be pathologically attached to his mother
and his sister, or spend his evenings and weekend afternoons watching one particular overripe *stripeuse* at the Concert Mayol, but the
most important woman in his life is now Madame Defarge. She no
longer counts guillotined heads. Now, as she knits, she dreams
stratagems to keep the Revolution going or, failing that, to impede
the enemy (almost everyone) by placing rocks for him to stumble on
and thorns to tear at him. She isn't dead at all; she is the concierge
with the square, homemade haircut and a large comb savagely
rammed into it, more weapon than decoration. Her clothing is dusty
gray-black, shapeless and discouraged. Like the witch she can be, she
goes accompanied by a cat with a demonic gleam in his slanting eye or
a bristling overtoothed dog. She doesn't have to put up barricades; she
is the barricades, broad, indomitable and noisy, that bar Jean from
the old courts of the Marais during his search for the house Mozart
lived in, that bar him from examining the organic intricacies of Art
Nouveau on the Square Rapp. As his very own Cerberus, she may decide to delay his mail or inform expected guests that he is definitely not
at home. This reminds him that he has become lax in the matter of
obeisances and tips. As the ticket puncher on the Métro platform, she
may insist, if he holds several tickets for himself and his friends, that
he fan them out evenly, proper face up, before she will touch them.
Among the pleasant, bouncy women who are bus conductresses, she
may turn up as the one who rules him off the bus because she disapproves of the bundle he carries or, once in, he may be subjected to
her stentorian criticism because he wasn't quick enough to give an
old lady his seat. In the museum, she is the shrew who will not let

him touch a booklet he might want to buy if he knew what it contained. Should he decide to buy it anyhow, she shuts her stall before he can do so, punishing him for being slow.

Because he is suspected of being a fool or a savage he must be taught constantly by the signs Madame devises in her literary moments. She keeps reminding him of the variety of acts that are *pénible*, *défendu*, etc., etc., and warning this madman that if he opens a Métro door between station A and B while the train is in motion, there is *danger de mort*. Never trusting him to settle matters amicably by himself, she posts signs in buses informing him that, should there be a conflict over whether a window is to be opened or closed, the passenger who opts against fresh air is the victor. Clear, calm walls Jean passes are defaced with immense letters advising that it is *défendu d'afficher* according to the law of 1881 and it doesn't occur to him, or anyone else, for that matter, that the antique law might be closed back into the books and the large, ugly lettering better replaced by the handsome gallery posters that enliven more permissive walls.

And then, there is the life of the Métro, once he has passed its Gorgon ladies. To reach the line of his *correspondance* he may have to run a tiled maze of dim tunnels, across the legs of crippled beggars, and at intervals, to be slapped by swordlike rods, hemmed in by spiked fences and imprisoned by implacable doors, all painted a proper poison green and decorated with the variety of words that shout "taboo." The doors set the mood for his frustrating day: they close as the train comes into the station and stay closed until it leaves. The practice makes sense; it avoids crush and confusion and storms of mutual insult, but it takes all the gamble and optimism out of subway riding. (Vaulting down the stairs, leaping across the platform and squeezing through a narrowing slit of door, possibly the sole adventure and victory of a Londoner's working day—or a New Yorker's—is denied the Parisian.) Jean must submit to the green door which, furthermore, tells him in large letters that he must submit as it closes on his face. He submits and vents his anger by breaking several of the regulations conspicuously posted in the Métro car. He sits on a jump seat although that is not permitted during the hours of *affluence* (rush hour) and stays in it, violating the priority list which informs him that the first claim on seats is for those with war injuries; then, those blinded or injured in the line of civic duty; then to pregnant women and people accompanied by children less than four years old. If he is to find out whether an injury or blindness stems from a military or civic cause or whether the poor, gnarled cripple was stupid enough to let himself be knocked down by a truck and consequently deserves no seat, he must ask to see the card the war-wounded carry. After his act of defiance—the show of the famous French independence that may simply be the "I've had it up to here," after enough restraints have enmeshed him—he gets out at a station which has the appeal and sparkle of an old section of sewer, or, worse still, one that has been tarted up with bright shop displays and reproductions of Impressionist paintings in glass, threatening with their manic eyes and big, glittering teeth to eat him.

John of London has learned to live with his weather because it is predictable, almost always variations of damp. Jean's winters, too, are clammy, gray shrouds, but the rest of his year is much more erratic, more menopausal, if we are to follow the literary custom of treating Paris as a woman. She can burst into plump, buttery bloom for three days, then become dull and heavy-browed, then weep and storm for weeks; she quiets down to sulking again, a day or two of trying to smile, then a lapse into bleak, not-quite-tears mounting to the full wailing assault.

August is Jean's cruelest month. If he takes his vacation then, and he is likely to, in spite of the government's urging that the *fermeture annuelle* be staggered, he may be imprisoned in his Breton cottage by icy rains. If he stays at home and his home is in one of the prosperous *quartiers* he is a wanderer in Pompeii, in streets that have the appurtenances of life—shops, houses, doors, windows—all shocked still, motionless and soundless. If he lives in a less noble quarter he still feels abandoned: there are too few people to talk with and about, too few foils with whom to play the Paris game of mutual abrasion. If the rains come and stay, the winter sweaters have to be dragged out of camphor, the shoes became shapeless and frail with constant soaking, new summer awnings drip bright indelible stains onto raincoats. Blisters of damp disfigure the walls, the old roof tiles admit a leak which spatters down on the dining table and the repairman is on his farm in Normandy. The children get feverish colds while all the doctors are motoring in Spain. The local drugstores which might ordinarily help with advice and home remedies are closed and Papa must walk to one some considerable distance away because all the taxis are in use by water-logged tourists making their gallant rounds.

It is, finally, a pretty day. The chrome and glass of the café windows blink back at the sun, the chairs and tables come back to the street. Now it is again time for a small coffee and luxuriant volubility. The Café is a big, smiling place conveniently situated for meeting a friend, back of the Madeleine, near Fauchon's. Jean arranges to meet his friend Paul there. The men have much to say to each other out of an old friendship nurtured through school and the small, neighborhood cafés of Batignolles where they grew up. Jean starts to speak but Paul's contribution to the conversation is "What? What did you say?" A covey of buses thunders around the church; motor-bikes drone and sputter in their jaunty, weaving flight through the clots of taxis, trucks and tourist buses. A thousand vehicles groan and bellow and spit exhaust into the café. Intimate revelations of love and money have to be shouted or left unspoken, light talk is not worth the effort it requires, so the men nod and smile at each other in a dumb show of amity and part.

Before he turns on the motor of his car, Jean puts on his gloves, slowly, flexing his fingers to make the leather lie smoothly. Tamping down each seam and joint he draws them on with the doomful purpose of a surgeon or a knight buckling for the Perilous Quest. The enemy is Protean: lights that impede his godlike flight, the irrational enemy flics, the survivor of horse and carriage days who wants to cross when he wants to cross and, waving his irascible cane, forces Jean to a screaming halt. There are too many other cars in Paris, he says, driven by sadistic fools out to impede his imperial course; they don't have to be out, they are only showing off. Why don't they fix their crumbling houses instead of buying those tin cans on wheels? No toilets, but a car, yes. Idiots. Beasts. And a list of scatological and sexual references.

At the Etoile (or the Place de la Concorde) Jean joins the supreme contest of sauve qui peut. Traffic zooms in and out of a dozen direc-tions, weaves itself together, meshes, unravels, knots again; paint-jobs kiss and scratch each other in a monstrous mating dance; separate, run in for another embrace. Two other cars zoom in to sever them, to assault each other, then change direction, and they all leap, career, zigzag their crazy different ways toward the releasing avenues. By the time Jean escapes into the Avenue Kléber he is un-strung and strung taut in spite of the taste of victory. Northward, into the starkness of Aubervilliers, his Quest leads him into a new set of dangers. A character out of Paul Bowles, boiling with anger and a long Saturday evening of wine, maybe clouded by a bit of kif brought in by a compatriot, thrusts a child in front of the car of a European. It isn't his child (families are frequently left in North Africa); it's a girl child, in any case, and if the European so much as grazes her, there will be hell and money to pay. If the adversary is wary and alert and avoids touching the child, the agonized screech of brakes and the terror on his face are almost reward enough.

Life is no less difficult for Jean as pedestrian. The Grands Boule-vards devised by Baron Haussmann—a public benefactor or a maniac and scourge, depending on whom one reads or listens to—cannot always be negotiated in one traffic light because cars tearing in from other streets won't permit it. The light changes while he is in the middle of the boulevard and he becomes a tiny island in the foaming, lashing traffic. Once in a horrifying while, late at night on a wide boulevard, a couple of young *sportif* types will appoint him "it" in a savage game: as he crosses the quiet avenue, seemingly free of hazard, their car will pursue him on a swift diagonal, cut off his path and scream a tight semicircle around him. The boys may or may not get close enough to hook his pocket with a door handle but his fear is good for a hearty laugh. Concealed passages spew out unexpected cars; the studded pedestrian walks are never to be trusted as safe ground. Jean begins to feel that rather than too many, there are too few cars in Paris; there is still too much space for burning spurts of speed, for jumping lights and roaring down on pedestrians. He wishes traffic were more like it is in Rome, so immobilized by its very numbers in ancient, irregular streets that a pedestrian can walk quite freely while the drivers fume and cars shiver in halted clusters.

Almost any simple, ordinary act can have a barbed edge. Rushing to the Métro in the morning, Jean is tripped by a bundle of wet rags, a soggy dark-brown mummy used by the street-cleaning department to sop up the flow from water outlets and a suitable mate for the besom of bound twigs, exactly like that used by Abélard's concierge, that is also present-day street-cleaning equipment. He can wait through interminable questions and discussions on a post office queue to find that there are no air mail stamps left; he will have to decorate his overseas letter with streamers of local postage. In the licking and pasting he forgets the last 5 centime stamp. Some days later the post office phones or sends him a telegram demanding that he appear to amend the error. He appears, states his business, his name and address to a series of people who consult with each other, separate to open and shut many sets of drawers, disappear in back caverns and reconvene for grave consultation. The diagnosis of his case has been made, it is serious; the letter has disappeared completely.

When the anachronisms and the inefficiencies don't annoy him, the legends may. The intellectual Jean must defend Paris as the still-fecund womb of great music and ballet although he has just come from a performance at the Opéra which could have been directed by no one but the Marx Brothers. He points to his many theaters but not the fact that they live off *Cyrano de Bergerac* and Molière, plus imports from New York and London and the brilliant views of cloacal pits by the Rumanian Ionesco. He insists that Paris has an intellectual class, which embarrasses him by its silence. The "thinking" French worker crosses him up by falling in love, just as does the United States primitive, with a new, attractive TV image who is touted as the "French John Kennedy" and for whom a substantial presidential vote is turned in, although very few seem to know anything about his provenance, his capacities or principles. Jean, the repository of fraternité and égalité, is unstintingly critical of Negro slums in Watts and Harlem but can neither forget nor acknowledge his Portuguese settlement that can be smelled two blocks off, or the North African workers who sleep like cords of wood in cellars meant for coal and wine.

He may come home one night to find his wife a boiling mess of irritations. She is checking the telephone bill, angered again with the high cost of antiquated service and infuriated because she has to check a London call on an arcane system of computation based on 30 centimes for 9.5 seconds per "unit" and she cannot figure precisely how many 9.5 seconds she consumed during the call. Furthermore her job as a biochemist has become a nightmare. The government has built for her and her colleagues a richly equipped, brand-new research center protected from the elements, theoretically, by a central air-conditioning system. Somewhere, in some office, the requisition for the air-conditioning equipment lies neglected or balked; the tight-shut showpiece is unusable for the time being and possibly an indefinite time longer. Furthermore, she has been coping with her difficult day in very high heels, as has her weary hairdresser and a snappish sales-girl she encountered in a glove shop.

In spite of its obvious physical and psychic advantages, a few Jeans now feel a bit trapped in the tradition that requires that they have both a wife and mistress. Jean can't afford a mistress, the cost of living is soaring and the little love token costs too much. Nor is it any longer quite as easy to find a young, attractive woman who will consent to passivity, fidelity and neglect. It is no longer the only career open to her; the girl who once considered the world well lost for love inclines toward the field, when it doesn't interfere with her job or her law classes. Divorce is less and less rare and why shouldn't she have the security to which he clings? Assuming he is lucky or irresistible, Jean has yet to cope with home pressures that require him to work a bit harder and later, that cut into his leisure and extra money. His blossoming daughter can't, absolutely can't, be seen in those old rags that smiled at her on the Rue de Sèvres last year; all the girls are shopping at the new Pucci boutique, please, please, be nice, Papa. Money must be set aside so that fourteen-year-old Robert can spend the summer with a family in Bournemouth to improve his English. The car is shaking itself apart, too far gone for repairs. Jean finds his wife, as wives go, pleasing enough to worry about. Is she spending her late afternoons as he does? He would like to give up the steady, orderly arrangement and settle for the light, fast landing and takeoff, like an insect's, but he's mired in the legend that no full male exists outside the old and more respectable triangle.

The final, most burdensome legend is that he is a logical, rational man sitting on his accumulated frustrations and worries and angers with philosophic calm, giving them only slight notice with a graceful quip. And that fiction, that last, large clamp, is the greatest irritant of all.

2 Monday

You will have seen the *Mona Lisa* (there is no escaping the insistent *La Joconde* arrows) and the *Winged Victory*, plodded through the Roman, Greek and Egyptian antiquities of which there are too many displayed in the 19th century manner when museums were dark, large rabbit warrens, not yet showcases of the choice. You will have dragged yourself through the large central painting galleries where Marie de Medici billows through her noble life as seen by Rubens (who, one hopes, disliked the job and was paid well for it) and where Napoleon had himself similarly deified by his painters. The rest becomes a colossal, frightening task, one it takes courage to leave in spite of glazed eyeballs and burning feet. Buy a plan or carry a Green *Michelin* which has one and sketch out an itinerary of what else you absolutely must see and can absorb.

Whatever that may be, try not to neglect the delights tucked away in side rooms as dignified and light as cellar pantries. Behind the acres of Marie de Medici and rarely disturbed by tourist hordes, one finds an invaluable cache of small Flemish and French paintings. Here hang Van der Weyden's masterful *Braque Triptych*, Van Eyck's *Madonna with Chancellor Rolin*, uncanny, clear-eyed Fouquet portraits—one of the fat Guillaume Juvénal des Ursins against fat golden pillars and Charles VII looking catarrhal and petulant. The nameless immortality of the Master of Moulins is held in two chaste portraits of children and the rich painting of a lady donor with Ste. Marie-Madeleine. Nearby, magical paintings by Memling, including his *Portrait of an Old Woman*; Quentin Metsys' famous *Money Lender and His Wife*, as much a portrait of an age as of a couple; the Anne of Cleves and the most famous Erasmus portrait by Holbein; the fat serene Elector of Saxe by the older Cranach and from the same hand, the sly Venus with small breasts and a big belly, dressed only in a big red hat and a necklace. Look for the group of Flemish cripples painted by the elder Breughel and the wonderfully narcissistic self-portrait of Dürer as a beautiful young man into whose elegant hands the world must inevitably fall. A crowded *Bal* painting is a literal document of interiors, costumes, jewelry and musical instruments found in the great houses of the 16th century. Near it, a superb Clouet portrait of an apothecary holding a book of pressed grasses, and the famous Clouet (probably) portrait of François I, splendid in his black cap with white feathers, his coat of white satin with gold sleeves, wearing a substantial amount of the crown jewels. Not the best by far, yet most mesmeric, is a painting of Gabrielle d'Estrées (a favorite of Henry IV and the mother of two of his children) who sits with her sister, both naked to the waist, both wearing earrings. One pinches the other's nipple as they look blankly out at the spectator; in the background a lady-in-waiting continues with her sewing.

Nearby, a collection of later small French portraits, almost miniatures, in enchanting frames, followed by small Dutch masterpieces: Rembrandt's luminous study of a skinned beef, his Holy Family in a carpenter's workshop; Metsu's lovely girl holding a goblet and wine pitcher, Vermeer's *Lace Maker*, Jan Breughel's graceful dream of an *Earthly Paradise*.

The above are, as you know, morsels of an infinite world of art, mentioned primarily to pull you into side alleys of the Louvre, too often lost among the more refulgent splendors.

WARNING: If you can, go to the bathroom elsewhere: the caretakers of this Temple don't seem to find paperless, towelless, dirty toilets inconsistent with high art. If you're hungry, eat elsewhere. The buffet has an old-oil stench (avoidable if you can get a seat on the open balcony, a rare event), the help is overworked and hasty, the list mediocre, meager and not cheap enough for quality or quantity. You will have reached the buffet, incidentally, via a vaulted hall with a noble set of stairs, lashings of gilt and paintings, a curious anteroom for a greasy spoon.

PALAIS ROYAL

One of the most retiring, unexpected places in central Paris, surrounded by and thoroughly separated from the shopping, the banking, the stock trading that surrounds it; now as sedate and pale as it was once regal, gay, raffish, crooked and depraved. It all started with Richelieu, who, on becoming prime minister, bought a large piece of land, made a number of profitable divisions on it and kept for himself a lordly section on which he built an immense establishment encompassing numerous courts, a theater and extensive gardens. (His south wall on Rue St. Honoré probably covered the spot where Joan of Arc was wounded as she tried to measure the depth of the water in the moat surrounding the English fortress.)

The Cardinal left his palace to Louis XIII, who died shortly after. His wife, Anne of Austria, brought the young Louis XIV to live here, as did later royalty. The Palais Cardinal became Royal. When dangerous winds blew, royalty fled it; when they subsided, royalty returned. Royal bastards were helped to birth by doctors led to the accouchement blindfolded and trusted ladies of the court whisked the infants out to be placed with wet nurses. There were exquisite suppers with intermissions of rare entertainment, particularly those arranged by the friends of the Regent, Philippe II, Duc d'Orléans, and his collection of mistresses. On his death of apoplexy in 1723, the Palais Royal became the property of his son Louis, the third Duc d'Orléans. He, in understandable reaction, preferred a monastery after the death of his wife, who died in labor on the way to Versailles, trying to comply with the cruel custom of the court that all princesses of the blood give birth there.

Through this time, the palace changed its original Richelieu shape to become more and more the structure one sees at present. Louis Phillippe I (the Fat), busied himself making changes continued by his son Philippe, Duc de Chartres (later the fifth Duc d'Orléans), who remains in history as Philippe Egalité, although that name didn't save *his* head, either. His thinking apparently more egalitarian than his tastes, Philippe was broke, always, and deeply in debt. To profit from his holdings, he built houses on three sides of the garden, a continuous, expensive row over galleries to be filled with shops. New streets were cut through for access to the houses and soon the Palais Royal became one of the busiest playgrounds of the city: wax museums, magicians, circuses, dance halls, cafés, shops—one of them sold Charlotte Corday the dagger that killed Marat—gambling halls and the French version of the "Beggar's Opera," the renowned "wooden galleries," as a fourth side to the clamorous rectangle. This was the market for all sexual tastes from little boys to extravagantly outsized women, the bargaining counters for crooked deals, a ripe field for pickpockets to reap, a playground for the vicious.

After the Palais became the property of the state in 1793 and was made the seat of several government offices by Napoleon some years later, the gallery excitements slowly abated; the infamous wooden galleries, fallen into disuse except by thousands of rats, were demolished in 1826 and the gambling houses closed a dozen years later. The February revolution of 1848 caused further destruction, soon repaired, and the palace was readied as a residence for the Bonapartes. With the fall of that empire, the royal enclave became once more the property of the state.

Walking through the stately, passive rows of colonnades and silent houses, untouchable grass and shadowy galleries, one still sees the signs of a number of government associations lettered on some of the boutiques and building entrances. What was once gaming houses and noisy cafés is now the quiet of rare-stamp shops, a few small antique shops, a small art gallery or two, one famous old restaurant, one brilliant boutique of modern international toys and ornaments, the rest blanked out and unused. The only vitality is supplied by the young mothers and babies who come to sit in the park, the proximity of the Théatre Français and the memory of Colette, who lived here for many years. Two plaques, one at the entrance of the passage to the Rue de Beaujolais and the other on the house itself, commemorate the fact. The rest is dignified resignation, unmoved by the whirling modernity around it.

NOTE: Although it is an important place to see, an essential of Paris, the Palais Royal does not absorb much time and could, therefore, be combined with the Musée des Arts Décoratifs, shopping on the Rue de Rivoli, the streets and passages to the north, or to the east, described elsewhere.

Monday Afternoon: Flea Market

Traditionally, tourist time at the Marché aux Puces of the Porte de Clignancourt is Sunday afternoon, a time when all the stalls are open and crammed with goods, when families are out shopping en masse and the solitary homesick men immerse themselves in the humanity and noise, something like that of their casbah souks.

Monday has a different cast; many Paris shops are closed Mondays and working women use this free day to do their bargain hunting. The stalls of jewelry and *objets d'art* are less crowded, the splendors of "antique" furniture disregarded; the concentrations are on the odds and ends that find their tired, rusty ways to the edges of the market. At the end of Rue Paul Bert, on rudimentary tables of planks on wooden horses, lie tangles of used raincoats, sweaters, skirts, dresses. Eager searchers like birds of prey swoop over each others shoulders, under elbows (no flutelike *pardon* or *je vous en prie* here), pounce, pluck, try on, throw back on the heap and start over again. Once in a while, a struggle over whose claws rounded on what treasure first, silent tugging, bitter eyeing and then the flow of harsh, shrill words.

If you can find it, though maps rarely bother about these streets, go into Rue Lécuyer and look at the assortment of junk someone cherishes—iron bits, nails, pierced buckets and dented tin platters, piled high in storage bins to be strewn on the unpaved walk for the day, piled back and locked up for the night. On the Passage Marceau, a gypsy family examines the blue jeans, the socks and shovels and slickers that wandered here from the warehouses of the U.S. Army. A pair of teen-agers finger a U.S. Navy peacoat considered chic (warm and cheap, too) among the Paris young. A young couple marked by his tweeds and her coiffeur as the 7th or 16th (currently the "best" arrondissements) linger over the dented brass and the china stalls of the Rue Jules Vallès, trying not to listen to the insistent muttering of a *Folle de Chaillot*, one of the considerable number still trailing their green-black skirts and torn coquettish veilings through the streets of Paris. A rack of men's clothing, not very old nor yet quite new, leads off with a gray shirt one of whose pockets is marked "Mr. Hogan," the other, "Housing Authority of the City of Patterson." It must have been an eventful journey.

The Marché Malik is a hidden village of bits of bits and yet, for the imaginative, capable of yielding something or other usable. The vendors are amusing, rather pleased with being in the pariah section of the market, especially the younger vendors who probably spend the rest of their week in studios and lecture rooms and enjoy the talkative, sprawling contrast.

Not too far away, in the alley number 10 of curvacious furniture and brown gravy paintings, you'll find a café. There are others easier to reach on the main streets surrounding the market and certainly near the Métro and bus stops, but not as stimulating. The place is not particularly neat or clean, the decor is its tables, chairs, bar and a niche which serves as bandstand, its size inconsequential. But when the music bounces against the narrow walls and the men at the bar argue about anything between bouts of teasing the resident gypsy fortune-teller, who can't play for long because she is trying to extract just a few more francs from the late shoppers and the market women, and it's cold outside and the place grows steamy with coarse wine and bonhomie, it achieves its own perfections, what a market café should be, was once, and rarely is any more.

MONTMARTRE

There were, it seems, two temples, one dedicated to Mercury and the other to Mars, on a height north of the Roman settlement of Lutetia. There is still argument, among those who argue these matters, whether the name of the famous hill derives from the "mount of Mars," or whether it derives from "the mount of martyrs," commemorating the miracle of St. Denis (page 145). The latter was the choice of the early Christian settlement, which was later expanded and ennobled by the Abbey of the Dames de Montmartre, whose power and piety are now remembered in an inconspicuous street, a small Place, a Métro station, and for one of the mothers-superior, the pagan Boulevard Rochechouart.

A witness and participant in ecclesiastical expansion and decline, a battleground of early struggles for power, a seducer of soldiers to its side during the Commune, the site of rapid population growth (particularly after the Revolution), Montmartre managed to stay a village into the latter half of the 19th century, when it became part of the city of Paris. It was then, to judge from numerous contemporary descriptions and paintings, still a place of fields and trees, country paths and gardens, herds of goats and country girls to watch them, vineyards and windmills and, in spite of the cabarets, a place that reminded the writer, Gérard de Nerval, of the Roman *campagna*. Subsequent exploitation of the combined charms of the bucolic and the wicked *vie bohème*, the unplanned expansion and the eager establishment at the southern foot of the hill—Pigalle, Place Blanche, Boulevard de Clichy—of a gaudy "Sin City" has changed all that. To quote Hillairet (who quotes an anonymous wit) : *"La butte sacrée a été massacrée."*

Not quite massacred; badly wounded but limping along gallantly in its mindless gait. As good a way of watching it as any is to circle around its eastern and northern border and then zigzag southward through the cat's cradles of streets. From the Place Clichy, the 80 or 95 bus trundles over a causeway that skims the spires and crosses of the Montmartre Cemetery and into the core and character of the Rue Caulaincourt, a minor Rue Victor Hugo (page 196) whose mood is *echt*-sober respectability, an almost Germanic solidity. Its elderly ladies are always black-hatted and spare, some of the shops and cafés shaded by tall canopies of trees still maintain their wavy glass and wood fronts. The neighborhood has good (but never outré in the showy Left Bank manner) antique and clothing shops; the beauty parlors are small, neat and quiet; the big corner cafés though modern and jukeboxed are rarely pretentious, never tinny. The restaurants are neither for big spenders nor impecunious students; their field is the unobtrusive, self-respecting meal for 10 to 15 francs. In and out of the candy stores run the neighborhood children in well-styled, sturdy coats, blue knees and cold-burned cheeks. Except for slum areas which don't care one way or the other, Caulaincourt, for some reason, shows its children more willingly than other parts of Paris. No Franglais is spoken here, no "quick" anythings, "breakfast" *or* "lunch"; the "ice-cream" is called *glace.* The most potent expression of the bourgeois-ness of Caulaincourt is the fact that its most opulent and colorful shops are the *charcuteries,* slightly overdressed and well-packed like the adjoining apartment houses with their coquettish balconies, garlands, and Greeky-Roman affectations.

The Square Caulaincourt opens for a monument to the painter and lithographer Eugène Carrière, badly served by the pigeons and the engraver who carved his legend in illegible "artistic" letters. Around the corner is the Avenue Junot cut through in 1909. Dispersing a colony of *clochards* and rags and old-paper dealers in filthy huts (it was called "le Maquis," oddly, in light of later connotations of the word), it became the terrain for houses of prosperous artists and followers of the arts, all devotees of the "avant" architectural styles of the 20's and 30's. It is an extraordinary collection of imaginative variations of white angularity and studio glass; some houses of staggered sections and zigzags of windows to accommodate modernity and the curve of the hill, others obscuring angularities with flowered balconies and playful trellises. The mood can be somber, or light, or shrill, but all the houses are in their different ways interesting.

About halfway up the hill there is an unexpected slit in Junot, a short narrow curve further narrowed by parked cars, named Villa Léandre for a Montmartre painter and crammed tight with little near-"follies" in various stages of collapse and renewal. A brave house painted orange, hung with toy balconies and gleaming white windowsills and another in Quaker gray with lemon-yellow awnings, jostle dark brick houses with deep eaves, buried in silent shade and ivy. One member of the community got as far as a peach-colored door with mustard trim and for a time left the rest in its old gloom, as if to symbolize the transition from drab elderly to young colorful.

Back on Junot, at about where number 11 would be, the street becomes a blank of wall. Behind it is the "Hameau des Artistes," a nest of solid studio buildings, ranged along a maze of paths. It is difficult to imagine starving and freezing in these garrets, if there are garrets at the top of a Siena-red Tuscan villa or a fortress-castle of gray cement, or a large, glistening box of glass. (Some periods and some styles of art must have paid, and apparently still do, quite well.) There are gates leading to the Hameau, usually open during the day. You may be told that entering is *interdit* by a boy of seven who has appointed himself dragon of the castle. Tell him you are an American cowboy—sex doesn't seem to matter—or better still an Indian (*peau-rouge*).

At the place where the Avenue Junot meets Rue Girardon and changes its name to Norvins, a Lutetian would have seen the Temple of Mars; long later, Renoir would have looked at the Moulin de la Galette. Now, the inhabitants of the studio courts on Norvins, on their way to the wineshops and galleries of indifferent to terrible paintings in the bent houses of Rue Lepic, pass the tired remnants of the many windmills that once turned on Montmartre. (Tasso in the 16th century coupled them with the stained glass in Notre Dame as the most remarkable sights in Paris.)

At this point a look at your map will show a web spun by a

psychotic spider—of streets, stairways and passages, short and clinging to each other so closely that it hardly matters in which direction you go. But you may prefer to follow these subitineraries in whatever order suggests itself: Go into the Rue St. Rustique, one of the few streets that looks now somewhat as it did two hundred years ago, for a view at Sacré Coeur as it threatens like a huge, invading balloon to choke the pockmarked walls and crush the geraniums of the ancient village path. Head for the white bulk in whose shadow you'll find the small dark church of St. Pierre, one of the oldest in Paris and considered by some absolutely the oldest because its structure incorporates four marble columns of the 6th century chapel, probably dedicated to St. Denis, which stood on the site. Added to, rebuilt, allowed to fall into decay and closed at the time of the Revolution, later revived by artistic rather than religious interests, it is a mixed bag of styles, though a few sections of 12th century Gothic, as well as Merovingian columns remain. It is a gloomy little church, more like an expiatory chapel, burdened with scummy sculptures and heavy, angular stone. Along the outside, through the grillwork, broad views of the city and close-ups of the gargoyles of Sacré Coeur. Back of the church, on the site of the ancient cemetery, an early 19th *Jardin du Calvaire*, a calvary past crypts of stone images surrounded by wax flowers, a prayer stool and a chromo of the Virgin Mary; then up a few stone stairs to the summit of the Crucifixion.

Ultimately, for its fame and central position one must land on the Place du Tertre; avoiding it takes careful planning and, in any case, it would be like visiting New York City without dipping into the carnival of Greenwich Village. Its once placid shape was marked out in 1635 as the public "Place" of the village, on land donated by the abbey. In 1790 one of its houses became the Mairie of Montmartre. In 1871 dozens of cannons used for the defense of Paris earlier, and gathered on the Place, formed an armory for Commune battles. Then there came the paintings and more paintings of its 18th century houses—the sloping picturesque corners, the modest wineshops, the bundles of children and washerwomen—followed by starers at the painters in their native costumes and lairs.

At the present place in Montmartre history, who follows whom becomes misty. Tourists flock to watch the painters who hope to sell to tourists the products of their factory of "Place du Tertre

Art." Part of the job consists of wearing, according to season, "artistic" pants and shirts and, as if it were a competitive game, the most startling cap one can find: a Scotch plaid tam, a feathered Alpine hat, a mangy Davy Crockett hat, a red hunting cap. The rest of the job is to produce the same two paintings that emerge from the easels next to, behind and across from yours. Recent production poured forth cute, big-eyed children suffering from either malnutrition or melancholia and equally cute Montmartre itself in pleasing flower colors with sunny streaks of thick yellow-white paint. It must take infinite patience to keep repeating these same paintings, but they seem to sell (the big-eyed waifs have, from time to time, stared out of Madison Avenue galleries) and it is healthy outdoor work—when outdoors is hospitable—in a market ambience of heavy-handed conviviality. Around these fixed stars, restless galaxies of soldiers on leave, a covey of nuns, girls in poke bonnets and hoopskirts advertising a local wax museum (page 46), policemen, Japanese ladies in kimonos, Japanese gentlemen in cameras, young Americans being French by tearing at baguettes of bread as they stroll, older Americans being French on too much wine and barbershop quartets of "Frère Jacques," homosexuals searching out confreres, elderly tourists plodding along on swollen ankles, well-packed German families in sensible shoes and practical raincoats, diehard English families occupied in their traditional job of not noticing the sudden chill.

Having seen as much of this operetta set as you care to, go to the top of the stairs that tumble down Rue Calvaire. At the side is a handsome studio, deep in trees and ivy, with one sparse, graceful decoration, like a Whistler signature, marking its tall facade. Below, clusters of other studio windows and the busy life of the stairs: boys galloping down, bumping women struggling up with heavy shopping bags, lovers glued to each other and a side wall, and lapping around everyone's feet, wavelets of babies practicing the stairs, toddling up and down one set, and then another, in uncertain unison.

A minutely different jog out of the Place du Tertre, through the turn of the Rue St. Eleuthère (along with St. Rustique, one of the martyred companions of St. Denis) reaches the Rue Chappe and its steep run of stairs, surmounted by a patch of green on a roof of the street below, enclosing a tiny apple orchard. (The door of this estate warns you of a "wicked dog," a wicked Chihuahua, judging from the space it must guard.) Beyond the orchard, a fall of skylight, like gentle waters, and the hazy distances of the city screened by the slender, light-leaved trees along the street.

North of the Place stretches the long Rue du Mont Cenis not now especially attractive except for a strong bold white tower and, from the head of the stairs, the dazzle of red chimney pots above the gray and grilled facades that course toward, fold into, and fly away from each other. At this point the street has stopped being a self-conscious annex of the Place du Tertre and takes on the steadiness of the Caulaincourt area, an almost "don't touch me or even talk to me" expressed by the Rue Paul Féval on a weekday afternoon at about 3:30. One sees nothing but silent houses, a cat, a lady with a dog, and hears nothing but the tinkle of the bell on the dog's collar and the hum of distant cars. Redone in a scourge of demolition and rebuilding about forty years ago, the Rue du Mont Cenis remains bare of any vestiges of its antiquity, of the processions livelier than the present march of gray walls that took place a long time ago, when it was the only road that led to the hill from the north. On this road there was a procession every seven years (until the Revolution put a stop to it) between the abbeys of Montmartre and St. Denis. At the head, according to Hillairet, walked four monks in red, carrying the head of Saint Denis which the nuns of Montmartre came to meet, to kiss, to make their devotions to, while Te Deums were sung. At the corner of Rue St. Vincent, a plaque indicates that Berlioz lived and worked there (or, rather, in a house that stood there earlier), and this, too, must have been a place of colorful processions considering the artists, composers and writers who were his friends.

Going west from the Place du Tertre on Norvins, past a group of white houses on a private park cut diagonally by a formal *allée* of trees, a hand-painted billboard advertising an "avant" movie and from a window above, the chords of a guitar behind indefatigable verses of a Kentucky lament, one sees the cones and bulbs of Sacré Coeur looming as a gigantic vanilla sundae. The Rue d'Orchampt crooks its elbow around the attractive Place J. B. Clément, then ends at a turn-of-the-century House of Usher, shrouded in stillness and ivy, heavily guarded by iron gates and stone pillars which permit only the narrowest slits of space for peering into a section of garden that must give on a fine view of Montmartre roofs.

A pleasant pause in the climbing up and down, especially if you've been lured by still another depth of stairs or snared in the loops and rises of the Rue Lepic, is to sit down in the Place Emile Goudeau—a bit of green, a "picturesque" yet reliable restaurant, still another replica of the Four Graces; a modest, poorish square of no distinction other than its calm after the brouhaha northward, and a low building with whitewashed walls. Early in the 19th century the site was a famous *guinguette* where Parisians came to dance and drink, sometimes to eat, in the shade of an immense pear tree. The pretty dappled gaiety came to a sudden end when the tunneling for clays used in local potteries came too close to the *guinguette*, threatening to swallow it. (The potteries closed soon afterward because the whole neighborhood was similarly endangered.) Early in the 1830's a young writer and his painter friend came to live in a section of the *guinguette* and with them, for a short while, the young Alexandre Dumas. Thus they established the artists' colony whose odd wooden dwelling, slapped together in the 1860's, became the famous "Bateau Lavoir" where Picasso worked for many years, accompanied by a model-mistress much of the time. Around the corner there was Braque and in adjoining studios, enough other painters of stature to give the plain wooden corridors the name "Villa Medici of Modern Art."

Down the Rue Ravignan (an ancient street once part of the only road from Paris to the abbey above), through the passage of sunless stairs and listless small hotels called the Rue André Antoine, one reaches the Place des Abbesses and its appealing church whose facade is elaborated in scallops, knots, florets, crossed with graceful arches and studded with ceramic bits, altogether like a heavily embroidered christening dress. Surrounding the main portal there is a flight of angels as windblown and sad-sweet as they should be for their neoromantic time, 1904. (In spite of, or rather to serve, its delicacy, the church is an important achievement in architectural techniques, architects say.)

A minute's walk away, at number 9 Rue Antoinette, just off the appropriate Street of the Martyrs, is the place where, supposedly, the region's three martyrs were beheaded. A small church was built on the spot and in its crypt Ignatius Loyola and his few cohorts took solemn vows to fight for the True Religion, thus establishing this inconsequential corner as the birthplace of the mighty Jesuit Order.

What next? The two museums of Montmartre (page 47)? Continuing on Rue Antoinette toward the funicular for the ride up and down (one bus ticket each way)? South to the Boulevard de Clichy between Place Blanche and Place Pigalle, among the touters of the sex temples and the buses to Longchamps for the races; the shouters of toys, sunglasses, waffles, crêpes and sandwiches; the crowds pushing into the vast movie houses, and the dark, homesick men searching, appraising the possibilities of all the women they pass, the pimply boys from the provinces trying to look hard and knowing? Or, sit at the Café Ronsard which faces the green hill below Sacré Coeur. Before you passes a group of Arab women with tattooed foreheads and an old Muslim gentleman whose beard is startling red with henna to show he has twice been to Mecca. Gypsies in long skirts and savage earrings, African women in beautifully wrapped cotton skirts and high turbans, a Punjabi girl combining two cultures with her good English sweater over the silk tunic of her pantalooned costume, women dragging babies and bundles of cloth from the market of St. Pierre (page 207), tourists from Caen, Osaka, Madras and Cincinnati taking pictures of Sacré Coeur while street photographers take pictures of them and, at the side of the funicular, the stalwart climbers of stairs who need the exercise or the price of the ride.

For those armed with Herculean energy and insatiable greed for Montmartre places, there remain many streets; the markets on Lepic; the affected cafés, the lusty cafés and the sodden ones; Montmartre's cemetery, entered via an anteroom carpeted with potted plants and grave flowers, called Avenue Rachel. You might want to pay your respects to Théophile Gautier, the brothers Goncourt, Stendhal, Madame Récamier, to the Lady of the Camellias and to Hector Berlioz who lies between wife one, an English actress, and wife two, an opera singer. To arrange this, he had wife one exhumed from another burial place and taken to Montmartre to wait for him. An eminently just man.

One of the details of the Place du Tertre (page 42) stage set— the girls in poke bonnets and hoopskirts—leads on by the combination of suggestion and overt signs to a wax museum that concerns itself with "Old Montmartre." The Impasse Trainée slopes toward a few low-built restaurants and studios fronting on a height over the city and down to the grouped images of local worthies in the history of the village. Wax, being the morbid medium it is, and the exaggerated foreshortening of the perspectives create an early di Chirico effect, in spite of the costumes and the scenes of the legendary café bonhomie.

After you've been guided through and out of the foolish, amusing waxworks (constantly reminded, in several languages, that your guides are students and depend on the tips you give although the entrance fee seems substantial enough to cover salaries), make your way to Rue des Saules which soon meets the Rue de l'Abreuvoir, a winding street of no shops, poised and interesting without bothering to be "artistic." Immediately ahead, on the Rue des Saules is the last of Montmartre's vineyards, carefully enclosed and guarded, and next to it, at 17 Rue St. Vincent, Le Musée du Vieux Montmartre. (Open from 10 A.M. to Noon and 2 P.M. to 5 P.M. Closed Tuesdays.) It is probably the oldest house in the area, although others claim the distinction. At one time (about 1680) it was the property of a well-known actor, who lived in an uncanny linkage with Molière; he not only acted in the plays of Molière, but played the roles Molière had played, wrote comedies too, and, like Molière, died during a performance of Le Malade Imaginaire.

The gardened rise accompanying the vineyard, the house and its location among streets that resist the permanent carnival nearby are the loveliest parts of the museum, of itself an easy pleasant compendium of Montmartriana. On the main floor, one finds the fine china made in the 18th century kiln of Clignancourt, a short distance to the north where now the disorder of the Marché aux Puces explodes each weekend. The upstairs rooms are hung with dreamy paintings of an idealized Montmartre by the M. Léandre of the Villa (page 41), caricatures by Daumier, André Gill and Forain, and posters of local entertainments in the good-bad old days. Toulouse-Lautrec's green-faced starvelings hang next to the more contented, charming drawings of Emile Bernard. A seductive old restaurant sign shows local views of a pretty house and garden and strolling couples. Near it, photographs of distinguished, or at least conspicuous local citizens.

A room cluttered with violins, pens, small pianos and a hat reproduces the place and atmosphere in which Charpentier probably wrote Louise and near it, the sort of café he might have frequented, with a gently curved zinc bar, zinc bottle containers, cane chairs and a piano with candle holders above the keyboard. On the walls of the café there may have been displayed the poster of the Folies Bergère starring Loïe Fuller and announcements of the appearance of the immensely popular Bruant whose commanding presence, sweeping hat and heroic scarf, as recorded by Toulouse-Lautrec, assure him the immortality his considerable native talents might not. There are photos and drawings of Marie Laurencin and Suzanne Valadon as their neighbors saw them and a view of the now frenetic Place Blanche in its 1897 guise as green and light, adorned with graceful long skirts and wide, confident hats.

With one last look at the spiny, febrile Jane Avril of the Lautrec poster and the actual photos of his Goulue, you might now return to the funicular and down to the furious presence of motorized Paris.

⋖§ Est-ce Que Vous Parlez Anglais?

There are too obvious advantages in speaking or even stumbling through the local language. If you can't manage for lack of time or inclination to learn or are one of those Anglos whose tongue and vocal chords are stubbornly xenophobic, take comfort from the fact that the usual tourist routes provide some sort of English. If you're the sort who prefers the offensive, present the challenge of the above little phrase vigorously, as if it were your due to be addressed in English. If you prefer a more subtle approach, carry your map and guidebook in a conspicuous manner. This often solicits a surprising amount and quality of English, or, at least, slows down the French. Where there is no possibility of verbal exchange, gestures can serve surprisingly well depending on one's degree of imagination and in inverse ratio, the degree of inhibition. And console yourself with the fact that a foreign language is like an opera libretto, more intelligent, beautiful and even witty if you don't know what is being said. The wide gestures, the passionate singing phrases, the conspiratorial whispers, the exigent repetitions are infinitely better as possible masterpieces than what they are, an argument with the plumber or a dispute over the "doneness" of a Camembert.

The lack of a language has to be paid for not only in bits of ego but in hard cash. Trying to understand the explanation for what seems to be an overcharge distracts you, unless you have godlike poise, from making the necessary calculations. And if your calculations prove correct—you have been overcharged—how are you going to argue, particularly when a big, noisy wave of foreign words comes crashing down on you? The likelihood is that you will pay and the cost should be anticipated, added to miscellaneous travel costs like overtipping, coins dropped into poor boxes, wine for *clochards*, the sweater that is cheaper in your local department store, the souvenirs that make overweight charges and later, accuse you of having been out of your mind when you bought them.

One of the very minor charms of our times is to see how the English language pushes up hardy little weeds in foreign soil, and how those weeds are distorted or enhanced into exotica. "Franglais," which has been abrading to shrillness the piping elderly voices of the Académie, with its "weekend," "smoking" (for the jacket), "breakfast," "snack bar," "lunch," "speekaire" (for narrator), "pullover" or, more simply "pulls" for sweaters, flourishes on in spite of the purists. Some cafés now make "Milk Shackes," modern household objects are sold in "Le Home Contemporain," one of the *bateaux-mouches* is called "le Hudson," an invitation to drinks is called "un coctel," and the newest, smart places to mash yourself against other people and tight walls are les "pubs" and les "drugstores." The shops springing up in great numbers full of young, hard, geometric clothing, as if a girl were a well-designed box or a tasteful page of print (or the other extreme, a limp, skimpy undershirt) are called "Bus Stop," "Snob," "Madd," "Le Knack," "Texas Ranch," "Minny," a name to which Paris has given a chic it lost or never had here. Shoes for this crowd are sold at "Flash." Men's shops are even more doggedly Anglo: "Auld Reekie," "Mayfair," "Today," "The White House" and hearty tweedy names like "Tedd" and "Bill" straight out of what we Americans know as Marlboro country, bursting with impossible and suspect masculinity.

Mixtures and semitranslations produce peculiar results, too. An eating stall which makes "le vrai hamburger" also grills the equally "vrai hot dog" or pushes them up in class as *"franckforts chaudes."* American Express (as nurse and sanctuary for thousands of Americans it should know better) bears signs concerning the "encashment" of checks, while one restaurant in Montmartre englishes coq *au vin* into "Cock wine."

A light knowledge of French teaches one soon that it can be a language of flourishes and hyperbole. "J'étais ravie d'être avec vous" means a pleasant, casual lunch and, "je suis désolé, Madame," is a compliment to your good manners when you call to cancel a restaurant reservation. The excess can take a sharp reverse turn and, become, instead, the most exaggerated of understatements. *Il ne fait pas chaud* means you wear all your sweaters in July. Someone who *n'est pas aimable* is a thoroughgoing louse. And watch the word *honnête.* It often describes an ordinary meal or an ordinary wine but touched by a fine talent for bending words and meanings, it casts an aura of painstaking virtue, a modest seriousness which may or may not really exist. Sometimes, the word "honest" acts as unspoken apology; if your host takes you to a restaurant which is cheaper than one he thinks you think you should be taken to, he extolls his choice as "honest." On the other hand, if you take him to a restaurant of his choice, too expensive for its zinc bar—old water-pipes decor and limited menu, he'll tell you the ambience and the lazy kitchen are "honest." A wine a cut above *ordinaire* and not good enough to be really good is *honnête.* As you can see, it is a useful word, somehow linked with money and usually the saving thereof.

3 Tuesday

(*Most museums closed*)

NORTHWARD WALK

The Métro station of Strasbourg-St. Denis leaves you at the corner where the 2nd, 3rd, 9th and 10th arrondissements meet, an indigenous core of working-class Paris and irresistibly alluring as a locus for Paris-singer nostalgia. It was not always exclusively working class; like other similar areas, it grew up in the style of feudal villages, as great houses set in low, redolent agglomerations of craftsmen, vintners, food merchants, abbeys, the working poor and the mendicant poor. The flow westward of money, given initial impetus by the decision of Louis XIV to establish his court in Versailles, left much of the east of Paris (and the north and south) long stretches of decayed grand houses and courts worn down to slums; blank, blind warehouses with teeming lost hollows hiding behind them; abattoirs, cemeteries and, farther north, the hard new sheen of industry.

Almost immediately as you leave the station, a huge ornate arch presents itself, the Porte St. Denis and a very short distance eastward, its twin, the Porte St. Martin. They were built in honor of Louis XIV within two years of each other (1672, 1674), both replacing the fortified old gates in the city wall built by Charles V in the 14th century. Though the gate of St. Martin bears, among its decorations, an unbelievable figure of Louis XIV as Hercules, dressed only in a club and a long, curly 17th century wig (Paris always enjoyed dressing up, or down), the Porte St. Denis is more splendid. It is covered with the symbols of the triumphs of Louis le Grand and marked grandly, LUDOVICO MAGNO, an improvement by Napoleon I who admired things Roman. Porte St. Denis is deservedly the fancier and more important gateway, leading into what is now the Rue du Faubourg St.

Denis, a long time ago the splendid avenue along which the royal funeral processions marched on their way to the basilica at St. Denis (page 145) and, in the reverse direction, for regal displays of victory and conquest riding to triumphal ceremonies at Notre Dame.

Now the intersection is a commonplace of shop fronts and traffic. The Boulevard St. Denis was and is one of the centers for inexpensive sex, probably a very old one since the gates of the city must have been a reasonable place to find strangers a long way from home, with money to spend. In more recent years, a certain amount of fame attached itself to the Rue Blondel, a small street just south of the gate, where knowing tourists—and Parisians— enjoyed the pleasures of imaginative brothels. Now they are closed, illegal, but their aura lingers on in the surrounding streets, and some of the unhurried women.

Find the Rue de Cléry and wander, for a few minutes, the triangle of streets between it and Boulevard Bonne Nouvelle. Stop to listen to the Babel of foreign languages that emerges from the small hotels on Rue Beauregard, to look at the almost derelict church, Notre Dame de Bonne Nouvelle, where Anne of Austria, the wife of Louis XIII and ultimately the mother of Louis XIV, prayed through long years of sterility, or more likely neglect, for a child and heir to the throne. Notice the stairs on Rue de la Lune, the metal uprights rusted and shaggy, the handrail kept smooth, black and shining with the polish of a million hands. Follow Rue de la Lune, a famous "sin" street now grown tired to the Rue de la Ville-Neuve. You are standing on what was once an artificial height (Beauregard got its name from the views it afforded) made of every kind of garbage that houses, mills and vineyards could dump. Houses and garbage mountain were razed in the early 17th century, and in order to lure respectable people to the famously noxious area it was advertised that craftsmen and merchants would, if they made "La Ville-Neuve sur Gravois" their neighborhood, be free of taxation. It must have been a powerful lure: by the end of the 17th century it was a quarter of the prosperous and intellectual. Corneille lived here, as did one of Molière's brothers who had kept the family name of Poquelin, and the banker Necker (from 1766 to 1789) and his wife whose literary gatherings each Friday included such guests as Diderot and Voltaire, and possibly the young daughter of the household, later to be known as Madame de Staël. The neighborhood also yielded to the guillotine its first victim, a householder of the Rue de la Ville-Neuve.

The Rue Notre Dame de la Recouvrance, like the others, flashes a noble bit of mansard roof and fine grillwork on old houses that hang onto each other, worn out by the nagging of time. The remains of these houses are usually inside silent courts but tenement street-floor kitchens and workshops, safe in the privacy of so narrow and forgotten a street, freely give out cooking odors, the cry of babies, the slap on the cheek of an older child.

Make your way to the bigger, more alert Rue Poissonnière (called that because it was part of the ageless route of fish and fishermen from the Channel to Les Halles), past the bakeshops and snack bars and, above all, the piles of inexpensive knitwear, each in its plastic bag in window after window, demonstrating that Paris is still a city of neighborhood métiers. Cross the Rue des Petits Carreaux to the Rue d'Aboukir, again crowded with knit goods and clothing houses, among them the house in which Napoleon lodged for a while before his flight into glory. His shadow appears again on Rue Réaumur, whose dull face won't tell you that Napoleon's Josephine lived here when she was Josephine de Beauharnais and that it was here that her son, later appointed viceroy of Italy by his famous stepfather, was born. On the north side of Réaumur strange angles and slices of small streets appear. The Rue du Nil, with scraped blue walls of buildings sloping inward and outward, the movement and color of sea, leads into the angled curve of Rue de Damiette and Rue des Forges, a no-man's-land of warehouses, blanked windows and tight grills. If you can see these alleys extending back through the present trucks and warehouses of France-Soir on Réaumur into the Place du Caire and proliferating into myriad warrens of hovels, you will have some idea of the extent of the most famous of Cour des Miracles, the meshwork of reeking paths and dens described by Victor Hugo in *Notre-Dame de Paris*. It was an academy of vice which teemed at night with the thieves and prostitutes, the fake blind, the fake crippled, the fake diseased—the "miracle" was the sudden cure they experienced each evening—who paid part of their earnings to a supreme chieftain, who obeyed only their own rules and even spoke their own language. (It was probably from the name of one of their illustrious tribesmen that the word "argot" was derived.)

In 1667 the first chief of police in Paris closed off all the approaches, sent the inhabitants to prisons or hospitals (fairly synonymous terms in those days) and demolished the web, soon to be replaced by new streets.

On the Rue du Caire (if you wondered, these streets were named in honor of Napoleon's victories in Egypt) there are several entrances to the Passage du Caire, one set of glass-covered shopping promenades fashionable and favored throughout the 19th century: the sun was filtered, the rain kept out, there was little dust and no traffic, the shops were close together and refreshment places handy for a cup of chocolate and a bit of gossip. Although it now holds an undistinguished set of shops, mainly knits and a concentration of flimsy *fantaisie* decorations like large papier-mâché sea horses, peacock feathers, tin trees and wax hydrangeas, it is an enjoyable ramble leading into and off several streets, particularly pleasing at lunch time in August, when you will have the quiet, glassy paths to yourself, the shops closed, no sound but your own footsteps. You might try to find your way out via Rue Ste. Foy, an unexpected small triangle of trees and, if you hadn't noticed before, Algerian names and faces, speaking and bargaining in Arabic and odd French, in odd dry voices.

Back through the fruit stalls, the fish and fowl and a few old, proud shops of Rue des Petits Carreaux, into Rue St. Sauveur, a curved, narrow run of small hotels you wouldn't want to stay in and small restaurants with big loud jukeboxes in which you probably wouldn't choose to eat. In a once-handsome court, which now seems to have been scooped out by a dirty hand, an old palace has been converted into a school for girls, offering music and design classes. Try to look in, but watch out for the little girl of about eight or nine who will chase you out, shouting, "Go! Now! Immediately! Get out!"—then demonstrating her contempt by peeing on the sidewalk before your eyes, continuing with, "If you don't get out, I'll have my father beat you up." They run out of gentility early here.

As you've walked these streets you will have noticed the kind of gnarled, indestructible aged such neighborhoods breed: slow, spare and dour, clinging to each other and to worn, never-full shopping reticules. The *clochards* prefer to cling, instead, to the handles of old baby carriages in which they carry their possessions and the paper and bottles they hope to resell. The carriage consists

of a body made of old boxes or torn cardboard cartons, the wheels
are of different sizes off different vehicles, the handle an improvi-
sation of broom handle and bits of old piping. It isn't usually
acknowledged but the clever workable carts may be the original
example and source of *Art Trouvé.*

If it means anything to you, go to the corner of Rue St. Sauveur
and Rue Dussoubs, where you will find the house in which Carlo
Goldoni, the Italian playwright and teacher of Italian to the
daughters of Louis XV, died at the age of eighty-six; or stay with
St. Sauveur and its small hotels at numbers 27, 29 and 33 trying to
picture who? what? how much? Rue Grenata is much like the
others except that it has a Tunisian pastry shop at number 52, and
a slatternly hotel, this time called by someone with a sense of
irony, Hotel of Industry, and a fruity history which encompasses a
hospice founded in 1200 for pilgrims and for those travelers who,
one way or another, were delayed, and found the gates of the city
closed. To judge from Chaucer, there were few as lusty and fun-
loving as a gang of pilgrims and voyagers and when, early in the
15th century, an acting company rented one of the halls of the
hospice for the performance of mystery plays, they turned into
bawdy farces within a short time. François I, he of the deceptively
humorous nose in the Clouet painting, closed the theater and the
high-jinks moved on.

Follow Réaumur to Sentier and then right on that street where
the businesses seem a little more prosperous, the houses more
recently painted and the scraps of past splendor larger; here a
protrusion of balconies covered in glass and ironwork, there handsome curly-haired, bearded old heads, sometimes a Neptune, sometimes a leering old Bacchus; at number 32 a 17th century mansion
whose majestic entrance is guarded by lions' heads. On this street
lived the future Marquise de Pompadour when she was still
married to Le Normant d'Etoiles. When she left him to become a
royal favorite he took another nearby house on this same street
and to his new house he brought an Opéra dancer, less flighty or
ambitious than her predecessor. She hung on as mistress until La
Pompadour died, when finally the man who at some time must
have been called the "Marquis de Pompadour" felt free to marry
his ballerina.

This might be the time to pick up a snack or sandwich in one of
the places on Réaumur (striving diligently to look like 42nd Street

in New York City) or in any one of the sea of chairs along the boulevards immediately northward. Depending on the usual tourist exigencies—time, energy, feet, weather or the heavy shadow of the Louvre not yet visited—there are several possibilities that open out of this area. You can hang around the busy boulevards to see what the movie houses are showing and watch the crowd, different from that of the Opéra complex and more varied. You can shop for undistinguished clothing on the Boulevard Bonne Nouvelle, one of whose awnings proudly displays a sign of Levi Straus and Co., San Francisco (California), U.S.A. You can stop in at the Concert Mayol (page 303) or continue westward to the banking area in the 2nd (page 35) or visit the Musée des Arts et Métiers in the 3rd or continue on into the 9th and 10th arrondissements.

The Rue du Faubourg Poissonnière, once part of the fish route from sea to market in a delightful suburb of vineyards and small dance halls among orchards, leads to the Rue Bergère which specialized in another of the local traditional métiers, this time furs, though the man for whom the street was named was a dyer. Off to the left, a couple of closed-off streets, actually large courts, which call themselves variously *cours,* or *squares* (an interesting word to try to pronounce in French) or *cités,* as in the angled Cité Bergère where Heinrich Heine lived for a while. On the Rue du Conservatoire stands the National Conservatory of Dramatic Arts, originally a conservatory of music (late 18th century) to which a school of drama was soon added. The music section was moved elsewhere early in this century (page 165), taking with it as director Gabriel Fauré, one of a distinguished line going back to the almost indestructible Cherubini. Continue on Conservatoire past several modest hotels used by Europeans who count their money carefully; some of them medaled with the badges of auto clubs and tourist organizations of Holland, Portugal, Germany, Belgium and one, as if anticipating the bright enamel plaques, suggests their design in classic, female heads veiled in bright yellow paint. Immediately on the left, on Rue Richer, one of the leitmotivs of the neighborhood appears: a star of David on a *charcuterie* sign, which in addition explains itself as *"Boucherie Cachère."* These butchers and grocers who advertise "Oriental specialties" are recently arrived North African Jews making a line, light in one area, heavy in another, from an ancient *Juiverie* on the Ile de la Cité northward through the Marais (page 110) and the shops around the Place de la République into the concentration around the Belleville Métro station (page 139). Passy in the 16th is an entirely other kettle of Jew, an astronomic distance from the bearded old men in the Marais or the sloe-eyed nimble children of Belleville.

Turn right under the crumbling arch and gates which once closed off the Cité de Trévise, a minor late Place des Vosges, cut through and built up over a hundred years ago, later collapsed and now being slowly revived with repairs and fresh paint. The street of small businesses and flats leads into a tiny square with a tight green bouquet of park from whose center sprouts a Three Graces fountain, the girls sandwiched between two ornate stone bowls in the airless Victorian style. Surrounding them stands an even row of neat houses eschewing the stone excesses of an earlier day, distinctly apart in mood from the Folies Bergère, its close neighbor. A couple of houses have been converted into hotels, one of which pleasantly echoes the solid Englishness of the square by maintaining a "Duke's Bar." A short jog right brings you to the curiosities of La Mamma (page 274) and on to the Square de Montholon, heavy with trees and flowers held together by a wilderness of grill-work design—arabesques, peacock tails, shields, free of taste or restraint, both square and the used-up elegance of decoration full of the sweet-sour odor of a place out of season.

Come back on Rue Montholon and look for a magnificent gilded key held forward by lovely curves of iron above a locksmith's shop. (A long time ago it was decided that these signs were to be flattened securely to walls because they dented too many heads in the crumbling of old brick, and the loosening—like old teeth in old gums—of bolts and nails. But this ruling was as lightly regarded as Louis XV's edict, repeated and repeated, that the city not grow beyond the limits he set; and the later edicts, exhumed and repeated through the years, that buildings be cleaned periodically. Only recently, with some recalcitrant exceptions, has this latter ruling been treated seriously.) Where Montholon meets the Faubourg Poissonnière, a curious anomaly for supposedly anti-Puritan Paris: a hiring and placing agency which has separate entrances for male and female employees; also, two medium-awful small hotels whose counterparts on Rue des Messageries have been brought up in class with fresh paint and bright red awnings, demonstrating again the magic of good makeup on a worn face.

Rue La Fayette is a large shopping street of no great interest, but it does lead into the Grands Boulevards to the west. If you head in that direction, you might notice the Cadet Métro station which retains its tall-grasses-in-high-winds 1900's style, the Hôtel Splendid La Fayette, smooth and assured in its dress of long windows and embroidery of sculptured stone and grillwork, remarkable only as the prototype of thousands of buildings which began to fill the city early in this century, maintaining some of the mannerisms of early houses and adding to them a bit of this and that. Near it the Restaurant des Diamantaires (page 282), whose bar is closed, the sign says, to all but regular clients, diamond dealers who conduct a considerable amount of business over an array of Turkish, Greek, and North African Jewish dishes. A shop of "Chine Antique" sits on Le Peletier off La Fayette and, as if in protest against the names on the surrounding buildings, and a Sephardic synagogue, the stationery shop of a "Widow Goy."

You might continue from Square Montholon northward to a large square which was named for Franz Liszt and, looming over them, the neoclassic bulk of the church of St. Vincent de Paul. Carefully balanced bits of park rise with the levels of the stairway, shaded quiet places for resting among the well-packed babies, the sensibly dressed mothers and the old grandfathers in berets talking together in an elusive combination of French and Yiddish. Entering the Rue d'Hauteville you will find a restaurant, the Nout-Bedaine whose name and flavors are distinctly of the area. Walk on into Rue de Chabrol, simultaneously a street slipping down and climbing up. KLM has an office here, and one row of newly painted houses glitters above the sloping, venerable Café au Petit Bougnat, attached in the usual Auvergnat fashion to its function of selling Bois et Charbons.

You should soon be at the corner of Rue de Chabrol and Boulevard de Magenta, very near the joining with Rue du Faubourg St. Denis. There are indications that this was part of a highway used in Merovingian times; it was certainly an important part of the route which led northward out of the city since early medieval times, passing a leprosarium (and its "Ferme," as the nearby passages recall) where the Hospital St. Lazare now stands.

Following the Rue du Faubourg St. Denis southward, you are in a long, vigorous marketplace, glistening with fish and piled with breaded pigs feet. It has a playground with honest-to-God sandpiles, clothing shops, cafés, a snack bar called Le Tout Alger and displays of sound, plain kitchenwares. And then one reaches the *pièce* of the neighborhood, the Rue de Paradis named for a house once occupied, the neighborhood legend has it, by a singularly happy family.

It begins rather modestly, in pallid colors: a couple of beauty salons, a small hotel, a shop of *Farces et Attrapes* very much like Broadway trick and joke shops, except that the scatological noises have a French accent, the fake sausage is labeled *Alsace* and the wax cheese stamped *Brie*. The shine of china and crystal and ceramics soon begins to appear and shortly becomes one uninterrupted dazzle of glasses, dishes, crystal, figurines, lamp bases in a wide range of prices and styles, from the unthinkably "twee"—as the British say—to the creations of Limoges, Baccarat and the stately glass and crystal ware of Daum, all of whom have establishments along Rue de Paradis. (That you are in a traditional métier *quartier* is indicated by the sign on number 30, Compagnie des Cristalleries de St. Louis, which occupies a court of well-kept houses bearing the date 1767.) Before you've reached number 30, however, and unless you're avidly bent on shopping, examine the splendors of a building marked "Choisy le Roi," a turn-of-the-century edifice made hysterical by glass, stone, urns, shields, gilded floral motifs. The gates may be closed, but it is still possible to see the dreamy, romantic fountains, the cupids, the languid ladies all done in ceramic tiles in the vaulted passage leading to the court. The glass-covered court itself has a grand staircase and more of the tiled murals, but the best is outside the gates, a muted, graceful arrangement of women, a bit misty and Japanesy, echoing Whistler.

A few paces away, at number 28, a ceramic tiles atelier shows what it really could and can do in its craft, using the window lintels, the street and its court as showrooms in an awesome display of subjects and styles. In the first court, a skillful bird panel, and a lovely flower panel of leaves and poppies, drooping upward, as only Art Nouveau can, and a set of butterfly panels. The inside court expands the range with Arabic designs in the rich deep blue once very difficult to imitate, an involved late-Renaissance pattern, a blue and white Chinese panel, the birds and flowers of a Japanese screen against a deep gold background, and two charmers of La Belle Epoque: a travel poster and an advertising poster in the

style of Lautrec—gentler though and unhampered by genius—
showing a cushiony lady holding a pink-petticoated lamp filled
with "Saxoleine, the reliable fuel oil."

As it began, the street dims near its end at the Faubourg
Poissonnière. Have a drink inside the stately wood and gilt lettering of the Bar l'Hirondelle on the corner of d'Hauteville or go
back the very short distance to the Cité Paradis and look across at
number 44 for still another example—if the idea is at all support-
able—of the millionth pair of plump neoclassic cliché ladies holding up a balcony. These are called Work and Commerce, stony
beauties of grimy black etched with pigeon streaks. The tempt-
ingly named Cité Paradis doesn't offer much among its ateliers
except an exit to d'Hauteville and, at its dead end, a surprising
facade with a classic pediment and full-length windows leading to
a few stairs, the back of a mansion built in 1776.

The fur companies and workshops continue on in the Rue des
Petites Ecuries, where the royal stables once were—hence the
name—and where Corot died in 1875 (number 56), and in and
out of a maze of passages, alike except for the Passage des Petites
Ecuries, a closed-off, isolated and self-sustaining small village, on
whose adjoining *cour* the legendary 17th century beauty and wit,
Ninon de Lenclos, was supposed to have had a country house. The
Passage has its big publike Brasserie Flo (page 289), the essential
wineshop with its bleary old man, its faded calendar, its pot-bellied
stove and the pile of coal in the back. There are lace-curtained
apartments and no-curtain apartments, a few warehouses, a box
maker, a button maker, a laundry, a grocer, a butcher and through
a narrow opening, the expansive presence of the Rue du Faubourg
St. Denis.

Before that, though, turn into Rue Gabriel Laumain at the side
of the Hotel Violet on the Faubourg Poissonnière which must
have been a place of grandeur once, since shattered by blasts of
doom. The narrow passage widens into a circular place with a
small, no-period chateau which houses what seems to be the
French equivalent of the Newspaper Guild on one side and on the
other, a surprising row of fine houses, now occupied by fur
workshops. Farther along, inside the court of number 30 is the
freight depot of Air France—if you have any doubts, there are
trucks marked FRET near the entrance—with the large dull space
and long counters one expects. But as you walk out you will notice

the regal entrance and experience the feeling that grows with enough walking in Paris: that the streets are stage curtains concealing a wide, vivid diversity of lives—working and domestic— playing out their hours and days in the courts, among the crumbling walls and splintered ornaments of disgraced palaces.

Any self-respecting map will show you that Rue du Faubourg St. Denis and Boulevard de Strasbourg are tied together by alleys. Resist them and make your way back to the station by way of either avenue. If you *must* explore more passages, keep away from the garbage-lined tunnels and go through the Passage Brady, a general shopping area under a glass sky, quite ordinary except for *"Produits Exotiques"* at number 59, where Vietnamese households buy dried mushrooms, curry powders, Vietnamese hot sauces, litchis in cans, tiny noodles and folds of rice paper used in cooking, and strange long transparent somethings that look like crystals. The way to the shop is via a murky stairway, your French and the political situation may make awkwardness; better to just look at the window display.

The broad Boulevard St. Denis, flanked by its arches, roars before you. Just as you get to the juncture with the Boulevard de Strasbourg notice a shoe shop called René. Its glass bends gently and so does the marble and the ironwork, a relic of a padded day when practically nothing had angles. Then order something at a café on the Boulevard, sit awhile and let the surrounding scene come to you; the huge, yellow gate impeding traffic, the traffic impeding pedestrians. To the left is the Théatre de la Renaissance, not one neoclassic ornament neglected: pillars and balconies, putti holding up flowery window frames, laughing masks, naked ladies sprawling and naked ladies whose bottoms are stuffed into stone vases, the whole works surmounted by a lyre. And what had been playing and playing and playing in the house which should have been built for Offenbach? The most angular play of the decade, *Qui a Peur de Virginia Woolf?*

In front of you a scene from an early French movie, those made long before the New Wave splashed and dribbled away. A dark young man in a closely fitted suit and lustrous pointed shoes walks toward the café with a sluttish, dull-faced blond girl, her young roundness already beginning to dissolve. He goes into the café to speak with a friend, leaving her outside. She lets herself be picked up, automatically, listlessly, by another man. Her master comes

out, whistles sharply. The new man looks surprised and foolish for
a moment, then loses himself in the crowd. She comes trotting
back, a shapeless, docile mongrel. He threatens to hit her, but it is
only a playful gesture; he may do it later on a less public street or
decide to be reasonable. Other men do, after all, pay for his new
well-starched shirts and big chunks of cuff link.

CANALS
(10th, 19th, Pantin & Aubervilliers)

The canals of Paris are to the tourist's Seine what the kitchen
and clutter, the sinks and ovens are to the poise and indomitably
starched linens of a three-star restaurant. They are obscure and
hardworking, sometimes shabby, sometimes fresh and charming.

The Canal St. Martin (which was for a while decorated with
a large plaster model of an elephant that Napoleon planned to cast
in bronze and place on the Place de la Bastille as soon as he had
conquered India) starts at the Seine under the north end of
the Pont d'Austerlitz, slips underground, then unseen and unheard,
it accompanies the northward march of Boulevard Richard Lenoir
and Boulevard Jules Ferry to emerge between the Quais de Jemmapes and de Valmy. It then parallels the Faubourg St. Martin,
ducks under the Place Stalingrad and the square that accompanies
it, comes up fatter as the Bassin de la Villette, mingles with the
waters of the Ourcq River to become the Canal de l'Ourcq, and at
the meeting of the animal market and the abattoirs, thrusts a long
finger northwestward, the Canal St. Denis. It leaves a bit of itself
in the Bassin d'Aubervilliers and rejoins the Seine near the suburb
of St. Denis. The l'Ourcq continues on through the near suburb of
Pantin, into the northeastern suburb areas with listless streets and
pretty names like Bobigny and Pavillons.

A glance at the map will show what a long, slow loop of the
Seine is avoided by the barges that ride the canal. Although their
number and the variety of freight they carry has diminished with
the advent of faster transport, they still convey a good amount of
building material and coal into the city, and a day saved is money
saved. The Seine in the center of the city can act as a less cluttered
tourist route for the *bateaux-mouches*, as raison d'être for the quiet
old bridges and the fanfare of the Alexandre III bridge, as mirror
and soft light for the stately beauties of the islands, the Louvre

and Notre Dame and as blue edging for the green of the Trocadéro Park.

The very beginning of the canal is of no great interest except if you come on it by surprise, unprepared for its existence, or if you can picture the images of history. Imagine it first as merely a moat (now the Bassin d'Arsenal) in the city walls built by Charles V in the 14th century. Then leap nearly five hundred years to the time of Napoleon I who caused the canals to be dug and to run along uncovered ramps. Napoleon III and his busy Baron Haussmann erased the slopes, dropped the waters and covered them with streets and squares where that was expedient.

The most appealing—almost winsome—section of the canals is the Quai de Jemmapes area from the Rue du Faubourg du Temple, near the Place de la République, to the Place Stalingrad. On both sides, the traffic rattles by, people dash around buying bread, newspapers and shoes in the shops below the uniformly gray, uniformly tall, uniformly shuttered houses. Where there might normally be thickened clots of traffic in the center of the avenue, suddenly rows of trees and benches under them. Babies in carriages, babies on leashes, little boys edging toward the water to see how far they can get before the maternal voice pulls them back, old fishermen still trying after fifty years of scratching the Seine's reluctant depths, the absorbed reader of yesterday's newspaper, the bum dipping up water with which to wash his face and feet. Two stubby, shabby concierges croon about the good old days, not wholly absorbed, though, because they have to watch the comings and goings in the houses whose destinies they control, as queen-wardens. (Police spies too, the concierge-haters say.) At frequent intervals the small, elementary bridges like pieces of construction toy vault the calm water. On the narrow passage a wide barge makes its leisured, dignified passage from lock to lock. No matter how scabrous its paint, or shaky its tiny house, or faded the pants on its line or shrill its inevitably shaggy dog, each barge is gentled from lock to lock as the fat lady of a circus is carefully taken up into a plane, or a baby grand hoisted to a new apartment. The precision and cossetting that goes into the moving this large, cumbersome and expensive object is cheered on by boys hanging over the bridges, stealing a few minutes from school or lunch.

If your progress along the Canal St. Martin with its city-country

lyricism and anarchronistic pace of barges and the slow hand-
turning of wheels to open and close locks becomes a bit repetitious, take the Avenue Richer to its meeting with the Hôpital St.
Louis. A large aggregate of restorations and additions, it still
strongly suggests the dignified style of its founding date, early in
the 17th century. The hospital marked the recognition, during the
plague of 1606, that contagion had to be isolated. In earlier
plague periods patients had been dumped into the already overcrowded Hôtel-Dieu, several in a bed, stretched on the floors,
heaped in corners, contaminating those not already plague-ridden.
Entertainment and music in the streets did not dispel the plague
or the fear of it, prayer and amulets proved feeble protection, so
Henry IV had an isolation hospital built and named it for St.
Louis (page 146) who had died in Tunis of the plague. (Returning
to the canal, you can walk an even more lugubrious route, the Rue
des Ecluses St. Martin, which marks the southern edge of the
square where the famous gibbet of Montfaucon, an efficient
structure which could hang several dozen men simultaneously and
dangle their rotting limbs, stood from the 13th to the 18th
century.)

At the other end of the Canal St. Martin, in the Place Stalingrad, stands the Rotonde de la Villette, a serious and massive
building suggesting a greater size than its actual bulk. It is one of
the few surviving tollhouses of a neglected master of architecture,
an original and a visionary for his time, the 18th-century Claude-
Nicolas Ledoux. Although it follows the neoclassic favored in his
time, the building bears, in the proportions of its rectangular
stones, its solidity and careful balances, the distinct stamp of his
individual style. Furthermore, it is a curious structure to find
partially concealed by trees, wreathed in noise and exhaust fumes
of surrounding traffic, unnoticed by the people who dash to and
from the Stalingrad Métro station to shop on the Rue de Tanger,
or the animated, small food shops on Rue d'Aubervilliers, to meet
friends in the plain cafés on Rue du Département or the couscous
restaurants, or to go to sleep in the scratched houses of alleys like
the Passage Goix.

It takes an ardent canal-lover to walk the whole meshwork.
Some of it can be done by car, some of it cannot, and the areas
closed to cars are increasing with the building of peripheral
highways around Paris and changes in the flow of traffic. The most

reasonable way to see the upper reaches of the canal (the meeting of the Canal St. Denis and the Canal de l'Ourcq and eastward) is to have a friend in Paris, with a car, with time, with the intrepidity to wander along a narrow unfenced path beside the bank and the control to back out along the same narrow path when it folds up into railroad siding and no place in which to turn around. He should also have the talent for arranging good weather. Riding and walking in the long oblique light of the setting sun of summer reveal a world of strange beauties: a high basin of water accompanying a bright, ugly red and white canal-tender's house, exactly like those at rural railroad crossings, and like those, with geraniums in the windows, fifteen feet below, another section of waterway flows past a tiny island park that surrounds a neat handkerchief of garden, shaded by two leafy trees. In the distance a fresh spur of building painted brilliant orange leaps into the gold-streaked blue sky. Huge bins along the canal sides glitter and blaze with the light reflected from their immense heaps of broken glass and the sandpiles along the canal take on the deep shadows and glowing peaks of sand dunes. Across the canal, on a grassy slope, a group of the neighborhood men share a bottle of wine and talk quietly. A short distance beyond them, a family and their dog are taking their Sunday walk; they walk silently and gravely, people in a surrealist landscape.

Returning to the Porte de la Villette, entering the suburb of Aubervilliers along the Canal St. Denis you come soon to the meeting of the Rue de la Gare with the Quai Gambetta. If you have the nose and stomach for it, this is the place to see Calcutta in Paris or worse, because Calcutta doesn't have to endure a Paris winter. Leave your car—locked—on the street and follow the children carrying water from the street pump or, if there is no business at the pump, follow the stench to a shamble of huts made of anything that might make a shelter: old doors, discarded slats of wood, tin, cardboard, bits of canvas, tied, pasted and nailed together in a low, stinking warren. An improved job or house-pride has painted some of the mean, crooked little walls and traced large house numbers and names on others. There are no toilets or outhouses; the canal and the edges of the tall sand heaps make both toilet and landscape for these Portuguese workers who do some of the foul underpaid labor which Frenchmen scorn. Unmolested by health and housing authorities who find it easier to forget about them, they make their lives in this reeking *Bidonville* (a *bidon* is a tin container, flattened for use as roof covering in this sort of colony), undepressed by it. On a pleasant afternoon the children are out scrabbling in the sandpiles, running in and out of the rambling secretive crevices between the shacks; a few men play cards on a crude homemade table, as small as everything must be in these cells, or throw coins in a matching game; the women gossip as they hang their laundry across two uprights stuck in the mud. One is appalled and moved by their liveliness—what must it have been for these people in Salazar's Paradise if they are so pleased to be here?

NOTE: As has been suggested, going by car is of course the best, but a combination of Métro, bus lines and stretches of walking will get you to these places; it takes map studying and a careful reading of bus signs when you get out at the Porte de la Villette or the Pantin Métro stations.

4 Walk on the Art Nouveau Side

Art Nouilles (noodles) they call it, but the Parisian took a new appreciative look at his old Métro stations when he found that the Museum of Modern Art in New York City was willing to pay a sizable amount of dollars for one member of the graceful family fathered by Hector Guimard. They may go in time, but neither being raised to "art" nor recent modernization in the Métro system has yet made much difference in the stations to the north where the whole structure retains its 1900 design, like the vaults of glass and iron that cover the elevated stops at Stalingrad, La Chapelle and Anvers and the flowing spaces of the Métro and railroad stations of the Gare St. Lazare. Art Nouveau buildings dot the city, particularly in areas like the 7th and the 16th where expansion and building were very active in its time and, of course, there is the superb gathering of Art Nouveau which is Maxim's (page 257). One charmer, cheap and easy to find, is the Hotel Céramique on the east side of Avenue de Wagram, about halfway between the Etoile and the Place des Ternes, a gently curved building espaliered with graceful ceramic greenery and flowers, a restrained effort of the architect Lavirotte, referred to later.

There is, though, a concentration on the non-Bohemian Left Bank that will give you the mild and sensible as well as the wild and genius-struck of Art Nouveau architecture, and a walk through one kind of bourgeois Paris. Like and unlike the others, it lacks the complacency of the 16th (page 130), is less self-conscious than the St. Germain classiness nearby and livelier than the slightly decaying, too-quiet Parc Monceau area.

By bus or Métro get to Les Invalides. Almost immediately west of the car-ridden Esplanade is the Boulevard de La Tour-Maubourg. Follow it from the Seine, peering wherever you can,

into the courts and grand houses like those on Rue de Grenelle
and Rue de Varenne, not far away. Rue St. Dominique curves
jauntily out of the Boulevard and reveals the sudden spray of the
base of the Eiffel Tower, the iron legs of the gaunt giant that
looms over the neighborhood. St. Dominique which has no particular character, except shyness, near the Boulevard St. Germain,
becomes one of the most amiable of streets west of the Invalides.
It has the welcoming ambience of the main street of a small, prosperous town which hasn't hurried especially to meet the 20th century. It abounds with well-dressed, well-fed children out with
Maman to do the shopping in cheese and butter shops tiled in turn
of the century designs. Small cafés and warm caves of wineshops
alternate with good busy greengrocers, one or two antique shops, a
tasteful gift boutique, many piled-high bakeshops. One of them is
a proud ancient with bright red lettering on a ground of gold:
"*Sp.té de Croissants Chauds à Toute Heure, Panification Hy-
giénique.*" At number 93, you'll find an arrangement that speaks
of the density and age of the city, courts beyond courts beyond
courts. Turn left, then, on the secluded Rue Amélie, a village
street, and return on St. Dominique toward and across Avenue
Bosquet. Suddenly, the very French provincial street turns Italian
at a minute heavy-arched square and its necessary Fontaine
de Mars.

The Rue Sédillot is a quiet street burdened with stone drupes
and drapes, neoclassic bits and a few touches of Art Nouveau which
reach astonishing and beautiful complexity in the Liceo Italiano
Leonardo da Vinci at number 12 by the architect Lavirotte. The
mansard roofs have been scooped softly into long shield shapes,
the horizontal wooden seam of the windows bent and curved into
sinuous diagonals. Long, slender stems climb the windows and end
in full, stone roses, ferns swell to thick, leafy brackets echoed in
the grillwork of interlaced vines and tendrils. The entrance rises to
a deep high cushion of ornament starting above the second floor,
so light in movement and grace that it appears to soar upward to
the pensive, sad Pre-Raphaelite lady who floats among her waves
and weeds and grasses of hair like the drowned Ophelia who seems
to have been one of the obsessions of this art.

The Avenue Rapp is a museum of Art Nouveau buildings,
among them an outrageous flight to the outer shores of the style
and maybe a masterpiece. From the Square Rapp, immediately off
the big Place, look down the avenue toward the creamy well-fed

curves, as organic as plump roast chicken or the baby fat on a round child. At about number 37, the paunchiness gives way to the contours of breaking waves and textured sections—possibly meant to suggest shore and sand—under the peaks of the billows. Now, turn into the Square Rapp. Some of it gone, leaving only its shadow on the wall, some of it going, there is—there was—an amazing spread of latticework in complex curves of *trompe-l'oeil* perspective, and guarding it, a once-beautiful iron gate, its musical turns and gestures sagging to the ground. (Coming on this wall at twilight when it has turned to cobwebs in a gray cave is terrifying.) The house at number 3 Square Rapp is emblazoned with stonework as Celtic lettering, as cobra heads, roots, and squat urns. The musical grillwork balconies like arpeggios appear here, inevitably resting on broad pedestals which are, in turn, held by a garland of fruits and heads (never to be omitted, either) and dwindling into long-stemmed roses. The corner of the building as it meets the lattice-work is a turret shaped like fluted scallions. It must have been an opulent gem of a building, especially when the deep, lustrous tones of a few remaining tiles covered the whole building. This one has everything, one thinks; where can you go from here, this summing-up of fairy-tale landscape in stone and iron? Walk around the corner to number 29 Avenue Rapp, an engulfment and best viewed from across the street or, if the trees aren't too leafy, from the outdoor table of a small café of a street that opens into Rapp at that point. The signature on the building is again that of Lavirotte, the date is 1901. There is something Victorian in the deep window frames overarched by Romanesque elements and separated by Egyptian columns. The dark brown stone, textured all over in coils and frenzies, breaks at one place into a large, stylized Chinese wave under a balcony which is itself a set of approaching, retreating iron waves. The patterns change from one section, one story, of the building to another; an agitated rush of metal boughs on one balcony gives way to the solidity of columns on another. The sculpturesque shapes of nature are used—a set of columns of endive and bunches of asparagus in stone. This vegetable garden nests two oxen, whose heads support a central balcony and numerous odd insects embedded in lozenges on the surface of the building. The king of the mythical insects is the entrance whose design in glass and wood makes an enormous mouth and eyes, those of an outsize ant or fly in a science-fiction movie. Around the doorway, the hair of the triste, lovely Art Nouveau lady shelters the pubescent nude figures of a girl and boy on either side of her. Above her, the surface of yellowish stone is inlaid, embraced, stroked and strangled by panels of darker stone reaching down from the upper stories. In short, the whole is an insatiable, manic structure, touched with genius and like the facade of the Cathedral of Orvieto, it works if you are indulgent.

Number 29 marks the peak of Art Nouveau architecture viewing. For more restrained examples of the style, one superb, try Passy (the 16th—page 132) or nearer at hand, the local streets, particularly the meeting of Dupont des Loges and Edmond Valentin, and that inescapable Art Nouveau fancy, the Eiffel Tower, always with you and particularly close from the Rue de Monttessuy where you can almost stand, like a corn, on one of its feet.

◄§ Des Belles Choses et des Curiosités

Paris polyphony from a street table among the sartorial, sexual and tonsorial varieties of the Deux Magots: directly ahead the sure, monolithic calm of the 11th century St. Germain tower. To the right, across the Boulevard St. Germain, the frantic warrens of Le Drugstore in the current style of white and gold innards arranged for the peristalsis of one-way traffic and ulcered with plaster eyes and mouths. Around the corner from it, the Supermag's racks of inexpensive T-shirts, very *ordinaire* wines, hillocks of cheese and sausage, *cassoulet* in cans and disturbing rods of *quenelles* frozen in thick, bellicose plastic. Toward the left, the ubiquitous fountain of the Four Green Graces, the gift of Richard Wallace (page 246).

In the patch of park at the side of the church, a Picasso head believed by many to be of Apollinaire, for whom a short, almost-adjoining street is also named. St. Germain is obviously the appropriate place for a street and statue of the poet, qua poet and intellectual, and because he lived on the Boulevard near the Rue St. Guillaume. But according to a Picasso ex-mistress, this is not the head of Guillaume Apollinaire at all; it is that of an ex-ex mistress thrust at an exigent "Commemorate Apollinaire" committee by the irritated master. (A close look at the legend will show that it is marked "to" Apollinaire, not "of.") Directly left, at the corner of the poet and Rue Bonaparte, a hirsute, androgynous café of long dyed hair on male heads brisk pants on female hips; the readers, the writers, active and manqué, the nonstop talkers and a young neighborhood mother in a Rue de Sèvres dress feeding her baby ice cream.

The long wicker baskets like large papoose carriers in which breads are delivered from the bakery to cafés and restaurants.

The 15th century porch of the church of St. Germain l'Auxerrois, once the burial place of royal favorites among sculptors, artists and architects, where church treasures and archives were guarded, whose bells signaled the opening of the St. Bartholomew's Day massacre, and now lost and unnoticed behind the Quai du Louvre, bears at right and left the large, printed stamps of "Liberte, Egalité, Fraternité."

Sunday afternoon on the Wagram side of the Etoile. Spanish maids, Spanish dishwashers, carpenters and roof-tilers meet to exchange news of home, to greet and advise newcomers and, as they talk they pace, unconsciously forming the circular route of the traditional Sunday *paseo* back home.

The sudden, framed view of the Tour St. Jacques from the opening of the Rue Adolphe Adam on the Quai de Gesvres.

The well-rounded French sphinxes that guard the triumphal column celebrating Napoleon's Egyptian campaign, on the Place du Châtelet.

At the Quai de l'Hôtel de Ville and the Rue de Brosse and at about number 100 on Rue de l'Hôtel de Ville, there are often window displays of remarkable, not too small, miniatures of wooden structures (one, recently, a reproduction of a Le Corbusier stairway). These are the work of an ancient society of craftsmen, Les Compagnons du Devoir, who used to—and clearly some still do—make these models as demonstrations of their finished skills, rather like the testing and proof in *Die Meistersinger*.

The obsolutely rigid, formal symmetry of the facade of the church of the Madeleine connecting across the Rue Royale and the Place de la Concorde with the echoing facade of the Chamber of Deputies on the other side of the river.

Crossing the Pont Louis-Philippe from north to south, the sudden astonishment of the Panthéon as huge, flat and unreal, pasted on a wide, flat sky.

The curious fancy of Ste. Geneviève as an angular modern buttress that guards one of the bridges of the Ile St. Louis. A number of the tenants of the island and other Parisians, dislike it as a compounding of nepotism with bad taste and, furthermore, the new Geneviève, they say, was as ineffectual in holding off the Germans as her ancestor was in her time.

The park of the Buttes-Chaumont in the 19th is a place of craggy promontories, rustic paths leading to miniature white temples, deep woods, rich rolling lawns (not to be stepped on, ever), a shaky, unused footbridge high over Byronic rocks, a few patches of the formal gardens essential to a Paris park and a small lake. Compared to the Tuileries, the Luxembourg and the Parc Monceau, it is a romantic wilderness, with sheltered glades for students and lovers, and companionable clearings where the neighborhood mothers and grandmothers meet to chat as they darn and knit, now and then releasing a busy hand to rock a carriage or tuck in the shirt of a little boy. For more festive divertissements than pacing the gravel, the children can take cart rides, buy and eat *gaufres* and watch the ducks and swans on the lake.

The ducks are either too proud or absent-minded to pursue pieces of bread or *gaufre;* they eat what is available at the moment and return to their arcane duck business. The swans are more Parisian, beautiful and aggressive snatchers of *gaufres* from the hands of mesmerized youngsters who giggle nervously and then, staring down at their astonished empty hands, begin to whimper. The thieving swans and the startled children provide considerable pleasure for an old habitué who has a strong feeling for the swans, less for the children and much less for the older boys who, he says, molest and injure the swans. It is his self-imposed role to guard the birds and he spends his days at the lake informing any one willing to listen about a swan that was poisoned, a swan kidnapped, a swan injured, recounting the baleful stories with precise details and dates, like an ancient bard recounting the chronicles of his suffering nation.

5 Wednesday

The **Musée de Cluny** sits inside the juncture of Boulevard St. Germain and Boulevard St. Michel, its entrance at the meeting of Rue du Sommerard and Rue de Cluny. Admission, 1 franc; free on Sundays. The hours are 10 A.M. to 12:45 P.M. (but the guards, savaged by hunger and boredom, will shout you out at 12:30) and 2 P.M. to 5 P.M. The elderly vial of vitriol who mutters curses over the cards and catalogues cannot brook the human face and voice for more than a short period at a time. If you dare, you might look at her wares—if you touch before buying she'll cut your hand off—between 11 A.M. and Noon and 3 P.M. and 4 P.M.

Remote and aloof behind its gates, the Cluny complex draws back in a privacy of age and privilege from the international looniness of its boulevards. Beyond the protective trees it shows first a massive ruined Roman face, that of a Gallo-Roman palace and/or public bathhouse. Probably built early in the 3rd century, it was destroyed in the subsequent invasions. The ruin was rarely completely abandoned, however, serving as cave dwellings and even shops until, early in the 14th century, the abbot of the rich and powerful order of Benedictines of Cluny in Burgundy bought the ruins and the surrounding land to build a pied-à-terre in Paris.

In later centuries the Benedictine house sheltered a distinguished roster of guests. James V of Scotland stayed here when he came to marry Madeleine, the daughter of François I. Mary, the sister of England's Henry the VIII, who had been married at sixteen to the fifty-year-old Louis XII and widowed three months later (the result, it was gossiped of her appetite and his debility), was subjected here to genteel imprisonment by François I who was afraid of her potential role in the royal succession. He arranged to find her with the Duke of Suffolk, forced them into a quick marriage and shipped them back to England.

Ultimately, an antiquarian named Sommerard brought his medieval collection to live with him in the Cluny. On his death in 1842 the state bought the house and collection and, under the supervision of the antiquarian's son, Edmond, organized the museum. It was opened in 1844 and has remained an eminently important and fascinating place for seeing the old crafts dedicated to uses of the church and the castle, worked by patient, awed hands with a passion for perfection.

Other than the Hôtel de Sens, near the Hôtel de Ville, the Cluny is the only medieval private residence left in Paris. It has been extensively restored, but the building surrounding the shaded court still speaks the flamboyant Gothic of stone lacework and finely sculptured ornaments. The interior, much changed, except for its too-medieval lighting, holds a wealth of beautiful silks and embroideries, fragile ivories, masterpieces of wood sculpture; objects for devotions, for the hunt, for war, for the table, for enhancing the female face and, almost above all, tapestries.

One series, made in France (about 1500) is a dream of high life, realistic in detail and remarkably fanciful in its conception, of the late medieval rich in Gardens of Eden—more populous, much more entertaining and considerably less innocent than the Biblical place. The Lady of this idyllic world sweetly spins, or accompanies on the virginals a gentleman playing a recorder. She strokes and kisses a bird while her friend whittles a twig of wood, or embroiders with the silks brought her by a lady-in-waiting. Her arts, her amorous discourse and gentle dalliance are all practiced against a *mille fleurs* background of fresh blue strewn with perfect flowers sheltering perfect little animals, perfectly spaced. Eden, though, takes on suggestions of Earth in a panel which shows the Lady in a bathtub nestled in a leafy bower. Except for the jewels on her neck and an ornamented hood, she seems to be quite nude. Privacy being a comparatively modern invention, except for hermits, the Lady is surrounded by attendants, male and female. The man who plays the recorder modestly averts his eyes, but a page carrying bread (a bath was apparently a festive, ceremonial occasion) appears to be staring, amazed, at the center of attraction. Early 16th century French though it may be, it makes a memorable scene for an old De Mille or new Fellini film, a fine example of the delectable excesses of those *other* disgraceful, lucky people.

This group is scattered through several rooms and in the search there are things which should not be denied a moment: Byzantine silks bearing vital hieratic figures, embroideries of subtle drawing and lissome elegance, among these a minute masterpiece, "The Dream of Merlin," which achieves the delicacy of fine ivory carving. In the tall, well-lit salon VIII, there is a gathering of extraordinary late medieval sculpture. Marie-Madeleine is a soignée, elaborately coiffed lady, her face long-lidded, lightly double-chinned, touched with disdain; surely a superb portrait no matter what the attribution. To balance her livingness is the very Spanish mask of the dead Christ, bled green, exuding decay and the Spanish love of death. The German influence shows in the agitated, spiraling movement and the vivid, coarse faces of *retablos* of the Passion.

The pride and prize of the Cluny are the Lady and the Unicorn tapestries on the upper floor, hung in a round room which serves to cut out too much damaging light and to suggest a tourney tent. Rather than the more common blue, the ground in these panels is red with the usual meticulous placement of flowers and small animals. However, the Lady, her lady-in-waiting, the unicorn and his banner, the lion with *his* banner, and a few pets are wafted into a further reach of unreality by disporting themselves on a little blue island in the red background. The theory is that the panels symbolize the senses—the unicorn is shown a mirror, listens to the music of an organ, and so on. This interpretation doesn't quite work, but it hardly matters; the whole is its own lovely excuse for being.

The "Treasury," on the same floor, contains priceless early enamels, the gold and silver and gem encrusted vessels and objects used in church processionals and court ceremonies. Look at the golden rose which was the traditional gift of the popes to kings, at the extraordinarily worldly and modern Gallic neck and arm ornaments of gold and the dazzling Visigoth crowns of beaten gold studded with large, crude stones.

Not everywhere well lit—and the personnel, as indicated, often as cranky as an ailing child, but go. It is one of the great museums and the time you spend in it will serve for missing a few miles of the overstuffed paintings dedicated to the greater glory of Napoleon and Marie de Medici, which the Louvre should retire for a millennium or two.

WALK IN THE FIFTH

First, the **Panthéon** (Place du Panthéon. *Open 10 A.M. to 4 P.M. in winter, 10 A.M. to 4 P.M. from April 1 to September 30. Closed Tuesday.*)

Quite ill in 1744, Louis XV made a vow that should he recover, he would replace the decaying old church of Ste. Geneviève with a magnificent new building. The King recovered and assigned the job to the architect Soufflot who planned the building in the shape of the Greek cross and, as style, hoped to achieve a synthesis of the classic and Gothic. It went very slowly, hampered by lack of money, revived by lotteries; a great deal of time and money had to be spent filling in deep pits made by Gallo-Roman potters; fissures caused by earth movement caused more delays. Ultimately it was completed, on the eve of the Revolution.

It was more churchlike then, but following the death of Mirabeau, the National Assembly decided to change the structure and dedicate the crypt to men of renown with no particular religious leanings. Religion bowed to patriotism. The cross on the dome disappeared, and the bell towers; the inscription on the facade read "To her great men, a grateful country." Voltaire, robed in purple, accompanied by children in togas and tunics and the grown-ups in the flowing robes of muses and ancient poets, was taken to the Panthéon in a magnificent hearse drawn by twelve horses to join Mirabeau who, however, was tossed out in the whirling of revolutionary sentiments, to be replaced by Marat who, in turn, was flung out. Napoleon I had the Panthéon changed back to a church —new inscription, cross erected, et cetera. Under Louis-Philippe it became a pantheon again, a church under Napoleon III, and to receive the ashes of Victor Hugo, in 1885, a pantheon once more and thus far, a pantheon still.

The large, tall space one first enters is religious in tone, not only because of its shape and structure but because the wall paintings deal mainly with the lives of the most famous of French saints. The varieties of style, dealing with similar subjects in what should be similar moods, make an interesting study. Some of the painters worked in muted, soapsudsy textures, others filled their canvases

with spears and horses (possibly imitating Uccello but not slavishly enough) and dense clouds as carriages for heavenly avengers
—the traditional bombast. By far the best group is by Puvis de
Chavannes who achieved combinations of delicacy and strength,
of simplicity and nobility in his murals of the life of Ste. Geneviève.

Except for a few unclassifiables, the Panthéon's crypt seems to
arrange its inhabitants in groups (ah, the logical French): generals
together, important Catholics together, the liberal Jaurès coupled
with the liberal Schoelcher. Hugo and Zola lie together and, quite
near each other, Rousseau and Voltaire, smiling his toothless,
immortal smile. (Did he never have teeth?)

This is a reasonable place to begin exploring the neighborhood,
the Luxembourg Gardens (page 78), and to look at the indefatigable Sorbonne, seven hundred and fourteen years old and
still, in spite of inadequacies and the justified complaints of its
student body, a commanding name though not—compared to
other old universities—much to look at.

Outside the necrology-hagiography of the Panthéon, one must
sense the Roman city of Lutetia centered on this hill, its vestiges
still clearly visible some short distances away, in the hoary stones
of the Cluny and the arena of the Rue Monge. Imagine the
temples, the theaters, the baths and forums; their ruins after the
barbaric invasions late in the 3rd century; the early abbeys and
churches, surrounded by a medieval city wall in later centuries;
their destruction during the Revolution and the later rebuilding.
Now, still threaded with frayed strands of its history, the neighborhood is a village of student life, a recent blooming of "antique"
and arty shops, a frantic renovation of old houses to make new,
costly apartments in the webs of ancient streets.

The views from the Panthéon portals make a conglomerate of
the scenes infinitely painted, photographed and reproduced to be
sent home on a million postcards. Directly ahead, looking down
the Rue Soufflot, the soothing line of mansard roofs repeated and
in the repetition, lulling, like the gesture of stroking a forehead.
Beyond, the tracery of the Eiffel Tower rising out of the low,
broad cloud of trees on the Boulevard St. Michel. Immediately
ahead, classic Paris neoclassic, the Law Faculty building, which
was designed by Soufflot, on the right, and repeated on the
left as the Mairie of the 5th arrondissement, a careful copy built

seventy-five years later. Although the arrangement is neat, both buildings suffer from the passion for matching and balancing that creates a cold stodginess, sometimes handsome, often forbidding.

Toward the right is the Rue Valette, a venerable street, one of whose wounded houses leans on antique wooden crutches. After coursing the broad avenues of modern Paris, it isn't easy to see it as a main thoroughfare called, for centuries, "Seven Roads" for the streets that converged on it, nor to see the houses now sagging with age as great mansions, one of them built over Gothic cellars where Huguenots hid during the Protestant massacres in 1572, another on the site of the 15th century college where Loyola and probably Calvin were schooled. Around the corner, on the Rue Laplace, a *couscous* house and a Vietnamese restaurant (reflecting local food tastes not so much for their exoticism as the fact that their prices can be met by students) and soft, fuzzy houses whose gutted shops and ateliers, covered with bright posters, hide courts and cellars older than the old facades. One of them—if it hasn't been torn down or improved out of reason—shows places of attachment for chains to bar the streets when local tempers and heated theological disputes got out of hand. At the end of the street, as if to remind one again of other powerful church companies that owned medieval Paris, a view of the towers of Notre Dame.

The Rue de la Montagne Ste. Geneviève, once a section of the Roman road that led to Lyons and on to Italy, and the Place Ste. Geneviève, are given over to "things" shops, inexpensive restaurants, the remains of a few ancient houses and courts and a cabaret, La Montagne, "La Plus Vieille Musette de Paris." The choices at this point are:

1. To examine the crafts, clothing and bookshops—practically one of every kind—and the Sorbonne on the Rue des Ecoles, then on to the Boulevard St. Michel and the Cluny Museum (page 73).

2. To walk down Avenue Soufflot to the Luxembourg Gardens through the formality of geometric hedges and bleached 19th century statuary of ladies real and fancied, to watch the serious young rolling rubber balls and propelling toy boats on the lake and the much more serious old propelling *boules* (you may know it as *palanque* or *bocce*), or to sit with a few foreign beats, a few indigenous beats, a few of the ancients who set the style, *les clochards,* or with the lovers at the side of a shaded pool full of big goldfish. On the Rue de Vaugirard there is the Parliamentary

Palace, an expansion of the Palais Médicis (although one rarely pronounces "s" at the end of words, hiss this unnecessary one distinctly). It was built by Marie de Medici in 1612 on the site of older houses and a section of garden she acquired from a nearby monastery. At the same time she bought the house of a nobleman, François de Luxembourg, which she gave, some years later, to Cardinal Richelieu to use while his great palace on the Right Bank was being readied (page 36). Inhabited through the years by a long line of royal luminaries it became, finally, the residence of the president of the Senate.

Marie de Medici saw to it that her architect incorporated Italian elements in her new palace but it does not, says Michelin contentedly, *"tomber dans l'exubérance italienne."* They are right; it remains incorruptibly a French palace. Once it was decorated with the enormous paintings of Rubens, commissioned by Marie for the greater glory of Marie (now in the Louvre), but she didn't stay long to enjoy them for she was forced into exile less than ten years after she moved into the palace. Later inhabitants saw—and made—some gaudy nights, particularly during the time of Louis XIV, when one of its tenants, the Duchesse de Berry, had the gates to the garden walled up so that she could, according to Hillairet, *"s'y promener la nuit en toute licence."* The Revolution took care of that sort of nonsense and turned the palace into a prison with a distinguished guest list (Danton and the painter David, among others). Early in the 19th century the building underwent considerable change, with a new facade and structural adaptations for its new purpose as governmental meeting house.

Going back to other possibilities of the neighborhood: you may not yet be bored by "amusing" shops; the Rue de l'Ecole Polytechnique is committed to them. You might follow that street up to the church of St. Etienne du Mont, built originally in the 12th century to serve as the parish church for the workers employed by the Abbey of Ste. Geneviève. It was, in the usual developments, expanded and rebuilt several times, taking its present style from a 16th century conception of the Gothic. If choir screens mean anything to you, see that splendid one, the only one left in Paris and important enough to serve as an example of *un jubé* in the Petit Larousse. At this point, the Roman road has changed its name to Rue Descartes, moving southward past the Lycée Henri IV which contains practically all that is left of the mighty Abbey

of Ste. Geneviève. The Lycée encloses 13th century kitchens and a
refectory and, more clearly visible, a bell tower named for Clovis,
king of the Franks at the turn of the 5th to 6th centuries, who
founded the abbey but did not build the tower; its sections range
from the 12th to the late 19th century.

The Rue Descartes is a crooked, eccentric little street, named
for the philosopher who found the irregularities, the unplanned
quality of these streets not to his orderly tastes. It leads down,
after changing its name to the Rue Mouffetard, to one of the most
ebullient of Paris markets. On the way, among houses of varied
antiquity, the *couscous*, the goulash and the blinis restaurants of
7- and 8-franc meals, there is a bookbinder who practices his
meticulous, anachronistic métier in a small shop with meagre
light and, at number 41, a younger anachronism, an Esperanto
bookshop that extends its proselytizing even to juvenile books
in the optimistic world-brotherhood language. At number 39,
the Verlaine Bookshop functions in the house where Verlaine
died, its commemorative plaque bearing a bitter stunning head of
the poet. Across the street, at number 40, a guitar maker who, on
occasional fine days, extends his atelier into the street where
sections of guitar can dry *en plein air* and the next door, a shop
that sells the assembled product and keeps aficionados abreast of
events in the plunking and plucking world.

Just about here, you would be standing, were it seven hundred
years ago, at the gate of city walls built by the ambitious, energetic
King Philippe-Auguste, a companion of Richard the Lion-Hearted
in the Third Crusade and his adversary in the struggle for the
lands of France. Below the historic shadow of the gate, a discothèque or two leads into the Place de la Contrescarpe, named for
the rise above the ditches along the medieval walls, now a place of
jazz and insomniac cafés that break the sleep of *clochards* who
once owned the Place, since ousted to constitute still another
group of D.P.'s.

Sooner or later, the modern chess sets, batiks, seed necklaces
and lamps made of pieces of rusty plow will move up the hill from
Rue des Ecoles, round the Panthéon and come down the hill of
Descartes-Mouffetard. But until that time—which may be this
very moment or yesterday—Mouffetard's wares are basic: clothing,
pharmaceuticals, hardware, wines and food for people of limited
means, the stores interspersed with houses covered with the fungus

of age, and one humorous junk shop, at number 36 (page 221). As you stand outside it on a warm day, admiring the fancy and courage of its collection, take in the Mouffetard smell, a combination of cheese, fish, bodies, discarded greens, overage flowers, urine—the smell of life in packed houses hugging a crowded market for centuries. Stink and name are antique and synonymous. "Mouffetard," derived from a word for "skunk," was what medieval wits named the street as they passed through the vapors from the workshops of the skinners and tanners at the edge of the hard-working, all-purpose stream (the Bièvre) that once flowed through the area. And almost as old as the stink are a few still-hopeful signs among the cracked hotels, the dark wine shops smelling of lees, and a few crusty ateliers.

As the street descends, a hum comes up to meet it and an increasing number of vegetable, fruit, fish and meat stalls begin to narrow the flow of the resolute stream of bulging baskets and canny shoppers, especially on Saturday mornings when the market glistens and gleams and shouts and pushes most fervently. But it always makes way for the plump man in a smock and beret or his friend in a vaguely Mexican-tropico costume who leads sweet, stupid burros laden with panniers full of lavender. The base of this spouting fountain of noise, color and, in season, a fragrance of peaches strong enough to drown out the fish, is the church of St. Médard, named for a Merovingian bishop who instituted the custom of rewarding girls of virtue and holiness with crowns of roses. This is not, however, the primary distinction of the church, nor are its 15th century nave and facade. It was a place of riot and carnage during the religious wars of the 16th century and two hundred years later, a stage for religious hysteria, attracting a large audience to watch and comment on the performances. François de Paris, a deacon of the church and a fanatical Jansenist who lived by ascetic denials, and probably died of them at the age of thirty-six, became the center of a cult after his burial in the Cemetery of St. Médard. His legend grew; he had been a saint, his tomb was miraculously healing. The blind, the crippled, the frightened, the diseased, the mad came to lie on his tomb or eat the earth around it. Driven by desperation and fervor, they inspired in themselves and each other spasms and distortions that the crowds of spectators found as absorbing as hangings. The excesses of *les convulsionnaires de St. Médard* and their audi-

ence were stopped, in 1732, when Louis XV ordered the cemetery closed. On the shut door, an anonymous versifier nailed a
couplet still quoted: "By order of the King, it is forbidden God to
perform miracles in this place."

Across the Rue Monge two small streets that run below the
surrounding sidewalks, the Rue de la Clef and the Rue Santeuil,
mark what was once the leather market, occupying the place of an
earlier orphanage for girls. What is now left of the tanning and
curing that went on near the tolerant Bièvre is a set of alleys
behind gates, secluded hamlets of carpenter shops, iron works,
some little leather, and minute houses hung with geraniums and
diapers, the color and flavor more Sicilian than *Ville Lumière*.

A few blocks northward, on the same side of Rue Monge,
bordered by the Rue de Navarre, is the Roman arena (*Arènes de
Lutèce*) destroyed in the invasions of the third century by the
barbarians and the local populace who had fled to the Ile de la
Cité and used stones from the arena to strengthen their ramparts.
Later, following the fate of other pagan monuments—the Colos-
seum in Rome, pre-Columbian temples in the Americas—sections
of the arena were used in house and church building. The rest was
lost under a cover of earth. At the time that Baron Haussmann
was reshaping Paris, street excavations uncovered what was
left of the arena, along with a number of artifacts. It was an
important archaeological discovery and several scholarly voices
insisted that the arena be fully explored and preserved, but money
was low, the site had been rented to a bus company which had
plans for a depot there, etc., etc. The arena was covered and
forgotten again for about fifteen years when the threat of a new
street which would cut right through it roused enough influential
ire (Victor Hugo got into this, too) to have the area once more
uncovered, this time yielding an unusually tall skeleton and a
section of sewer which carried waste to the Bièvre, already a
useful stream in Roman times. The arena had, naturally, to be
much restored and, although the steps on which its neighbors rest
from the excitements of a *boules* tourney and the Métro sign in
one of the exit tunnels are of recent vintage, the plan is authentic
and conducive to imaginings of gladiatorial contests and performances of Plautus' comedies.

Via the Square Capitan and its imposing fountain and down the
Rue Linné which continues as Rue Geoffroy St. Hilaire, into
Daubenton and the unusual apartment buildings in the section,

one comes to "La Mosquée," a sizable model Muslim village, whiter and fresher than the usual real thing with pretty courts that recall southern Spain, a minaret, an Arab restaurant and a coffee-house. (Open to visitors, except from Noon to 2 P.M. every day except Friday.)

This may be high time to look for a bus or Métro station on the Rue Monge. Or, let us assume that you dislike markets, Romans and Muslims, and still stand, hesitating, on the Place de la Contrescarpe. Walk into Rue Rollin and look for number 14. Here Descartes lived on his visits from Holland where he spent many of his years. His death in 1650, however, took place in Sweden, followed by a singularly long, peculiar series of burials, especially unsuitable to so neatly rational a man. Seven years after his death, he was exhumed and his body brought to France, first to one church, then to another and finally, to St. Germain des Prés. That was the body only, the skull suffered a more restless fate. In the course of the exhumation, another skull was substituted for that of the philosopher while the authentic one traveled from owner to owner, each of whom wrote his name on it and then passed it along for a bit of money. More than one-hundred fifty years after the exhumation a Swedish scientist happened on the skull and sent it along to his colleague, Cuvier, who gave it to the then science museum in Paris. It wasn't, however, until 1913 that a noted anatomy professor, comparing the skull with portraits of Descartes, decided it was the one worthy of the philosopher and it was put on view, with its label of authenticity, in the Musée de l'Homme (page 167) where it may still be resting after its centuries of wandering.

From the long dead to the fervently living is a short walk across the Rue Mouffetard into the Rue d'Ulm, a street of schools, and students, of their cinémathèque and cafés, of the Curie Institute and its young scientists and a Lebanese home and Maronite church for students from the Near East. Crossing Ulm and a view of the south side of the Panthéon you will enter the Place de l'Estrapade, another Paris Place that grabs and holds forever. It hasn't any of the regal perfections of the Place des Vosges or the Palais Royal, or the miniature elegance of the Cour de Rohan, or the faded tristesse of a Place des Victoires. It is much more comfortable, much more quartier than any of them, and that might be its appeal, this sense of safety among full-paunched houses in metal curls and stone flowers and a gleaming old butcher shop framed in gold and fresh flowers; a *pâtisserie* deep in irises under a tile ceiling of flowers and birds on a field of celestial blue, reflections of a tough, bitter time, one thinks, to be so effulgently sentimental. In the afternoon students flock to their accustomed places and companions at the cafés or drop into the Délices du Liban for a bowl of yoghurt, a piece of syrupy baklava and the thick, aromatic coffee of the East. Nothing in the almost bucolic calm relates the present Place to its name, taken from the Italian *strappata*, a device for punishing malefactors by hoisting them, arms tied behind backs, to a considerable height and then dropping them to a jerking stop just before they reached the ground. A few such drops dislocated both arms and legs and if that didn't do it, heavy weights were tied to the feet of the victim.

The more innocent Fossés St. Jacques, built over a section of the ditch outside the medieval city wall, narrows and snakes down past shops and cafés and a keymaker's establishment whose sign is in elaborate wrought iron, one of a number you may have noticed over locksmiths' shops, about the last métier which indulges in this engaging tradition. There were many more—and more old door knockers, and brass edges on shop windows and metal ornaments—before the Germans collected as much metal as they could find to send home for melting down. Near the keys a shoemaker sits in his little glass box squarely fronting the street to catch the last of the thin light. At the Rue Malebranche, the street splits into two levels of printers and carpenters and you are back at the Rue Soufflot, here meeting the Rue St. Jacques at a large modern international bookshop, and soon among the pallid rebellions of the Boulevard St. Michel.

❧ *And the Armor*

Having decided that the giant isn't *that* big there is still the waspishness to cope with, and money is not quite enough. The fortunate few with sturdy interior structures pay no attention to it and go on to enjoy Paris despite some of its population. Those of stuff more frail will find, on a stay long enough, that the small brutalities, like a series of cold showers and stiff workouts, produce their own counter-strengths.

Shout back, in any language; if you hit it lucky you might find an English phrase with a close and easily comprehended French equivalent, like "stupid beast." Or, if you prefer a more secure attack study the impolite phrases they didn't teach you in First Year French. An additional joy to roaring back in French is that you can wallow freely in what would be obscenities and possibly actionable accusations back home. *Merde* is as natural as breathing and as inoffensive. *Emmerdeur* and *pédéraste* are common coin in the exchange between clashing taxi drivers and the epithet thrown by a spattered pedestrian at the spattering car is frequently what our books used to spell as "old c — — —."

If you can't talk dirty, talk tough; if you can't do that either, think tough. It may not be the best balm, but it helps to think about things like: "This pricking and scratching and slapping is a good toughener for Americans who assume that they are lovable, expect everyone to love them all the time and are desperately hurt when they aren't." "So the French have a highly developed interest in food. So do infants." Or, "Why does anger exhaust most people, except Parisians who batten on it? It exhilarates them. Do they have some malfunction of the adrenals that requires stimulation so frequently? If that is so, too bad; if they didn't spend so much time and energy on temper, what a race this might be." And "In spite of their cars and television sets, a lot of working class Paris still seems to be fighting the Revolution. Someone should tell them that few American couples are Louis XVI and Marie Antoinette." And, "How far is greed from begging and where does one draw the other line, the division between greed and thievery?" (This is a thought that may occur to you elsewhere, since Paris has no monopoly on greed; it is the summer dress worn by too many places.)

"Can it be that the decorative art of verbal fussing is for bolstering a failing amour-propre? Is that why a platitudinous American Western film can be encrusted, embroidered, fretted, lace-edged, until it becomes an important structure, which it must become since the intellectual Westerns addict cannot confess to a simple, open-mouthed pleasure but must make a philosophic, aesthetic system around the conflict between the good guys and the bad guys? Few other people have quite this talent for surrounding a small, indifferent picture with an immense Baroque frame of verbal decoration to convince me and himself that we have been confronted with an important entity.

"The Frenchman finds dozens of descriptive names for lengths and shapes of bread ('string,' 'wand,' 'bastard') and each of dozens of little cakes has an individual name, but he forces me to go through finger counting, like a child, for ninety-seven (four twenties, ten, seven) and seventy-nine (sixty, ten, nine) while the rest of the Latin world and the

French provinces of Switzerland follow the easier more logical pattern of *septante, octante, nonante.*"

Like all tourists, you hate them, you loathe the word and you might be willing to put considerable effort into avoiding the label and the feeling. Even though the distinctions among big city people are almost nonexistent since we dress alike, live in similar houses and think and avoid thinking similar thoughts, you still don't want to take a chance. A few suggestions: Learn the difference between Montmartre, the northern border of tourist Paris, and Montparnasse, the southern limit. Learn the sizes and denominations of coins (a confusing business—see page 183) and count them out slowly and carefully. Avoid the tourist tendency to keep changing bills because he can't sort out and add up coins, thus accumulating a Gibraltar of coins which makes things even more difficult. Don't say of a 10-franc note, "it's only two dollars"; treat it with the native's respect.

If you want to melt into the atmosphere more thoroughly you might disguise yourself in any of the following modes of dress: The summer look for young women is to wear a black bra under a transparent white or pastel blouse, no slip to interfere. Wear no or little lipstick, plenty of eye-makeup and a Hermès or quasi-Hermès pocketbook—the belted one, with the lock. Weigh your scarf down with a string of pearls, or, if the weather is very warm, knot it—chiffon preferably—high around your throat. To add an egalitarian touch, carry a shopping bag of cotton mesh, a battered small plaid valise or a canvas holder with bread poking out of it.

For looking like a Frenchwoman of "a certain age" pluck your eyebrows very thin, wear a dark suit of durable, dull material cut straight and square. Wear a stern expression and always, always wear gloves, no matter how hot the day may be. You might, for a touch of dash, tie a silk scarf to the handle of your pocketbook. Blending with tenement life can be achieved by taking off all makeup, bras, girdles and nylons, cutting one's hair in a merciless style and donning the dour concierge costume elsewhere described. Do not bathe frequently nor bother with deodorants and let nature take her sweaty course during a heat wave, when Paris becomes one monstrous armpit.

A young man can look French by trying to look English. The vogue among those who have grown tired of jeans and sweaters like dried moss is to wear dark trim suits and high collars, to carry a tightly furled black umbrella and gloves in one hand, a newspaper in the other. The bowler hat has been slow in crossing the Channel, but it will come; the outfit cries for completion.

Unless he wants to look like an elderly nationalist or a Spaniard, a man never wears a beret in Paris.

To resemble a pair of Paris lovers can be pleasant but not necessarily easy. It takes some loosening of cultural restraints to kiss deeply, drowningly, to clasp and hold breathlessly while a busy world mills about, jostling love. After enough necking, if there is such a thing, the young man must put his arm around the girl's shoulder, leaning heavily on her, his hand drooping over her breast. She must appear to be carrying him and happy to do so. When she admits exhaustion, he can vary the gesture of affection by grasping the back of her neck firmly, ready to lift her as if she were a kitten for drowning.

There are, of course, defenses that require no disguise and little play-acting. For instance, smiling or being smiled at are not common occurrences. Ergo, smiling at a shopkeeper disarms him pathetically. He is unprotected, aghast, like a guinea pig when one blows into its face. Slowly, very slowly, an abashed smile creases his reluctant face and he is yours, courteous and genial, for the moment. If you are a prowler (and a good traveler is) you will often find yourself peering into a Paris courtyard and the lowering face of the concierge thereunto attached. As she emerges from her cell, call out in the lilting bird song you must learn immediately as you touch French soil, "Bonjour, Madame. C'est très joli, votre cour" (not hers at all but she insists it is and you must maintain the fiction with her). Ready for a fight, or better still, expecting to see you flee her Medusa head, this stuns her and may keep her speechless long enough for a good look around. If you need more time when she comes to, "Je suis artiste," a phrase which still evokes some respect in Paris. As you saunter out, "Au'voir, Madame. Merci mille fois. Vous êtes très gentille." She isn't nor need you be so grateful, but you can afford to be generous in victory.

Finally and most importantly, always remember the beautifully direct and simple action of money. It won't buy civility in the street or the bus or Métro or supermarket, but it must in good shops, restaurants and hotels. The lavish cost should cover minimal politeness, part of the "service," as it were. Demand it or leave. Our century has achieved, among its other peculiar contributions to civilization, systems of facsimiles—exact, reasonable, unreasonable. The absolutely unique object, other than a work of art or achaeology, is extremely rare and you can usually find the thing you want, or a close relation, in another less irritable shop.

Finally, don't call those Art Nouveau street flowers of iron with human legs pissoirs. Use pissotières, the chummy term of which Larousse disapproves, or if it suits you to appear gentleman-of-the-old-school, the archaic Vespasiennes, and as often as you can remember, complain of a crise de foie.

6 Thursday

WALK IN THE 6TH AND BITS OF THE 5TH AND 4TH

The airy well-lit house (6 Place Furstenberg) in which Delacroix lived, worked and died can be the beginning or end of meandering through narrow, irregular paths of the mighty Abbey of St. Germain des Prés, in its time so powerful that it considered and conducted itself as answerable only to the Pope.

As witness to the life of a successful, productive painter who traveled and enjoyed a lively social life, the house and studio are remarkably uncommunicative, in spite of sketches and African souvenirs. To approach it via a set of lovely and almost artificially perfect "Paris" views brings to the house the interest and charm it lacks intrinsically. Behind the church of St. Germain des Prés runs the Rue de l'Abbaye, a short street leading to Rue de Furstenberg and into a view of streets closing in on each other, a heaped cubist rise of roof to roof, that rhythm answered by the staccato of windows cut at haphazard levels, quickening in a tattoo of chimney pots. The rhythm mellows at the Place Furstenberg; at its center a cluster of five milky, round lamps, not an artifact of recent "camp" but legitimately indigenous, surrounded by four full trees whose dark leaves hold patches of the pale light as it fades toward the shuttered houses that hug the tiny Place.

Off the Boulevard St. Germain, the Rue des Ciseaux, where, undoubtedly, a maker of scissors once lived and worked, is a Villon alley, shut off from the light and explosive movement of the permanent performance on the stage of St. Germain des Prés. It doesn't invite lingering in spite of its 16th and 17th century houses but impels one into the equally old, still vigorous Rue des Canettes which saw the struggles and play of the characters of Murger's *La Vie de Bohème* a hundred years ago, now imperfectly replaced with the vaguely similar habitués of a wineshop grocery (the shop also a rare anachronism). Its neighbors are a nightclub of the size and density of a rush-hour Métro car that pours into a warm summer night the sounds of Arabic, Israeli, Mexican and Greek folk songs, and on the corner, a restaurant wrapped in the stripes of a Mexican sarape and hung with a Pancho Villa hat, proclaiming itself the first Mexican restaurant in Europe. Across from that, an Italian restaurant that proclaims itself in no way but just goes on living as if it were still on the back street of a forgotten Renaissance piazza in Rome. Among them, hopeful modern shops, all glass and freshly waxed woods, heaped with a tasteful carelessness of avant "young" clothing and clever international tricks of household decorations.

Between the Rue Bonaparte and the Rue de Seine, the Rue des Beaux Arts is of the mixture as before and around except for the presence, at number 13, of the hotel in which Oscar Wilde died. Immediately south of that street, one comes to the Rue Visconti, not quite as forlorn as the Rue des Ciseaux yet hardly a gay ribbon and one tends to use it only as a short cut between the brighter streets. Its retiring nature may have attracted the colony of Huguenots who took the street over in the 16th century. Later tenants, hardly seekers for the quiet, inconspicuous life, must have had other reasons for choosing the street. Racine lived at number 24 and died there in 1699 of a combination, to quote a historian, of "dysentery, erysipelas, rheumatism, a liver complaint and, possibly, the chagrin of no longer being in favor with the king." It was a street of actresses in the 18th century, among them the famous Adrienne Lecouvreur, the subject of Cilea's opera. A century later, the young Balzac established his print shop at number 17, had an unsuccessful time of it and moved away to devote his life to novels. Delacroix moved into the same house a few years later (1836), choosing a brighter, bigger atelier, and if it weren't for the noise and fumes of buses and trucks on the bordering streets, one might still hear the voices of Chopin and George Sand arriving to sit for their portraits.

The Rue de Seine finishes at a treed triangle and a very white wall, large and almost windowless, then plunges into an arcade of the Institute and the happy surprise of the Seine with its green flourish of the Vert Galant at the tip of the Ile de la Cité. Another archway, a short distance eastward leads into a faceless, still street, the Rue de Nevers, that sounds of carpenters' saws and the clack of small printing machines, and into bits and corners, hardly large enough for street signs. To stand at the angles of their joinings is to be in medieval Paris. The Rue de Nevers marked the western boundary of the monastery of the Grands-Augustins and hasn't changed shape, nor altogether its houses, since. The scrap of street called Nesle takes its name from the local tower in the wall built by Philippe-Auguste, a scene of scandalous medieval goings-on later used as material by Alexandre Dumas, and repeats the name of a great château, the Grand Hôtel de Nesle, that stood inside the wall.

Touching the Rue de Nevers at the Seine is the Rue Guéné-gaud, an African primitives mart that shields another medieval tower, which is extant but quite hidden. For the peace that African masks shatter, one must walk into the street of Jacques Callot, the 17th century master of etching who sketched in-numerable commedia dell'arte figures. Whether the name works its suggestion or whether it is an intrinsic characteristic, there is a look of an Italian square about the street, an outdoor room off a minor canal in Venice where a troupe might perform to the calls and applause of the locals standing on the benches of the corner wineshop, here and now a pleasant, tawny café with purple awnings and to complete the picture, a timbered, unpretentious arch at the side of a wood-and-tipsy glass *papeterie* which may have supplied Balzac's printshop with paper. To the east, just before one reaches the Place St. Michel, the 12th century street called Gît-le-Coeur, a corruption of the name for or of a cook. Where there is now a Corsican restaurant (page 282) there was the fine house François I built (mid-16th century) for his mistress, of the earthy name of Anne de Pisseleu, Duchesse d'Etampes. As fit both their stations, he surrounded the lady who was spoken of as "the most beautiful of learned women and the most learned of beautiful women" with rare paintings and exqui-site *objets* in the palace that occupied also the splinter of street called Hirondelle where reproductions of the Salamander, the totem of François I, were carved in the walls long after the original house and its symbols were gone.

South of the Place St. André des Arts, the Rue Hautefeuille, where Baudelaire was born, continues the walk through the shadows of antiquity. At number 5, the narrow aisle puffs out a toy tower in Renaissance style, the embellishments of a building of the

16th century in which a number of Italian artists lived, imported by the Medici wives of French kings. A century later the tower frequently saw the famous *empoisonneuse*, the Marquise de Brinvilliers, whose lover and teacher of the poison arts lived there (page 163).

Rush as quickly as the crowds permit across the honky-tonk of Boulevard St. Michel at this point and its "picturesque" annexes of *couscous*, jazz, pizza and Greek lamb, across Rue St. Jacques into the Rue Galande, the start of the Roman road which ran through the Rue Descartes (page 79). The once noble street, holding onto vestiges of its past—a medieval bas-relief of St. Julien l'Hospitalier, his wife and the rescued Christ on the way to or from an early Gothic chapel on a bank of the river and a 16th century slope of roof—is now a repetition of the local mélange (though not as avid) of attractive "artistic" shops, a *boîte* or two and behind them, slum. It takes a considerable act of the imagination to see the Rue du Fouarre in its 13th century importance, as an open court where classes of the University of Paris were held. The lecturer sat on a bench or wooden rail while the students sat on the ground or on the little piles of straw which gave the street its medieval name. In the imagined group of scholars from everywhere in Europe place Dante's Italian profile and, at the ends of the street, the chains strung across the street by Charles V in the 14th century to contain student disorder, or maybe to keep out the rebellion and ribaldry of the plaster workers who lived on the Rue Domat. That is an extraordinary street whose swaying houses and half-sunken, half-raised walk might have the charm of its venerable contemporaries if it weren't for the forbidding small hotels, the decrepit houses and ateliers, and the black mouths of alleys leading to the houses of displaced Algerians. One of the paths that turns to the river, the Rue des Anglais, takes on the present mood of its neighbor though it must once have been a gay exotic street, brightened by the high voices and blond hair of English students who came to study in the greatest of medieval universities.

Scholar's Latin continues to buzz across the river and into the streets behind Notre Dame. One hears Abélard disputing a point of canon law as he walks with a fellow scholar along the Rue des Chantres—the street of the cantors of Notre Dame—or arranging some matter with the school authorities in the buildings that once

occupied what is still a fine Renaissance court hidden in the street
of the canoness (Chanoinesse). The Rue des Ursins thunders with
the voice of the 12th century St. Bernard inveighing against the
worldly students who, he said, had no time or interest for psalms
but would rather listen to the tinkle of their jeweled accouterments. The shadow of Gothic rests on the windows of a house at
the opening of Rue des Ursins, then gives way to an earlier shadow
at its end, Rue de la Colombe, which stands where once stood
the Roman wall built to keep out the barbaric invasions. Around
the corner, the return flight into the present-day Paris of household wares (mainly Japanese and Scandinavian), cafés and *pâtisseries* and souvenirs, the leaden bouquets of Notre Dame, the
Eiffel Tower and the Panthéon crammed together on one tiny,
metal island. Or, to stay with the medieval, back across the
river to the Square René Viviani and its church of St. Julien le
Pauvre (almost as old as Notre Dame and the only Romanesque-
becoming-Gothic church left in an area where there were many),
the witness to an eventful past and a treasure of present charm.

WALK — MONTPARNASSE — LEDOUX —
CITE UNIVERSITAIRE

Lunch at the Coupole (page 270) in Hemingway country. Then
look for the Rue Boissonade that runs between the Boulevard
Raspail and the Boulevard du Montparnasse. At number 45, you'll
find a relic of an individualism now lost to houses and people. The
gated courtyard of studios is a blast of strong tastes: red, yellow,
orange; round roofs, angled roofs, shallow, deep-eaved, the giddy
colors and shapes of a costume party of houses.

One emerges at Raspail possibly for a look at the lively American Student Center at number 259, the art gallery next door and
the covered subway grating, once a dormitory of *clochards* who
needed the warm air of the Métro below. One of the diehards of
the neighborhood remains, a talented beggar who saves her drinking for the evening, full of tragic probity during the day when she
works on the softened wills of visitors to the Montparnasse
Cemetery nearby. She has slipping, rolling false teeth that fasci-
nate and garble her chronicle of woe. She has no work, it is hard
to find in Paris, but fifty kilometers away there is a job waiting for
her. She has no money for train fare, no place to sleep, nothing to

eat. You know, of course, that there is public assistance for which she can apply—slow-paced, long-winded and mired in official papers—and she doesn't have to starve in Paris. However, your judgment and vocabulary slide away as you watch the teeth dropping, rising, joining obliquely, and when she lashes them with an adroit slap of her tongue, coming together straight and hard, like the teeth in an old dental sign. She has you, or at least her teeth do, and then she drains your heart and purse with "When one is old, it is best to die."

This might be the proper mood in which to turn to the Montparnasse Cemetery if you haven't been to Père Lachaise (page 136) or, having been, still remain an enthusiast of lugubrious terrains. Approach it via the Rue Froidevaux which, like most of the surrounding streets, is full of chrysanthemums and wreathes, particularly on Toussaint (All Saints' Day).

Montparnasse has few trees and too much gravel per grass, but the fallen leaves and the usual late-autumn rain, acting out the suitable pathetic fallacy, temper the crackling ground, and the improbable art of some of the tombs. One remarkable monument consists of a family bed. An angel perching on the headboard gazes down at Papa who is sitting up in bed, fully dressed, keenly staring out at the world. Mama lies next to him, very dead, cloaked in a rusty shroud. In chaste contrast, the Saint-Saëns family tomb, exactly the same as most others except for the presence of a lyre and, in more dramatic contrast, the grave of the sculptor Henri Laurens marked by an impressive large, black mourning figure, a grateful relief from the sentimental *kitsch* around it. César Franck and Guy de Maupassant lie near each other, across the Rue Emile Richard from the monument for Baudelaire, derived of a long line of agony out of stone, from Michelangelo through Rodin. The poet is shown bound in death like a mummy, his spirit a male Fury pulling out of the obdurate rock with agonized, clenched hands.

The Rue de la Gaîté, a short, vivacious street a block from the western edge of the cemetery, is wholly dedicated to the living flesh. Stand after stand of waffles, crêpes, cakes, chestnuts, candies, cafés to eat and drink and talk in, shops of shoes and clothing, a famous music-burlesque hall, a discothèque. It displays an engaging variety of faces from Spain, Italy, Morocco and the French Congo, and the neighborhood girls in their fall costumes of tight,

tight pants, sleek boots and bulky short coats that are precisely burlesque length—and don't think the girls don't know it; this is a neighborhood of professionals.

If you and your day are still fresh, walk southeastward (or take a bus on the Boulevard Raspail) to the Place Denfert-Rochereau, named for the *barrière d'Enfer*, the place, in the 18th and 19th centuries, for the inspection and imposition of taxes on goods arriving into the city from the direction of Orléans and the scene of the third act of *La Bohème*. It is now a good-looking generous square, guarded by the Lion of Belfort and still, fortunately, the possessor of two of the remaining Ledoux buildings, 1784 to 1787, which flanked this opening to the city.

It is in one of these buildings that the trip through the catacombs starts. You might, however, postpone bone-viewing for the immense supply in Rome and instead take the bus marked 68 to the Porte d'Orléans where the Boulevard Jourdan will lead you the short distance to the Cité Universitaire and the Parc Montsouris. The park, more relaxed than most large Paris parks, probably because it was built quite late (1870) by Baron Haussmann, when styles were free enough to suggest the romantic planned wilderness of a *jardin anglais*.

The other side of the Boulevard Jourdan borders the Cité Universitaire, literally a small city, literally of students, from a diversity of several dozen countries. This vast aviary of variplumed young birds living in nests somewhat styled to their nationalities shelters them from the assaults of the big city for long enough, usually a year, to venture out comfortably, leaving their places for newcomers. It was inaugurated in 1925 and added to, chalet after temple, after "stately home of England," after sensible Scandinavian, and in 1936, a large International House encompassing a theater and recreation halls that cost John D. Rockefeller, Sr., an Everest of dimes. Two of the buildings are the work of Le Corbusier, the Swiss Pavilion of the 1930's and a much more recent house for Brazil, a joyous, playful house, rampant with clever tricks, the toy devised by an old master for his own fun, like the songs Rossini wrote for his dinner parties.

Le Musée Artistique et Historique de l'Assistance Publique de Paris, 47 Quai de la Tournelle. *Open 10 A.M. to Noon and 2 P.M. to 5 P.M. Closed Tuesdays and holidays.*

The Public Assistance Museum is part of a 17th century house where, in its time, abandoned children were sheltered by an order called "Filles de Ste. Geneviève," not quite nuns, not quite only charitable ladies, headed by the owner of the mansion, Marie de Bonneau de Miramion. Like so many *hôtels particuliers* and religious establishments it was made public property by the Revolution to become later the central pharmacy for city hospitals.

As one looks at old etchings and hospital rosters and official letters, it becomes clear that there was little difference between prison and hospital. The latter was often both. From the earliest etchings of the Hôtel-Dieu (the first hospital, which once stood in the space facing Notre Dame) with its assortment of ills, male and female, several to a bed, to those of the unspeakable madhouse of Salpêtrière, to the plans of the immense yards and dungeons of Bicêtre (page 157), the lesson is that the sick, the mad and the criminal shared the same hells. Of Bicêtre it was reported, for instance, that "it was for two centuries a veritable caravansary, at the same time hospital, an asylum for the insane and epileptics, for those with venereal diseases, and a prison." One engraving shows a mass of men behind high fortress walls watching as others are put in irons, possibly among them the Marquis de Sade or the false dauphin. In another part of the room there is a register of women's names and ages (sixteen to twenty-six) which represents the girls who, like Manon Lescaut, were sent to the American colonies as possible wives for colonizers and soldiers. Some were thieves, some were prostitutes, but the record is that of a hospital, so one must assume the sick were shipped out, as well.

Less desperate matters are dealt with, too: the enormous locks used to shut the hospital-prisons; pewter syringes and porringers; medicine vials from Roman times on; identification bracelets and medals, very old and quite new. In a side room there is a model (only the amiable, lonely guardian may operate it) of the turning towers of nunneries that welcomed unwanted babies. A bell was rung, the tower turned so that its accepting opening faced the street; another ring and the baby was turned to a room where the nuns had food and linens ready. If the parents suspected they might have second thoughts, they pinned half of a paper, irregularly cut, to the child's garments and, in order to claim the baby, had to present the matching section.

The upper floor of the museum is section on section of apothe-

cary jars of different times and provenance—all French. A few
heavy, glowing copper basins stand near old glass jars and small
stacks of ornate prescription blanks, some of them edged in gold
leaf. The guardian will point out chunks of marble scraped to
make powder for moist baby bottoms and if he is in the mood—he
usually is—will let you smell tea that is over a hundred years old
and still has its scent, and the bitter odor of antique opium.

On the way out, sit for a moment in the vestige of the once-
large garden—a place improved, grown *à l'anglaise*, through neglect
and look for the sad tub of a M. Beaujon, whose former gold and
decorations were boiled and scraped off during the long years it
was used for washing institutional vegetables.

Le Musée Historique de la Préfecture de Police, 36 Quai des
Orfèvres. *Open only Thursdays from 2 P.M. to 5 P.M.—if Thursday is not a holiday.*

The Police Museum makes itself hard to get in two ways: its
rare hours and by being perched at the top—via countless
flights of stairs—of one of the police buildings. Cheered on by
sympathetic gentlemen who move briskly from office to office on
the interminable floors, and guided by the coo and flutter of
pigeons who roost in the eaves, you reach an ordinary door marked
"Musée." At your touch it gives off an enormous sound and you
expect to be flown at by a group of full-uniformed gendarmes. No
one. And after a long time, no one, except a young gentleman who
takes a shy, furtive glance at you now and then. There are other
visitors once in a while but usually the absorbing collection is yours
alone, disturbed only by the dusty full-size wax figures of gendarmes with mangy crepe beards and depraved pallor.

The museum's arrangement is rather musical, progressing from
allegro to andante to an agitato movement to a grave adagio,
finishing with a scherzo. The opening is figurines and drawings of
the people on whom the police had to keep a watchful eye; water
carriers, fruit vendors, repairmen and the girls who delivered
bread in long papoose carriers (not too different from the cradles
now in use); carriage drivers, flower women, knife grinders. Street
scenes occasionally appear in juxtapositions that seem to make a
sociological statement like the brutish, vivid crush in a section of
Les Halles next to the crinolined ease of 19th century ladies and
children among the flowers on the Quai aux Fleurs.

The next movement is dour: documents of crime and punishment and graphic representations of the punishment. Of 1563, there is a precise print of the quartering—drawn by four horses— of the assassin of the Duc de Guise. In 1591, a German engraver put down in attentive detail the hanging of a number of dissident aristocrats. An attractive subject for contemporary sketchers was the hysterics of St. Médard (page 81); a particularly inclusive one shows people praying, lying on the tomb, a few seemingly mad, one clearly in convulsions and the crowds of spectators watching them through barred windows. Next to the engraving is the decree that caused the cemetery to be closed.

Out of ponderous old Conciergerie tomes marked in graceful scribe's lettering faded to sepia, rises the attempted assassination of Henry IV by a Jean Chatel who had crept into the room of Gabrielle d'Estrées (page 35), the king's mistress. Later, the 1610 report of the assassination, accompanied by an engraving of the event, of the killer and a later photo of the knife he used. The antique hand-lettering tells of the infamous Marquise de Brinvilliers (page 163) and of the famous affair of the collar that involved Marie Antoinette, Louis XVI, a Cardinal de Rohan, the Comtesse de la Motte and court jewelers. An order that the pillory be removed from Les Halles (1785); announcements of royal birth requesting that merchants and householders illuminate the facades of their houses and that shops be closed in celebration; dooming lettres de cachet that opened with *"De par Le Roy il est ordonné. . ."* Orders for the arrest of Dr. Guillotin in 1795, of Josephine de Beauharnais in 1794, of Beaumarchais in 1792, of Louis-Philippe-Egalité; the order that Louis XVI be handed over, the account of the murder of Marat by Charlotte Corday and two broadsides issued within a short period, one headed *De Par Le Roi*; the other *Au Nom de la République*.

If you can tear yourself away from puzzling out who ordered whose death and when, in the sanguinous turning of the Revolution's kaleidoscope, there are other bloody matters in store: photos and documentation of the assassination of Jaurès in 1914, the gun and the bloodstained book carried by the murderer of President Paul Doumer in 1932. An entire case is devoted to Rimbaud and Verlaine including the famous portraits from the group by Fantin-Latour, the statement of the attempted murder by Verlaine of Rimbaud and a police report stating that Verlaine was taken home by the police from a writers' banquet, too drunk to make it on his own.

Surmounted by caricatures and early entertaining numbers of the local "Police Gazette," there is a group of cases exemplifying the shrewdness, inventiveness, patience and ingenuity of man intent on murder. Knives of all kinds, including one that pops out of a lady's fan; sticks, hooks, hammers, clamps, handcuffs, guns, blunt pieces of metal, a strangling string made of twisted paper; metal "knuckle-dusters," whips, big keys, a sleeve covered with spikes and two correctors: a large medieval "sword of justice" and the actual blade of a guillotine used in the Revolution. Portraits of a few noted killers and labels explaining their achievements accompany the instruments. Two may stay with you. One was a monster who devised a periscope through which he could watch the agonies of his victims, and the other was Antoine Léger who raped and killed a twelve-year-old girl. Faced with the problem of what to do with the body, he ate it.

A small, restrained display that deals with the German Occupation—a torture post, a few leaflets, photos of the last barricade in Paris and the Liberation—leads back toward the entrance, past pictures of public fetes and horse-drawn omnibuses named "Citadine," "Bernaise," a "Dame Blanche," a "Berline du Delta" and yet another document or gravure dealing with prostitutes, a leitmotiv that runs through all the periods of police activity. An early ordinance forbids merchants "to rent, for money, by the day or otherwise, clothing and accessories to the families of girl or women prostitutes." Scattered etchings record periodic roundups of women, their transport to prisons and hospitals in large open carts, the farewells of women about to be deported and as if for relief, an ebullient scene of 18th century police breaking into a brothel, sending frothy skirts and curls and ribbons bouncing around the room and out the window.

LES HALLES

The tradition insists that you go to Les Halles at four o'clock in the morning and get right into the core of the fleshly, lusty market life of Paris, then finish up with the ritual bowl of onion soup in one of the local restaurants. It is a fine thing to do, but there are a couple of hitches. You may be too tired after a day of sight-seeing to wait up that late; the restaurant you choose may be mobbed, particularly during the tourist season. Why not try it at other times?

During the daytime the inner iron markets are locked and have that strange mood of waiting, almost threatening stillness, the mood of the brooding canyons of Wall Street on Sunday and the frozen circle of Ferris wheel in a December fairground. Outside the central buildings, the shops and restaurants keep busy, buses lumber around the area and as night deepens, the prostitutes gather in the hallways and cafés on the Rue St. Denis, if the police aren't bothersome, to wait for the truckdrivers and vendors who might want refreshment before the night's work begins. They make curiously beautiful groups in a brilliant diversity of costume, gathered around café tables or on hotel stairways, boxed like paintings in the spots of light along the dark street. Crimson hair plunges toward a high-necked purple sweater and tight black trousers in cruel boots. On the step below, leaning against the black knees a pink graduation dress and a stack of baby-yellow hair; flanking them, a long orange dress and a wilderness of blue-black medusa hair. A few solitaries solicit from shadows and if a couple or a group passes, invite them to a *"partouze"* or a *"surboum."* Nearer the market, on Rue aux Ours, one group favors the giggling school girl approach to attract tourists coming through.

A good time to go is about 11:00 to midnight on an August night (not Sunday) after dinner at one of the local restaurants. Because so many people are away, the loads of food being delivered are lighter and because it's still early, you will not be jostled and turned by the stacks and heaps mounting around you. There is less to see, but it *can* be seen and, if your French is up to it, there is the possibility of conversation with the informative *commissionnaires* who supervise various sections. For watching, there is the hypnotic rhythm of meat delivery. The men wear wide, white bloody smocks, white caps whose visors are turned to the back, and carry big hooks; they look like surgeons in old horror films. One man lifts a whole calf (two hundred and fifty pounds or more) out of the truck and onto the shoulders of a man waiting below. Jogged by his steps, the calf wags its tail, kicks out his shiny, skinless leg, bounces its headless neck and falls back to motionless death again after it is impaled on a market hook. Only the tail resists with one or two feeble swings. When all the shining dead are in neat rows, two men—one to hold and one to saw—cut off the cheaper sections to be stacked in another part of the market while the heads are swirled in a rhythmic flow of arcs out of the truck, through the air, into a waiting bin.

When you've had enough of impaled flesh and thumping heads, go into the vegetable sections, through landscapes of green lakes of parsley, tomato mountains and hillocks of golden-yellow squash and on to the fruits, a luxuriant outpouring of plums, pears, apples and wild strawberries. Look for the section where the aristocrats of fruits, those meant for places like Fauchon's, the food shops on Avenue Victor Hugo, the starred restaurants, are displayed like jewelry. Exquisitely matched apples and perfect pears, each labeled, are placed in careful rows in plastic-covered boxes, the covers prettily sketched in gilt. In August, though, it is the peaches of Provence one goes to see and to smell in Les Halles—golden, pale or blushing; small, medium, enormous, boxes on boxes of them, the massed chorus of countless peaches giving off a perfume that is literally intoxicating.

Diagonally across the market, is the Square of the Innocents, nicely named for the blandness of butter and eggs concentrated there, although that was actually the name of the local 12th century church and a cemetery, the potter's field for medieval Paris, as it was for Roman Paris. The growing population of the city and cemetery required that a charnel house be built also. Limited by the houses that grew up around the cemetery square, crammed with the remains of too many people, the charnel house gave up in the late 18th century. The bones of over a million skeletons were moved to the Catacombs (under the Place Denfert-Rochereau) and the cemetery covered by a market surrounding a Renaissance fountain brought here from a nearby corner. It was the work of two masters, Pierre Lescot and the sculptor Jean Goujon, mainly, although later hands were also involved. Paradoxically, the copies of the Goujon sculptures in the Musée des Monuments Français (page 160) are much more satisfying than those in the old charnel square where dirt and weather have battered and darkened the ripe grace of the figures.

⊷§ *Parisian Contours and Stances*

Among the difficulties a traveler has with or about the Parisian Frenchman is what he looks like. Most Italians look Italian, north or south, and enough Spanish have the national pallor. The English fre-

quently look "English" and even the Jacob's coat of American back-
grounds is producing a distinctly American face, but what is the
French face? Is it Brigitte Bardot's Pekinese or Jeanne Moreau's
brooding? De Gaulle's all prow and no ship, or Malraux's screened
face? The round plump baker's assistant who should be talking Dublin
brogue, the curly-haired, smoky-eyed Berber owner of a wine and
coal shop, the short, skinny Cockney who collects bus tickets, the
Sicilian matron knitting on the Métro are all French. One likes to see
an identifiably national face; it is disconcerting to search for a
stamp and find none. So one tries the clothing. But a chic Parisienne
turns out to be a visitor from Rome, and the girls with the tightest low-
slung pants, the loosest hair and the most Scandinavian of sweaters
are German au pair girls. For easy Parisianess you have to go back
to old photos of the Belle Epoque, even earlier costume prints, the
children in their smocks and the one-strapped aprons of the waiters in
market bistros.

Another area of Parisian failing—to the traveler—is that he is not
moving. As a national character he is not amusing, as the Italians can
be; no pitying fury wells up here as in India, except for the rare weak
clochard in a race of indomitables. The Mexican can tear your heart
out and make you laugh at almost the same time. The Spaniard
earns a certain awe with his sallow taciturnity. The English refusal
to change—or even notice—myriad inconveniences like drafty windows, marshes of dough and white sauce as food, the diffuse, undis-
criminating radiance of the working class, "dear" and "not to worry,
duck" are vastly endearing.

The Paris face is guarded indifference. The famous French tolerance
is a facet of not giving a damn about what you do, the je m'en fichisme
which is the blanket attitude toward anything that isn't of immediate
personal interest. The Africans who live in pustulant slums (and often
look and act as if they did) don't interest the Parisian much as social,
economic or epidemiological problems, although the newspapers often
explore them. "If they don't like it, let them go home," without thought
as to who will collect his garbage and clean his streets if they do. The
clochards lying on Métro stairs with newspapers as blankets? "They
like it." "All of them? The women, too?" "Of course, without a doubt."

The indifference and guardedness which offer privacy and the right
to be eccentric yields also a lack of curiosity and a staid dullness.
There is little awe or reverence, no singing or whistling in the streets.
The Parisian rarely runs, except to catch a bus. He is stiffly decorous
in public, when he is not necking. Nor is he given to warm laughter,
unless food and wine glow in him.

There is little that can distract him from his blinkered course

whether it is going to work or sitting in his café. It might be a
golden afternoon. The Boulevard St. Germain is alert and busy—
people getting on and off buses on the Boulevard, on the Rue du Bac.
The Bac Métro station swallows passengers and disgorges a few into
the deepening shade of its trees. The clients of the local cafés lean
back in their chairs to face the last slanting rays of sun. Women with
market bags guarded by the cannon mouth of a long bread loaf
march briskly along the Boulevard. Children accompanied by mothers
and nurses run, stop, and swing their briefcases at each other in the
release from a long school day. Overhead, the cloudless sky is
etched by the sky-writing of three small planes. They are writing
nothing intelligible, just weaving back and forth, crossing, turning,
drawing white calligraphic designs on the spotless blue. One spectator
stands on the busy junction staring up and continues to stare at the
changing, fleeting patterns in the sky. Then he looks around to
see if anyone else is watching—the children surely must be. No. No
one else looks up although they must notice his craning posture. He
continues to look alternately up and around him for about five minutes. No one else, not one child watches the show.

The saddened sky-watcher must go to renew his love of Paris to
the bank of the ageless Seine and watch the failing sun gloss over the
facade of Notre Dame and linger on the chimney rims of crooked
streets.

7 Friday

Musée Carnavalet, 23 Rue de Sévigné (3rd). *Open 10 A.M. to Noon, 2 P.M. to 6 P.M., April 15 to September 30; rest of year to 5 P.M. Closed Tuesdays, some rooms closed Saturday P.M.*

The name derives from one of the early owners of the house (then considerably smaller), the widow of a Sire de Kernevency, later known as Carnavalet, who bought it in 1577, thirty-three years after it was built for the then-President of Parliament. A century later, Madame de Sévigné rented the house and lived there for nineteen years, until her death. She loved the house, its gardens, its courts, its elegance, its pure air and the neighborhood particularly. As Michelin puts it, having been born in the Place des Vosges, baptized in the church of St. Louis-St. Paul, married in St. Gervais, *"elle se trouvait ici dans son quartier,"* a more fervent statement in Paris than it might be in New York. The *quartier* was, and in many areas remains, the larger home of which one's private dwelling was the dormitory. After running through a career of less distinguished uses, as the fashionable moved to the Ile St. Louis and later to the Faubourgs of St. Germain and St. Honoré, the Carnavalet was established in 1880 as "Le Musée Historique de la Ville de Paris."

The house itself is a glorious museum piece of lordly space, colonnades, tightly coiled arabesques of gardens and an abundance of decorative elements, from wreaths and arches, heads and shells to lions and ladies. Especially ladies; as seasons, as winds, as symbols of plenty; plump, dimpled, cushiony ladies, the forebears of the caryatids who support half the buildings of Paris and swell the canvases of Renoir.

To know or even lightly examine the total of the Carnavalet would be as Herculean a job as really knowing the Louvre or the British Museum and furthermore (as of 1966), no diagrams of galleries are available from which one might arrange a budget of viewing. Nevertheless it should be dared, not all of it necessarily and, preferably, early in your visit. This is the parade of people, incidents, styles, commemorative objects, prints, paintings, furnishings, souvenirs that witnessed the evolution of the streets you walk, the houses you see, the people you will encounter, the attitudes that may charm or repel you.

Much of the lower floor is given over to two brighteners of Paris streets, shop signs and vendors. An early 17th century *charcutier* let his presence be known by a portrait of a suckling pig; a carpenter's sign was a large, painted tree; a sheaf of golden wheat naturally led to a bakeshop; a hand with a swollen thumb was the sign of an itinerant bread seller. Some of the signs were demonstrations of a craftsman's skill, like those of the locksmiths whose signs were wonderfully wrought keys in ornate scrolls of iron. Royal insignia shedding an aura of class seem to have been the choice of modistes, one of whom worked under the shield of Orleans, another protected by the shield of a Duc de Berry. Saints, too, lent confidence: St. Batiste has his shops and so does St. Antoine. St. Denis, very large, stands for a vendor of novelties and St. Crespin sits and cuts leather in a pretty ecclesiastical enclosure hung with shoes and boots.

The sketches and engravings of *Les Cris de Paris* are portraits of beggars, workers, craftsmen and vendors from early in the 17th century to the middle of the 19th century, carefully observed and cleverly put down, making a number of these *"études prises dans le bas peuple"* works of art, especially those of François Boucher who translated and charmingly falsified these "low people" into the stylish, graceful figures of boudoir and pastoral paintings, rather as if Madame de Pompadour and her ladies decided it would be a great lark to be portrayed, not *again* as shepherdesses, but this time as vendors of milk or laces.

The enormous rest is, as has been indicated, all kinds of things. Inevitably one finds the heroic paintings of which old cities have too many, groups of gentlemen in thickets of wigs attending royal celebrations and great banquets. One engraving depicts the triumphant reception in Paris of Louis XIII after his defeat of the Huguenots and is dedicated to the king as "the Very Christian King of France and Navarre, invincible, just, debonnaire, strong through his virtue, clement through his piety"—hardly the picture his neglected wife would have drawn of him. The iconography goes on and on, with portraits of people, bridges, quais, churches, and the famous Places as backdrops for spectacles, fetes and fairs. It roams through the lives of French writers, with a particularly beguiling display of things pertaining to George Sand, including a small portrait done in her youth, when she was still Aurore Dupin, sweet and possibly not too bright, and later portraits as the dashing writer, very bright and not too sweet. One caricature has her surrounded by friends some of whom look like snakes, others fish. Chopin is a red-winged, strong-beaked bird who sits in her lap while the long-haired pale Liszt kneels before her in supplication, or adoration.

The theater section exhibits scenery, costumes, portraits of actors, commedia dell'arte figures (the Comédie Italienne was very popular for a long time, its presence still remembered in the name of the Boulevard des Italiens), Watteau paintings of a *danseur* and *danseuse* of the Opéra and probably by Watteau, a group of Italian child actors.

Furniture, fans, plates, pottery, clocks, carved wall panels (a number brought from local houses), more portraits, one of them of Madame de Sévigné and of the daughter to whom she wrote the famous letters, a sundae of bows, transparencies, curls and pearls, alluring and aware of it. We march, or totter, on with Paris time, possibly to pause at a piece of popular art commemorating the birth of the Dauphin in 1681. In bulbous strophes it depicts the joy of the French people, the jollity of the public entertainments arranged for them and the royal accouchement in which all the participants—a considerable number of them—are hugely classic or, at least, winged, watching the royal baby nursing of a solid, peasant angel. More egalitarian celebrities are represented by Benjamin Franklin in sculpture and painting, Rousseau's inkpot and book of herbs and grasses, the letters of Voltaire and medallions, statuettes and sketches of his lively, testy, toothless face. The Revolution is exceedingly well documented and includes, if you've wondered what it looked like, models of the Bastille.

A tasteless *Apotheosis of Napoleon* by the usually chaste Ingres leads into a collection of numerous objects that belonged to the Emperor. Since there appears to be an inexhaustible supply of these in many places, you might prefer to concentrate instead on a picture of the Galerie des Variétés as it appeared more than one hundred fifty years ago and an engraving of the galleries of the forlorn Palais Royal (page 36) when it echoed with the calls and chatter of soldiers, prostitutes and gamblers, early in the 19th century. It was, almost naturally, the Italian Giuseppe Canella who recorded Paris of the early half of the 19th century best, in a series of fine, precise paintings of streets, buildings, river front and markets.

We learn, as we go, that there was a café for the blind in 1840, that the actress Rachel liked to wear embroidered red slippers when she was not on stage in classic sandals, that Daumier's palette was as messy as anyone's else and that a show of Delacroix' works was an event of red-walled, red-draped splendor. A print of an enormous fete on the Place de la Concorde shows a confusion of floats and costumes, a number of busty girls, a gaggle of drunks and at least one transvestite. *Plus ça change* . . . Later, with the help of photography, the city was documented more widely and exactly, though the painters remained undiscouraged and still enamored of painting restaurants, *guinguettes, pâtisseries,* theaters, parties and personages as if amassing, consciously, witnesses of a robust, passing time.

Where does one call a halt? At the rosetted, garlanded, be-eagled, be-lionclawed, mermaided, puttied, enamel-plaqued, leaf-and-scroll ornamented, royal-crowned and royal-shielded cradle of the Prince Imperial, presented to Napoleon III and Eugénie by the city of Paris? Or maybe the time to cry, "Hold, enough," is after having seen the vitriolic sculpture caricatures of Jean-Pierre Dantan. No one was safe from his demon's eye and fingers. He took on politicians, foreign dignitaries, writers, singers, and professors, and found a rich lode in musicians, reducing Verdi to foolish drapery, Rossini to nothing but girth and Liszt (who seemed to have asked for it) to a small monster with lank hair dripping onto starved arms and legs and carrying a saber marked "*Peste.*" Malibran, Grisi and Rachel were sculptured simply and affectionately. The poison spared them was darted instead at their audiences in a caricature as dense as a German carving of a loge crowd of snoring, yawning, dyspeptic, coyly flirtatious music-ignorers.

FAUBOURG ST. ANTOINE

(Bus or Métro to Place de la Bastille)

On the surface the main streets of this quarter just east of the Place de la Bastille are hardworking and ordinary, in no way revealing that it was, to quote a historian, "the crater from which the lava of revolution escaped most frequently."

To pick an arbitrary place in its belligerent history: it was the scene of battle between the king's forces and those of dissident princes and dukes in the middle of the 17th century. A span of peace was marked, in 1660, by a lavish welcome arranged for Louis XIV and his new young bride as they and a large, operatic escort made their way into the city. An enormous throne was set up and decorated for the royal couple at the end of the Faubourg St. Antoine. Then called the Place du Trône, reasonably, it later became—and still is—the Place de la Nation. Still on the lighter side; one of the earliest balloon launchings—which also launched a world of prints and balloon-decorated fans, boxes, dishes, cloth, etc.—swayed and rose, in 1783, out of a garden adjoining the workshops of the famous wallpaper ateliers of Revéillon in the area.

Only six years after the balloon floated off, the same ateliers were burned and pillaged. Although the immediate cause was the rumor that wages were to be lowered, the Revolution was on, and the fact that government troops killed and injured several hundred people hardly calmed the fury. Time after bloody time it was the place of the most volatile encounters and of the thickest, most numerous barricades—possibly helped by the easy availability of wood in this furniture-making quarter.

In 1848, the barricades went up again (the reports range from twenty-seven to sixty-five on one main avenue alone) and in that conflict, a considerable number of army, church and government functionaries were killed along with the anonymous.

The neighborhood undoubtedly has its fair share of Communist Party membership, although the revolutionary spirit—what there is of it—seems to inhabit the industrial north of the city more intensely. But the interest to the visitor is in its present and ancient role of guild center for furniture making, selling, repairing and the tangential crafts that go with furniture, métiers centered here as early as the 14th century and greatly expanded when Versailles began its insatiable absorption of furnishings.

Having arrived at the Place de la Bastille, find Rue de Charenton and walk past its small shops and look inside them at the elixirs, the waxes, the oils, and the *eau merveilleuse* which nourish polished woods. Extraordinary brushes, bits of metal railing, tassels and cording follow as you turn into Rue St. Nicolas, where one goes to have a leather chair-seat stamped in gold classic design, or modern table-legs turned to the elaborations of a century ago. As one must always do in Paris, for one reason or another, look up and notice that the heads peering out of the windows are by and large, elderly. Many of the ateliers are in apartments, sometimes inhabited by daytime workers only, sometimes functioning in the old style of shop and house, a combination scorned by the young.

Up and down on the Rue du Faubourg St. Antoine, allowing no interruptions except for an occasional corner café and a tiny park, shop after shop after shop of furniture; low tunnels of shops, queenly, well-lit and overstuffed shops, frosty dignified shops; jumbled, frantic shops where one finds a few genuinely old pieces picked up at a flea market and dressed in new lacquer.

Since neither prices nor styles nor age are alluring enough to go through the colossal expense and trouble of shipping this perfectly good, perfectly ordinary furniture home, head for the alleys which, your map will (or should) show you, make a beehive of the quarter. Choose whichever appeals to you with its listings of the ateliers inside the court—or to your nose, with a combination of oils, woods, leathers and glue. If only one will do, take the Rue de la Main d'Or (commemorating a gifted craftsman, one likes to think) into its 18th century maze of anachronisms. Passing the shops of upholstery material and drawer pulls and hinges one comes to abandoned courts surrounded by broken paper-stuffed windows, obviously long-unused ateliers. Still functioning are surprisingly high-vaulted deep yards on whose floors lie immense trunks of trees, almost like sequoias in contrast to the narrowness of its passage. (How trucks large enough to carry a number of such hulks maneuver through the alleys makes a nicely unimportant problem to ponder.) Only one or two men seem to be involved in cutting the trunks; here, too, things aren't as busy as they should be in a bustling trade, to judge from the countless shops on the Faubourg. A pleasant man in a nearby workroom, carefully applying a stain in the traditional manner (a wad of cotton or soft cloth wrapped in another, dipped into the solution and rubbed and rubbed, gently, patiently into the wood) explains the abandoned factories and the quiet lumberyards by the fact that manufacturing is cheaper in the provinces in spite of the cost of carting the finished work to the city. Also, he says, the government's moves to decentralize industry have discouraged if not depleted the area. The next reason he suggests is the most telling. Stroking, stroking an 18th century chair as he talks, shaking the ashes off the cigarette growing to his lip, he speaks of himself, rather proudly, as one of those who are "dying," soon to be altogether gone. He feels fortunate in being able to supply himself and one assistant with livelihoods as repairmen for a leading hotel.

A short distance along, before you reach Rue de Charonne, you will find a bright, small furniture showroom. If your French is up to it, and you are genuinely interested in any of the well-made pieces, try to involve the manager in a discussion of woods, polishes, techniques. He is, though young, steeped in the craft and he may take you through some of the workrooms, room after room of a small apartment building where the chests and tables stand in several stages of development: the wood inlays being delicately applied, the diagonals of grain matched and then opposed in geometric patterns, and the strange lovely purple-gray of one tropical wood waiting for a more conventional stain to be applied are displayed and the processes explained with enthusiasm. But in spite of the enthusiasm and expertise of the people one speaks to in the alleys, there is an indisputable dyingness, the sense of a crafts tradition fading out and forever.

Rue de Charonne will lead you back to the Faubourg or, via a ramble of alleys, one of them the Rue de Lappe of Apache and brothel fame, now sapped and colorless, to the Place de la Bastille again. A half-hour's walk or less to the eastern limits of the 11th would take you to Père Lachaise Cemetery (page 136) and if you decide to do it that way, you will be passing what was the home and business of an extremely practical member of a practical race. A short distance from the meeting of Charonne and Avenue Philippe Auguste there was, in the late 18th century, a sanitarium run by a Dr. Belhomme. Here the doctor of the sunny name sequestered potential victims of the Revolution as if they were ill and needed treatment. Neither Royalist nor sentimental he took immense amounts of money from them for their safety. Those who couldn't pay were thrown out to hide elsewhere, if they could, or resign themselves to the Terror. The good doctor's turn came to stand at the end of a pointing finger and he, in turn, hid in another's sanitarium while the family business flourished on the

Rue de Charonne. After a period of touch and go, he returned home and many years later died a rich old man.

THE MARAIS

One of the early blossoms of the Paris summer is the poster, one year a 17th century ornament, the next a Japanesque abstraction, advertising the Festival du Marais (page 247), a June-July season of concerts, chamber opera and plays performed in great refurbished palaces, until recently corpses lying in scabrous slums behind diseased walls. The "what to see in Paris" listings always include "The Marais Illuminated" for an evening's entertainment. Yet, other than to the large plastic-bound tourist buses that whip around the Place des Vosges (this year's model looks like a transparent lumpy worm pregnant with two-legged larvae whose ears are hearing discs), a few visitors to the Carnavalet Museum and a few music-lovers at the Festival concerts, the Marais is relatively unknown. Many Parisians dismiss it as a depressing slum although those who love it, love it inordinately.

In spite of the fact that it is an easily accessible part of the city—north of the Hôtel de Ville and the Ile St. Louis, between Les Halles and the Place de la Bastille—a newcomer searching the indispensable map finds no Métro station, no local street name to pinpoint "Marais" (marshes), the centuries-old name that describes the area after a branch of the Seine that ran northward disappeared into the surrounding earth.

Riding through its main boulevard, the Rue de Rivoli, as it becomes the Rue St. Antoine (sharing both names at one place) one sees a broad busy street of shops, markets, a movie house, cafés, slits of alleys and a trustworthy symbol of a working-class area: a merry-go-round that whirls splendid planes and buses at the Métro station (St. Paul, in this instance) and when that goes on to a station in the 20th or the 13th, replaces them with a gaming wheel. The hypothetical bus rider may have noticed a freshly cleaned handsome house front that guards, unknown to him, one of the most beautiful French Renaissance palaces (the Hôtel de Sully, built in 1624) whose court is hung with luscious stone ladies lightly disguised as the elements and the seasons, and behind that, the former garden, now an outdoor auditorium, fronting on a broad, gracious facade. A hundred years before the palace was built, the site was a vast court where, in the early summer of 1559, Henry II gave a magnificent fete to celebrate the royal marriages of both his sister and his daughter. In the course of jousting with a captain of the Scottish guards, the King was struck in the head (some reports add the grim detail of a pierced eye) by his opponent's lance and died shortly thereafter. The later history of the place, when it was mansion, never witnessed the death of a king but enjoyed, nevertheless, a parade of colorful events, as most of the luxurious old houses did. To pluck out for display one tenant, the Duc de Sully: He was seventy-four years old when he bought the house in 1634 and married to a young woman who made no secret, nor even a gesture of tact, of her lovers. He hoped, however, to embarrass her—a futile try—by counting out household money to include the item, "this much for your lovers," asking, in return, that she keep them off the stairs. Still later, the old *cocu*, probably tired of adorning lovers, began to adorn himself with ropes of diamonds, jeweled rings and collars of gold in which he strutted through the arcades of the Place des Vosges, then the Place Royale, amusing his tough, regal neighbors.

The man on the bus will by now have passed the church of St. Paul—St. Louis, designed in Jesuit style (after the Gesù in Rome), where the first French chapter of the Order had placed its chapel and houses in the 16th and 17th centuries, up to the time that it was expelled. Madame de Sévigné, an enthusiast and indigene of the quarter was baptized in St. Paul, as was the first child of Victor Hugo whose house is a small museum of Hugo iconography on the Place des Vosges (page 118).

To the bus rider the streets will appear ordinary, poor, at times brutish, attractive only for their vigor. The Marais takes exploring, peeping behind makeshift fences, burrowing through discouraged old streets and undiscouraged old streets, peering into courtyards (*visite-conférence* trips help; see page 297) to find the many-layered mélange of past and present, decay and rehabilitation, the ancient mixture of rich princes and poor Jews, the evolving mixture of Parisian intellectual and newer poor Jew.

How does one plunge into this mine of dross and gold? Which tunnel does one use first? Via the Ile St. Louis, across the Pont de Sully, into the street called Petit Musc (a corruption of its 14th century name, "Where the Whores Hang Out") and the Rue des Lions, where Charles V, the Wise, and Charles VI, the Mad, kept a menagerie? Should one go to it through the banter and shrewd play of the clothing market at its northern edge, near the Place de la République and descend to the ghetto streets? By way of Les Halles, the "belly" of Paris, to use Zola's word? From the Place des Vosges, still something of a mourning goddess not yet consoled by her fresh paint, the green dress of too-many trees and the tinkle of bright new shops? From the historic belligerence of the Faubourg St. Antoine?

Catching hold of two dominant threads of the Marais texture almost simultaneously might be as good a way as any: off at the St. Paul station of the Métro and into the Rue des Rosiers to buy a thick chunk of Jewish cheesecake in one of the bakeshops near the Rue des Ecouffes. From station to cake you will probably have passed the Rue Pavée which shared with the Rue du Roi de Sicile, in the latter half of the 13th century, the pomp of a royal château built for the brother of St. Louis, Charles d'Anjou, after he was crowned King of Sicily. Still partners centuries later, the streets held two prisons, one of them for ladies of easy virtue regularly rounded up in screaming, cackling, cursing bundles. The girls and their playmates were replaced by political prisoners at the time of the Revolution when, during one month of 1792, over one hundred fifty persons were put to death here.

Where knights once jousted and the blood of their descendants flowed there is a graceful facade of an Art Nouveau synagogue, built by Hector Guimard of the Métro entrances and used by the people who also use the ritual baths on the Rue des Rosiers, who cook and serve Polish style—too sweet—gefilte fish (*carpe* or *poisson farci*) in their simple restaurants, who make and sell *pain azyme* (matzo), the twists that Parisians buy as enlarged brioches, greeting cards in Hebrew and Yiddish, Israeli records, prayer shawls, and keep shabby little cafés that serve kosher wines and *couscous* to the recently arrived Moroccan Jews visiting from the tenements between St. Paul's and the river. (One of the cafés, incidentally, is the descendant of a place Lenin frequented.)

"Rosiers" of course means rose bushes, those that grew inside this section of the medieval city wall of which a tower remains, covered with white plaster and hiding in a local courtyard. Another meaning of the word, according to some authorities, was local slang for a piece of money, appropriate for the Rue des Rosiers which was a shopping street as long ago as the Middle

Ages, when Jews from the Rue de la Juiverie (now gone, or its name changed) of the Ile de la Cité came to this quarter to sell and trade and later to settle. Rue des Ecouffes is an intensification of ghetto where old black-coated, long-bearded men teach in the store-front religious schools and conduct services in the minute synagogues behind splintered great doors and up the stairs of crumbling 18th century courts that bear government notices about what to do about rats. Beyond Rue des Ecouffes, Rue des Rosiers breaks into a minute square of butcher shops, a seller of choice *saumon fumé*, a shop of Hebraica and old tomes and a government school for *Israélite* children (the word *"juif"* is considered unkind), then narrows into the Rue Vieille du Temple, a name that suggests in its present context a modern locution for synagogue though it has nothing to do with Jewry. It marked one side of an immense estate of the order of Blancs Manteaux (a name still remembered in a church and a street) established in 1258 by St. Louis after his return from the Crusades. The white-robed mendicant friars, "Serfs of the Virgin," somehow annoyed the Pope who suppressed the order and supplanted it with black-robed friars, the Guillemites of the street that crosses Blancs Manteaux.

At number 47, on a narrow section of Vieille du Temple that has the look of an interim place, a path to somewhere else, there is a magnificent set of doors ornamented with large figures of War and Peace and, among other figures and medallions, two vivid Medusa heads. This Hôtel des Ambassadeurs de Hollande was an important place in the history of Protestantism in France because it was one of the few sanctuaries (the chapel of the embassy of a foreign, Protestant power) where Protestants could meet in safety for services after the Edict of Nantes was revoked. The Hôtel is now the offices of a charitable foundation and cannot be seen except, possibly, the first court, if the guardian is in the mood. If he is, one can see the figures of Romulus and Remus being fed by the wolf carved on the inner face of the entrance and on the walls, the remains of curious mathematical drawings and projections, the work of a priest-scientist. The rest of the courts and rooms, paintings and decorations (*"si beau, si riche et si orné, qu'il est inhabitable,"* according to a 17th century writer) are not viewable. It helps suffuse the unknown and unseen with life to know that late in the 18th century, part of the house was used by a Spanish company, organized with the support of the French and Spanish governments, whose function was to supply arms and monies to the American colonies in their struggles against England—less altruistic than it appears to be when one considers Hispano-Anglo and the Franco-Anglo relations of that era. At about the same time in another set of rooms, Beaumarchais may have been working on the *Marriage of Figaro,* a delightful and courageous play which might nevertheless have stayed in France, to be performed only by the Comédie Française or a Marais troupe if it weren't for the child genius who had come some years earlier to astonish the court at Versailles, and who had lived with his father and talented sister in a Marais hotel a few hundred yards to the south.

At the corner, Rue Vieille du Temple, as it meets Rue des Francs-Bourgeois, opens to a broad Marais view of broken walls, striped with shadows of abutting lost houses and dependent lost roofs, slid or pushed into desuetude through the years. At the corner of Francs-Bourgeois an enchanting little late-Gothic tower is all that is left of an early 16th century palace and at number 38, behind an unprepossessing door, a passage of houses that lean toward each other, almost touching, where Louis, Duc d'Orléans, was assassinated by the Duc de Bourgogne in 1407.

If one had to choose a single street to exemplify the wealth of the past in the Marais it might be Francs-Bourgeois. A part of the street was known in medieval times as the "street of the spools" for the spinners and weavers who lived and worked in its houses. The present name derives from an almshouse, now numbers 34 and 36, which sheltered a group of the respectable poor held free (*franc*) of taxes of any kind. Following a common tendency, it became a hotbed of low life and was closed by the authorities; only the name remained. It takes a slow, curious eye to see that the street was a palatial row. A few of the houses are being restored, but a number still wear their masks of abuse, revealing only by a broken decoration or the shape of windows in a court, their aged glamour. The Hôtel d'Albret, at number 31, built in 1550 and restored in 1690, housed a number of lively tenants, from a commander of the king's forces (the Montmorency whose name was Anne which did not inhibit his martial exploits), to a young woman later known as Madame de Maintenon, the governess of the children of Madame de Montespan and Louis XIV, who married her in a secret ceremony after the death of his Queen. The Hôtel de Lamoignon, one of the oldest (1584) and most imposing, is in rapid restoration and will soon be ready to show at least its noble white court when and if it becomes a library of historical material. Westward, at number 60, sits the Hôtel de Soubise, a younger house in less sedate style, which shares the National Archives with its neighbor, the Hôtel de Rohan (87 Rue Vieille du Temple), a house of cardinals and bishops, one of whom was believed to be the son of Louis XIV with the fertile— eleven children—Princess Soubise of the family next door.

While the numerous dead palaces (marked on maps posted in several streets) languish, waiting for help from an active com- mittee dedicated to restoring the Marais (and then Les Halles and then, etc., etc.), the ghetto streets work and talk and eat and shop for delicacies on the Rue de Bretagne where glistening fish and plump chickens and an exuberance of vendors and customers make a lively Friday morning. There might be the time to visit with an aunt who is keeping an eye on her grandchildren in the Square du Temple while their mother is minding the stall in the adjoining Marché du Temple, calling her wares among the other women who sell furs, dresses, sweaters, pocketbooks and children's clothing. There is nothing timid or distant about these *mar- chandes*; if you say you have no money for a fur jacket (it is fur, but whose is sometimes hard to determine) they offer to lend you money. You are stopped, confronted, beckoned; bags dangled before your eyes, a sweater slapped to your chest as the perfect fit. No one minds if you don't buy; the conversations go on over and around you, bouncing off the ceiling and ricocheting through the basketball chutes on the wall. (The market is market in the mornings only; basketball court in the afternoons.) Rue Dupetit- Thouars takes care of the male wardrobe; racks and racks of suits and coats ranged on the sidewalks and manned by fast and many- tongued gentlemen, at least one of whom will try his English on you and tell you he has relatives in Brooklyn.

There are other brilliant markets in Paris, however, and you may want to continue on Francs-Bourgeois, past or into the Carnavalet Museum, and on to the Place des Vosges, the core and magnet for the palaces. The Place had been a horse market that the energetic city-planner, Henry IV, thought first of converting into a village of silk workshops, then changed his mind and began the construction of a large court for tourneys, dress parades and festivals. The first section, the Pavillon du Roi that fronts on the Rue de Birague, a regal stand of pink brick edged with white stone, steep roofs and deep arcades, was finished when Henry IV died—assassination again, a specialty of the neighborhood. The rest was finished by 1612 and opened with a fete of supreme luxury to celebrate the marriage of Louis XIII to Anne of Austria and that of his sister Elizabeth to the future Philip IV of Spain. Two hundred fifty musicians played, over a thousand gentlemen danced, ten thousand spectators watched while the cannons of the Bastille boomed. (A contemporary drawing that tries to get it all in, down to the last horse tail and window, must surely be one of the most crowded works of art.)

Although the royal family never lived in its pavilion, the neighbors were distinctly the upperest of crusts, great names and their families and mistresses who later abandoned the Marais when the Faubourgs St. Germain and St. Honoré became more fashionable. They were replaced by a minor royalty of writers among whom were Théophile Gautier and Alphonse Daudet and, as mentioned, Victor Hugo. Recently brought back to a look of health and again somewhat exclusive—this time money, not titles—it is still an inconsolable place. Neither the benches nor the baby carriages nor the gendarmes harrying sleeping bums, nor the peculiar equestrian statue of Henry II, can quite substitute for the sound of trumpets and the glitter of lances. Nor can the hopeful new shops and busy cafés that overcharge tourists mercilessly, nor the bright blue wall of an old *blanchisserie*, nor the stained glass of a Swedish-modern Jewish center, expunge the grooves on the disconsolate face.

Across the Rue de Rivoli, the St. Paul station marks the end of the Rue François Miron. Among the *produits exotiques* (which means Jewish, primarily, though it may include Indian curries and Chinese teas), a Franco-Polonaise bistro, a few secondhand miscellany caverns, cafés where Hungarian, Yiddish, Arabic, Russian and French newspapers are read, there are battered mansions, surrounded, cut apart, hanging on to a few pieces of Renaissance, a few deep Gothic caves, a few spans of garlands and masks. One such house, the Hôtel de Beauvais at number 68, not yet restored to the full radiance of some of the others and showing deformities introduced by 19th century owners, is yet a beauty, a great yellow set of pillared and balconied curves. A series of heads, all carefully different, indicating possible portraiture, lead to a plaque which informs that Mozart, a seven-year-old brought to

dazzle the court at Versailles, lived here in 1763, a short distance
from the house of the Couperins, at number 4.

The house was built about a century before the Mozarts came to
Paris, by a lady-in-waiting and trusted favorite of Anne of Austria,
"sans doute," says Hillairet, *"du fait que c'était celle-ci qui lui
administrait ses clystères."* Neither good-looking nor charming, she
managed to collect a Monsieur Beauvais as husband as well as a
number of lovers. To this knowing lady went the honor of teach-
ing Louis XIV, then sixteen, what it meant to be a man. The
grateful Anne made Monsieur a baron and a court counselor and
saw to it that her former lady-in-waiting had enough money to
build a palace and disport herself as a *baronne*. A century later
an envoy of the Duke of Bavaria, continuing the rakish legend
of the house, used it as an exclusive gambling den. Then came
the few months of the Mozart family, then the Revolution, then
private landlords who crammed families into jerry-built subsec-
tions. Now it is the property of the City of Paris, still a tenement,
though with renewed ambition.

Among streets like discarded crusts that lead to the river, there is
one called Geoffroy l'Asnier, which gives onto Piranese views of
blind, shattered portals and a superb lion's head over a great
archway of the Hôtel Chalons-Luxembourg, partly visible from an
adjoining handball and *boules* court. Diagonally across from it,
there is a fresh modern building with a stone screen of repeats
of the Star of David and near the entrance a huge, bitter caldron
whose only ornaments are the letters that spell out Belsen, the
Warsaw ghetto, Auschwitz, Treblinka and names of other concentration camps in a stark terrible band. Inside, dark marbles,
hushed inserts of bronze disks set around a great center Star of
David, held in light reflected through the drum above. In the wall,
six bronze sets of tablets, on which are inscribed the names of
thousands of known victims, repeating the unit of six for the six
million Jews murdered.* There is a hideous rightness about the

* A more literal, theatrical monument to the "Unknown Deportee," is
sunk into the ground behind Notre Dame. A narrowed prow of rough stone
with a barred opening over the water and hideous wedges of metal over
the opening, a set of cells scratched with legends imitating the laborious
awkward writing on stone prison walls, and a long, narrow, closed corridor
with a minute light at the end, apparently to suggest hope—distant, dim,
nevertheless there—distinctly tell a terrible story; but after the first shock-
ing impact, it is the other one returns to for the deeply moving, sorrow-
ing dignity.

monument and its place, among the worst and oldest of the Marais ruins and tenements, where Jewish refugees from North Africa now live in the houses where once lived a large number of the thirty thousand Jews rounded up and shipped out by the Germans.

Picking up a brighter thread of the Marais fabric, we reach the Hôtel d'Aumont on the Rue de Jouy, a calm broad splendor by Mansart on the river side, a simpler, narrow facade on the forgotten inner street and inside that, a lovely Le Vau court. As one listens, or doesn't, to the sophistries of a Marivaux play performed here by pretty girls and swashbuckling men (none of them blazingly talented) and catches glimpses of painted ceiling—an angle of pastel sky out of Tiepolo, an arch of gold-lozenge, a strip of decorated wood—and lets the eye rest on the 17th century garlands, and forgets the lowering sky and the hard benches and the irritation of no program unless one buys the expensive catalogue of Marais activities, the time is again the 17th century, the seats covered with silk brocade, the intellectual young ushers now in satin breeches and wigs and on the stage, a company of players hired for the amusement of oneself and one's rustling, amoral friends.

VICTOR HUGO HOUSE

Musée Victor Hugo, 6 Place des Vosges. *Open 10 A.M. to Noon; 2 P.M. to 6 P.M., April 1 to September 30; otherwise, 2 P.M. to 5 P.M.*

Although the peripatetic Hugos occupied only the second floor, the whole house is now given over to Hugo souvenirs, a mixed bag of the prayerfully inept (like a terrible plaque of the apotheosis of Victor Hugo flying off on Pegasus) and the powerfully adept, a set of Daumier caricatures depicting The Master in a series of political stances. One finds, too, in the usual excess, drawings, engravings and paintings of the novelist's characters, with particularly repetitious emphasis on the smoldering, gypsy dancer, Esmeralda, admittedly an attractive subject. There is furniture, there are documents, including Hugo's public proclamation against the death sentence, letters, an elaborately ornamented and designed passport, busts and paintings of Hugo, ancestral portraits, paintings of his wife and children, and sketches of Hugo grandchildren.

Photos, watches, medals, jewelry, locks of hair—the usual witnesses of a distinguished public life and the sentimentalities of the private life, except for one significant omission.

Near his death chamber, as it was in the house on the street now called Avenue Victor Hugo, there hangs one of the last photos taken of the author, an extraordinarily moving one. He looks very old and yet ageless as if he had crossed the boundary of years, significant and, as some men are in old age, beautiful.

Among the furnishings there are two important curios: a table ordered by Madame Hugo for a charity affair in Guernsey where the family lived as exiles after Napoleon III came to power. It is a quadruple writing table, each of the four corners bearing the names and autographed notes of four illustrious hands: George Sand, Lamartine, Alexandre Dumas and Hugo. (No one in Guernsey wanted the table so M. Hugo bought it.) The other oddity is a playful chinoiserie dining room—no Peacock Room, but effective —decorated by Hugo himself for Madame Juliette Drouet in Guernsey. This is the only mention—a taciturn label (no photos, no paintings, no mementos, no letters) of a patient, devoted and enduring mistress, and the erasure of her existence in a French museum is surprising.

The best for last: a considerable number of sketches and watercolors, a few fairly large, a few as small as postage stamps, by Victor Hugo; all of them at least skillful, many of them poetic, lovely things, very much worth a visit for themselves alone.

ILE ST. LOUIS

While Henry IV was rebuilding the horse market in the marshes across the Seine he cast his restless eye on the two bucolic islands (once a unit as it is now until it was cut in two by a canal in 1360) and decided that they also could use some city planning. He would join the islands and build great houses on them as a near suburb for his Place Royale. After his death, his wife Marie de Medici and their son Louis XIII gave body to the project. The islands were joined, cleared of the grazing cows that gave one of the islands its name, and of the laundresses and lollers under the trees and among the flowers. Soon the mansions began to rise along its edge.

A logical approach to the Ile would be via the Marais which

touches it with three bridges, permits it to use Marais Métro
stations (there are none on the Ile), two of her bus lines, the same
arrondissement number, 4, and shares with it a number of moods
and much history. The Pont Marie leaves one at the meeting of
the Quai de Bourbon and the Quai d'Anjou. Examining the
plaques on the Quai de Bourbon will give some idea of who lived
in the houses behind the worn doors (like the Marais improving,
but more rapidly since there is so much less to do in the tiny area).
At 13 there lived a Commander of the Regiment of the Queen; 43
was built in 1635 and used successively by a Grand Master of
Waters and Woods (1680), in 1730 by a man who supervised
water conveyances and in 1770 by a Treasurer of France, concerned with mills.

Very few of the interiors or even the courts can be seen except
with a *visite-conférence* group, but a house-proud tenant or a
concierge might let you into a court that opens into depths of
house and further courts, some of it rag-hung, some of it revived to
stately mansion. The Hôtel Le Charron, at number 15, for instance, has a gracious court gleaming with many-paned long
windows, delicate ironwork on the stairways, a memory of a tower
and an ancient well. At number 19, the Hôtel de Jassaud, of the
same period (the middle of the 17th century), there is a deeper
court with the ghost of a park, regal stairways and on the street, a
rich facade. On the way to the Quai d'Anjou, at number 1, the
cabaret Au Franc Pinot now functions more peaceably than it
once did behind the jollity of grapes and vines on its grillwork sign.
Early in the 18th century its cache of forbidden pamphlets was
discovered and the cabaret closed for a while. Later in the century,
the daughter of the owner was guillotined for the attempted
murder of Robespierre.

The Quai d'Anjou repeats the patterns of monumental doors
guarding courts, of rare ironwork balconies and stair rails, of the
ubiquitous garlands and masks in several stages of decay and
revival. One of the simplest facades is that of number 17, the
Hôtel Lauzun, now used by the City of Paris for official receptions.
Nothing on its quiet face betrays the interior of golden nymphs,
whipped-cream amours and leering satyrs, Pompeian walls and cut-
velvet walls; a ceiling that is flights of masks, garlands, allegorical
figures, vases, flying putti, arabesques and curlicues tossed in a high
wind, a welter of golden gaud that goes well with its past. It was a

house of nouveau riche money, built by the architect Le Vau who seemed to have had the building monopoly of the Ile, for a man whose wealth and power grew from the money his father had made out of the pockets of customers like Molière, La Fontaine and Racine in a café on the Ile de la Cité. The owner lived in it with his wife (their elaborately interlaced initials appear on the stormy ceiling and elsewhere in the house) for about five years before he was arrested for overzealous manipulation of public funds. Shortly after his death the house was bought (1682) by the Comte de Lauzun, a small, fair man with giant appetites and a mercurial temperament who occupied only a slim tangent to French history but figured weightily in records of his time because he was so irresistibly colorful a subject. The big, equally tempestuous cousin of Louis XIV, the famous Grande Mademoiselle, was crazily in love with Lauzun, six years younger than herself. The King, sensing a threat in such a marriage, had Lauzun imprisoned and kept him locked up for ten years while the frantic Grande Mademoiselle raged, pleaded and politicked to have him released. She succeeded ultimately and they were secretly married. She was then forty-two. The couple moved into their Ile *palais* and proceeded to tear its walls apart with their titanic battles. They separated after a few years and the house became the property of another couple who also separated after some years of high life which left them broke and hating each other. Worn and sick, the house was passed from hand to hand, as it were, until it became the property of a collector and connoisseur, in the mid-19th century. He began to restore it, earning some of the money by renting apartments to Baudelaire, Gautier, a painter friend, a journalist, who formed the nucleus of the "Hashish-Eaters" Club, a free-form, nonstop circle that seemed to forget about floating on drugs for long periods of talk and women.

Daumier, less given to exotica, lived a few yards away, as did other artists of the 19th century and as does Marc Chagall on his infrequent visits to Paris. Farther along, near the Pont de Sully, below the quai, one sees the marks of filled-in arches that were once the river entrances of the houses. Above, surmounted by a high terrace, stands the Hôtel Lambert whose superb, courtly entrance is around the corner on the Rue St. Louis en l'Ile, behind a massive, sculptured doorway. Reputedly the most beautiful and richest house on the island, it too had some fascinating tenants:

the Marquise de Châtelet and for some time, Voltaire, her lover.
Later, a royal Polish émigré family, friends of Chopin and of his
friends bought the house, and their descendants still own it.

The Rue St. Louis en l'Ile is the Broadway of this smallest of
kingdoms. (To say you live on the Ile though it may mean a dark
cell and a toilet in the hall is to add a title to your name.) The
sign at number 12 boasts *"Gaz à Tous les Etages,"* a commonly
observed sign, still a distinction in some neighborhoods. Additional meaning surrounds it at number 12: it was the house of
Philippe Lebon, the discoverer of the use of gas for light and heat.
Across the street from Lebon's house is the Rue de Bretonvilliers,
remains of a village within the village, owned once by a family who
fancied the Place des Vosges and emulated one of its entrances,
still standing.

Down the street a golden clock juts out from its tower on a
brace of ironwork doodles. The church attached to it, St. Louis en
l'Ile, encloses naturally enough a full-length figure of the Saint-
King in his chain mail and crusader's sword surrounded by a
splendor of square pillars and gilded stone, a large, golden glory
over the altar and in the corners attractive pieces of religious
art. On the doors of the church one still sees the impress of the
fleur-de-lis erased during the Revolution and near it, carved into
the walls, the words *Loix et Actes* which headed a board for
affixing declarations of the Revolution.

At number 51, an almost grotesquely ornate door leads into the
Hôtel Chenizot. The first court, in restoration, reveals a beautiful
head and an enchanting plasterwork fan of cornucopias and ferns
dancing above the archway that once led to gardens and the river.
Now it opens on a broken, clammy second court inhabited by a
low, meagerly lit atelier that produces *Carcasses d'Abat-Jour*.

After a stop for a dish of ice cream in one of the unheard-of
flavors invented by a small, teeming ice cream parlor, you might
want to look into the few cross streets of the island for more
vestiges and skeletons and Lazarus houses, interspersed with shops,
a few modest restaurants and one or two immodest. Or, walk
around to the Quai de Béthume whose stately doors close off
apartments with back gardens to which the 18th century sometimes returns as exquisite, very private musicals arranged by the
tenant-proprietors. Then, down along the Quai d'Orléans into a
Paris watercolor of domes and spires, a boat on the Seine and
a velvety matting of ancient streets in the Latin Quarter.

⊷ *Des Belles Choses*
et des Curiosités

Sitting on the Rue de Rohan, looking toward the Place du Théâtre Français and its bubbles of lights, the white columns surrounding the theater and marching into the somnolent depths of the Palais Royal eastward and to the south, the strong arches surmounted by stone worthies and seals on the Rue de Rivoli. Then, seated on a local bus that plunges under the heavy blackened vaults to emerge into the broad green of the Louvre–Tuileries gardens and ahead, the river and the bridges and the slopes and domes of Left Bank roofs.

For an idea of the comparatively minute size of the 14th century royal residence that Charles V made of the Louvre fortress built in 1200 by Philippe Auguste, go into the most appealing and oldest of the present Louvre courts, the Cour Carrée at the eastern end. Having enjoyed the graceful power of Pierre Lescot's architecture and Jean Goujon's sculpture, look for the markings in darkened stone of the dimensions and shapes of the toylike towers that stood there centuries ago.

An invisible curio: According to a trustworthy Paris newspaper, twenty thousand buttonhole insignia, designating the wearer as a speaker of a foreign language and willing to give advice in it to foreigners, have been distributed in Paris. Haphazard though wide investigation concludes that no one has seen such a button on or off a wearer. The plan includes similarly invisible windshield stickers for 1967.

If you can get and hold a seat on the terrace of Lipp's at about 7 P.M., wait for the parade of the Garde Républicaine on its way back to the barracks at 7:30. Superbly, anachronistically showy in blazing helmets and plumes, mounted on the finest of matched steeds, they ride like kings of the world until a small red light stops their triumphal progress.

The dome of the Galeries Lafayette, an immense turn-of-the-century confection of gilt, glass and color, ringed with elaborate balconies and broad bands of peacock color which gather to brilliant peacock fan spots and then burst into curly extravagancies at the top.

The street musician of Paris has several guises, each visage for its own neighborhood. Working class Sundays and fair days (like the "Iron Fair" on Boulevard Richard Lenoir in early October) perform their *boules* games and *palanque*, their café verbosity and wine-drinking against a musical background of family groups of costumed musicians from the Auvergne who wander from café to café grinding and pumping their lovely mountain airs out of lute-hurdy-gurdys and bagpipes. Solitary ladies in layers of torn sweater held together by the female proletarian flag of large, dust-colored apron, quaver old love songs. In Montmartre, an accordionist in a heavy blue cotton smock and beret accompanies his lonely walk up the rise of the Rue Lepic on a bleak Sunday with old *bal musette* tunes. The blind find their way to busy shopping areas on Saturday afternoons or major bus stops like that of the Place des Ternes where a blind woman, guided by a somewhat sighted man, tootles on a flute controlled by a small piano keyboard.

The boulevards St. Michel and St. Germain are the terrain of *clochards*, semi-*clochards*, the guitar-bearing young and the shaggy, theatrical young, only some of them indigenes. Under the trees of the darker, calmer stretches of Boulevard St. Germain, toward the Palais Bourbon, Portuguese students enveloped in black fringed cloaks (each tear, ultimately fringe, means a kiss wrested, they say) pull *fados* out of their guitars as the wind makes black wings of their capes. Occasionally, what is left of the once enormous Russian colony get into the old flowery headdresses and side-buttoned shirts to play and sing for the crowd at the Rhumerie café east of the church of St. Germain on the Boulevard. Lipp's is the territory of an old lady in an innocent Salvation Army shaped bonnet whose head and hand and mandolin shake along with the shaking voice attempting a militant, rousing "Marseillaise." The rest is bearded and sneakered, in wild flight from the baths and neatness of Surrey, Darien, Stockholm, Hamburg, plunking and wailing unrequited Appalachian love—born in Renaissance England, strained through Southern Negro blues-spirituals, propelled by the driven beat of Harlem "race" records, tempered to current respectability with a phrase of "protest," ending on the sidewalks of Boulevard St. Michel. Or in the timid junior college voice that sings for a few embarrassing centimes at the Coupole on Montparnasse. (The sight of these young, so far away from home, so exotic, so full of *je m'en foutisme,* moves an occasional *clochard* rich on a lucky haul of negotiable soda and wine bottles, to fling the singers a few coins out of his dirty, majestic hand.)

The Passage des Panoramas and its extension across the Boulevard Montmartre, the Passage Jouffroy, are tunnel grab bags of shops, among them North African souvenirs, an Italian trattoria, old books and new, a tottering centenarian of an engraving and paper establishment, a once-popular wax museum, two hotels, rubble and memories of a bubbling beribboned past preserved in Carnavalet prints.

Paris animals:
Although a taste for horse meat depends on habit or penury, the horse meat "hippophagique" appeals universally. Its golden heads rearing out of bright red store fronts—sometimes two, sometimes a trio, with and without halos of golden horseshoes, inevitably evoke the frail petulant music of a far-distant carrousel.

The snail, too, sits well for its portrait; its big round coils of bright gold are one of the favorite emblems of the streets of Les Halles. Butchers prettify calves' heads and pigs' heads with a sprig of flowers stuck in the ears or placed as rosettes on bovine foreheads. Less dead and yet not much alive, the burros and donkeys whose drooping heads and lank tails nod across the Concord bridge, a set of magic-lantern silhouettes against the twilight, making their way home after a long day of pulling carts and children in the park.

The prime mover of the crashing, thumping, whirling success of the *pompiers'* ball of July 14th, 1966, on the Rue du Vieux Colombier was a lady of about sixty or more, wearing studious glasses over a witch profile. She was the leader of the three-piece orchestra. No; she *was* the three-piece orchestra. First, she played the saxophone, sweet or hot, or both, lifting and lowering the horn, bleating out key rhythm patterns to drag along the reluctant, shapeless tinkle of the piano. She was good and she was confident; she knew how to make music and how to make dancing. But it was when she tucked a fiddle under her chin and began to soar and trill and swoop throbbing gypsy tunes that her mastery became supreme. Launched on a Viennese waltz she gave it all the singing and swift grace that Strauss meant it to have. Some of the older members of the crowd showed off their agility to the young, the young stared at the elderly maker of music as impelling as their Yé-Yé. The pianist tinkled a chord or two and gave it up to listen, the drummer brushed the drums soundlessly, like a somnambulist. The fiddler went on through repeats and variations, exalted and transfigured, until she came to an exhausted halt.

She is possibly a *pompier's* wife or spinster sister, had possibly won a fourth prize in her Conservatory, probably ekes out a living by performing at just such engagements and giving a few inexpensive lessons to neighborhood children, but on the night of July 14, 1966, she was Paganini.

In the park adjoining the Bon Marché department store, there is a monument commemorating two charitable ladies, one of them the wife of the founder of the store. Both are large, fur-bearing and grimly bountiful under the streaky depredations of rain and pigeons. They cosset, in a formal, aristocratic way, a poor child while his ragged mother, a baby in her arms, looks on not very hopefully. Farther along on the Rue de Sèvres, at the Vaneau station, stands a stone Egyptian frozen in something like a tomb niche. He extends two urns in a hieratic, pouring motion, though the water finds its way out of the mouth of the inevitable lion. The oeuvre hardly merits searching for, though it may be a curio left of the rash of triumphant symbols (street names, too) that decorated Paris after Napoleon's African victories.

8 Saturday A.M.

Saturday, A.M.

Musée Marmottan, 2 Rue Louis Boilly (16th). La Muette station. Phone TRO 12–80. *See Note.*

Like a number of the small museums in Paris, the Marmottan is a private house and represents a family collection. They had a passion for Napoleon and things Empire (a fact which may serve as either lure or warning): furniture, a sea of busts and objects, a number of very good portraits, a number not quite so good, and a number which simply echo the art approved at the time, like several panels showing Napoleon and Marie-Louise, both lithe and young, going to the hunt, riding on a boat, etc., in landscapes of Elysian fields under creamy, untroubled skies.

Earlier matters, considerably pre-Empire, help to fill the large, gloomy house that sits between the park strip of Ranelagh and its parent body, the Bois de Boulogne. There are early 16th century tapestries of the life of Ste. Suzanne, a series on Alexander the Great, whose flesh (and the flesh of his hordes) has faded to an appalling gray, more like a Doomsday rising than conquering armies, and a more lively set of tapestries concerned with ladies and gentlemen languidly playful after the hunt. The lower galleries are hung with Italian, Flemish and Spanish paintings, among them a Canaletto and one Dutch portrait of a girl whose composition and distribution of black and white suggests Rembrandt's *Lady with a Fan.* Along with the paintings, some Italian Renaissance chests, Spanish faience, an enchanting set of German Virgins and a forbidding group of *Fourteen Petitioners,* saints with various afflictions literally rendered, in the German manner.

At some point, a member of the family decided he'd had enough of the Empire and the Renaissance and began to buy Impressionists—a few Monets, Degas, Renoirs, a Pissarro, enhancing an already odd and interesting (if you dash through the acres of Napoleon) miscellany.

NOTE: The recent legacy from the Monet estate, a sizable collection of Monets and paintings of other Impressionists, should have been installed in the Marmottan. In that case, the hours for viewing may have been extended. Phone to check.

For the area between the Marmottan and the Balzac House see page 130.

Musée Balzac, 47 Rue Raynouard (16th). Passy or La Muette station. *Open 1:30 P.M. to 6 P.M. from April 1 through September; from 1:30 P.M. to 5 P.M. the rest of the year. Closed Tuesdays.*

So simple a house for so flamboyant, extravagant and successful an author? The simplicity was probably dictated by the ruinous expense of the house he had built near Sèvres; he couldn't afford anything more luxurious, and it was in some ways a symbol of reform, this simple cottage set in the quiet village of Passy where one lived modestly and worked hard. And a good place to avoid process servers, creditors and exigent editors to whom one had made overambitious promises. The plainness of the house—its exterior, at any rate—and the obscurity of its position stimulated the writer's theatricalism. As Balzac wrote his Polish love, Madame Hanska, he was to be written to as "M. de Breugnol"; persons with permission to visit were given a password which they had to speak to successive guards before they were admitted to the presence of the personage himself. Should an unwelcome creditor break in despite these precautions, there was a trapdoor through which the writer could reach a tunnel leading to escape at the bottom of the hill behind the house (now the Rue Berton).

The larger than life-ness, the vivid, human, Titanic quality of the man caught immortally by Rodin in his innumerable studies, reflected itself in his work habits too, long periods of a few hours of sleep in the evening, a session of work from midnight until midday—or later—the hours kept alive by gallons of coffee. The costume for pumping out of himself the great many-peopled novels was a monk's robe ("one-time white" as a visitor put it), and for interior setting, the expensive baubles and *objets* he found necessary, and always sound, reasonable buys. A publisher of one of the leading magazines of the time wrote an account of a visit to Balzac in Passy. After going from one guardian to another by asking for "Madame de Bri," he was lead to a large, female presence, "Madame de Bri" herself, ostensibly, who then led him to *le sanctuaire* where, M. Solar (the publisher) tells us, Balzac sat. He was caressing a porcelain cup designed by Watteau, bought in Germany and miraculously joined with a saucer found in Paris, the set worth 2,000 francs (1840's value). Then Balzac showed him a Giorgione for which the Louvre had offered him 12,000 francs; refused, of course. And a painting he was sure was a Raphael, a piece of furniture that had belonged to Marie de Medici, a rare Greuze portrait, antique Chinese vases, figurines by Cellini. Balzac put a price on these, too, 400,000 francs for the collection. When M. Solar suggested that it would take another Louvre to hold these treasures, Balzac replied, "I'll build it. Yes, I'll build it."

The treasures are gone. Three years before his death in 1850, Balzac had had enough of the quiet of Passy, money enough and renewed credit to build a mansion on the present Rue Balzac. There he placed his treasures, subsequently to become the property of Madame Hanska, who after a long, peripatetic romance became Madame Honoré de Balzac shortly before the writer's death. On her death, in 1882, the auctioneers came into possession.

Immediately on entering the Passy house, through a small glass box, one is confronted by a heroic bust of Balzac, this surrounded by photos and engravings of houses in which Balzac lived or visited, including the Saint Petersburg house where Balzac met Madame Hanska after one of their long separations. Beyond, the undistinguished rooms whose major charm is that they are many-windowed and hung with a diversity of portraits, drawings and caricatures of Balzac; more busts, portraits of his friends and lovers, a number of the latter accompanied by pieces of Balzacian prose honoring the ladies; the famous coffeepot, and an 1842 daguerreotype of the writer, now faded to almost total dark blank.

From almost any room one can walk into the narrow, long garden, rather like the prow of a ship, cutting through the wave of land rising as Rue Raynouard at the crest. Back in the house, more portraits and in the dining room, a cast of Balzac's hand and

the figurines which helped him remember the hundreds of characters whose lives he invented and followed. Also, the documents
that marked, brightened, or threatened periods of his life: a
diploma, a passport, the first letter to Madame Hanska, his
nomination to the Legion of Honor, bills, bills, bills, for laundry,
for the purchase of a watch, for antique furniture, for the repair of
the famous turquoise-studded cane. Finally, funeral and death
documents, and in an adjoining room, heavily marked and
changed proofs, sections of notebooks, sets of illustrations and
examples of early editions.

Plans to furnish the house may have taken concrete form by the
time you get there, but if they haven't it will be of little importance. There is enough of the immense and wonderful greed for
things, for people, for theatrics, for work, for life bellowing
through the plain, small house, as it is.

WALK IN THE 16TH

After, before or between the Balzac house (page 128) and the
Marmottan Museum (page 127), have a look at the melding of the
villages of Passy and Auteuil which became the core of the 16th;
something like London's Hampstead for its proximity to green,
though not anywhere near as intellectual; something like New
York's Park Avenue before the glass towers took over, though
considerably more varied.

Should you start at the Marmottan, sit down on a bench of the
Ranelagh green on your way back and watch the children of the
16th at play. The young mothers wear English cashmere sweaters
and Italian shoes, while the young daddies wear Italian pants and
Scandinavian sweaters. The children, though, the babies in handmade, hand-smocked billows, the little girls in long-waisted,
exquisitely cut dresses, very short, with a pleated flounce below the
waist and the boys in perfectly tailored pants, so short and tight
that one wonders how they can run. It is the French children who
maintain the "French look" from which they stray as they grow
up to the "Italian look," the international "beat look," the
"Chelsea look," the "California look," and, if they can afford it,
the most coveted "look" of all, that of being terribly *sportif*: hairy
sweaters, tweedy leather-patched jackets, serious shoes, glorious ski
suits for an aggressively athletic appearance to counter the fact

that they are among the least athletic people of the Western world. Have a drink at the Café Rotonde near the Muette station for a close look at the powerful, poised *grandmères* of the neighborhood and a row of balconied houses across the avenue and then start eastward on the Rue de Passy, best, of course, as all shopping streets are, on Saturdays, though this estimable neighborhood keeps its shops busy all week.

Out of the Balzac house, on Rue Raynouard, you are practically face to face with the house in which Franklin lived and set up the first lightning conductor. Follow the street a short distance to the right, for a set of stairs that lead down to the Rue Marcel Proust which continues as the Rue Berton, an astonishingly rural alley that leads in turn to the Rue d'Ankara, named in honor of the Turkish Embassy nestled in what remains of an 18th century park and château. A short distance away, the Rue Raynouard becomes the Rue La Fontaine. If such things still hold your interest (see page 67), look at the house at number 14, one of the most inventive pieces of Art Nouveau architecture, yet restrained and almost classical—if these terms don't contradict the essence of the style—built by Hector Guimard.

If Art Nouveau repels you, follow Rue Singer to the small Place Chopin (the streets of the 16th, you have noticed, are a roster of the arts: George Sand, Gautier, Rodin, Proust, Delibes, Pergolesi, Goethe, Bizet, Lamartine, Greuze, Mérimée, Boilly, Rossini, Heine; a major street for Mozart and for Victor Hugo, a deep-treed avenue of choice, expensive shopping), and follow the shadows of the village of Passy in and out of Duban, Lekain, L'Annonciation, into the Place de Passy and across it, through the paths that lie between the Rue de la Tour and the Rue de Passy. You will have seen among the garages and shops a polished old *Bois et Charbons* and wine shop (Rue Nicolo) and its tall two-wheeled cart, once laden with sacks of coal and dragged by a sooty coalman, now dragged by a sooty man whose cargo is oil cans. On the Impasse des Carrières you will have passed ateliers of billowing glass held in old wood and, hidden behind the Rue de Passy (at 48) the Hameau de Passy. The narrow passage opens to a treed walk along ivied walls surrounding low elderly houses and leading back to a studio-apartment building, 1920's to 1930's in design and behind that still another house, all hiding from the enterprising street a few yards away. (A recent survey of city populations by

UNESCO revealed that Paris was the most densely populated per square yard, a startling fact when one thinks of Indian and Eastern cities; less startling when one begins to explore the houses behind houses behind houses which make packed cubes of Paris blocks.) You have passed, on Rue Lekain, the scrap of green that remains of the cemetery of Passy and the church it surrounded in the 17th century and on the street of the not-impossible two-wheeled cart (51 Rue Nicolo) the ghost of a great courtesan. She was the Comtesse de Castiglione frequently referred to as the "enigmatic Comtesse de C.," who did solace, to use the gracious medieval phrase, a royal horde including Victor-Emmanuel II, a number of princely Poniatowskis of Poland, and Napoleon III, from 1859 to 1870, her halcyon years. Later she banished every mirror in her house and slid into long, tormented rusting and death in 1899.

Passy was a sensible place for *l'amour*; not too far from Paris, not too near, and romantically rural beyond the parks of the great châteaux. A skillful stone's throw from the Hameau de Passy there was a house which belonged to one of Louis XV's councillors. It was this house that the king rented in order to install as his mistress a young woman whose beauty had attracted him and who bore him the only bastard he permitted to be baptized as a Bourbon.

Amour may still be a major preoccupation of Passy, but what shows is a passion for shopping and the wherewithal to indulge it. Passy's drugstore is the nearest thing to an American drugstore on New York's upper East Side, well-arranged windows, neat counters and that rare and wondrous thing, space. The small department–Woolworth–supermarket store has humane aisles, good color and pleasing arrangements of wares quite unlike the careless grubby warrens of similar places in other—not necessarily poorer—parts of Paris. It has good clothing shops that design the well-dressed inhabitants but above all, it has *food*. The cheeses are enormous, the fruits and vegetables spotless, perfectly sculptured and petaled, the meats and fish beam contentedly on marble counters. The *charcuteries* gather imports from every part of the world. They stuff their sausages with truffles or pistachio nuts, design artful rococo galantines and sell pâté de foie gras in large, economy-size containers. At 4:30 the cake shops fill up with children and mothers who engulf a few of the staggering varieties of cakes and then take a mound home for dinner.

The overstimulated salivary glands can be calmed by a drink in the *café-tabac* where the Rue de Passy and the Rue de la Tour meet the street of Benjamin Franklin. A zesty, modern neighborhood café, it is especially amiable at about five o'clock when everybody comes in to hang around the zinc bar for a while, or clutter the tables. The kids come in from school for the touch and smell of the great world between school and homework. The middle-class gentlemen, in no hurry to get home either, stop for a drink and a spot of politics with a friend. Young sporting bloods and workmen hang over the ticker tape that tells them how they've done in the races, while a quartet of disputatious card players slam out a few hands of a game, leave, and are replaced by the group that had been kibitzing. There is nothing distinguished about the café, but a half-hour over a slow aperitif (if you can find a table) will give you more of Paris than hours of pouring over guidebooks.

Saturday Afternoon Shopping Fair

The above phrase does not mean that *you* will be able to shop; rather it describes a route of middle-class shopping that can have, if the weather favors it, strong elements of the fairs that seem to remain as lively folk memory. At about two o'clock, alight at the Place de Clichy, somewhere near an *académie de billard*, at 84 Rue de Clichy, probably a converted 1900 dance hall to judge from the fancy mirrors and "classic" ornaments inside, and outside a pair of those ubiquitous stone ladies without whose strength Paris would collapse. You might arrange to enter a match—2 P.M. daily—or saunter around and down the Rue d'Amsterdam, past a number of rug and carpet stores that are not all of them treasure troves but reliable witnesses of what much of Paris aspires to in house decor. Rugs are followed by secondhand furniture, objects of varied and questionable provenance, a miscellany of used or unusable or inconsequential things, and homeopathic drugs among respectable clothing shops and a restaurant that studies and produces the many possibilities of cheese.

At the bottom of the hill, by the side of the Gare St. Lazare, the heart of the neighborhood begins to beat vigorously. The pace speeds up, the shoppers more numerous and avid, jostled and crushed by the crowds weaving between the station and the terminal hotels and cafés named Calvados, Havre, Normandie, etc., to suggest a touch of home to travelers from the north who use the terminal. On the Place du Havre working girls and their stocky aunts in frizzy permanents and stiff square suits, down from the country for a weekend of shopping, cram the deep stalls of inexpensive bags and the surrounding shoe stores. On the Rue du Havre, a group of musicians, all blind, play and sing in a small clearing marked out for them by an impressive dog. On the Boulevard Haussmann, the shops Au Printemps or the Galeries Lafayette will have found some reason to deck themselves and their adjoining street booths in the streamers and colors of birthday cakes. The booths flow nightgowns, bras, stockings, yard goods and bathmats, supervised by stern wicker torsos dressed in corsets. To catch some of the massed, almost immobile trade a few freelancers set up big red umbrellas filled with cheaper stockings and handkerchiefs. The gentleman with the panniered donkey has moved up from the morning market of Rue Mouffetard (page 80) with his supply of lavender replenished, again heaping.

If the weather is good you will make no progress—and why should you try?—between Rue Caumartin and the Rue de la Chaussée d'Antin, nor will you be able to converse. The spielers are going at top decibels, slapping the sides of the newest, most economical of toasters, calling for you to watch the perfect new grinder reduce meats and vegetables to pulp. They implore you to examine the efficient charm of plastic flower-holders and to buy, to buy: yard goods, candy, sandwiches, ice cream. The crowd watches, buys, stands, eats, pushes for a closer view, drips ice cream onto the street and into its shopping bags. Outside the big Café de l'Opéra, the black-coated elderly from the suburbs sit blankly watching the shoppers and the spielers, the cars and buses, and the drunk who plays the Clichy area on weekdays (he likes the number 30 bus), flashing his hideously reasonable facsimile of a gray rat in the faces of young women. As the girls recoil shrieking attractively, they almost topple an ancient pair of beggars trying to get to the corner for a foothold from which to sing their tuneless quavers in the din. But nothing in the vivid, restless, roaring scene before them unfolds the tight-shut mouths and dulled eyes of the people in the black coats.

Take a look at the shops on Chaussée d'Antin and then—courage!—back through the crush of Boulevard Haussmann (there

may have been a spieler and gadget you missed) to Rue Caumartin and look up at the horizontal band of people moving
through the high glass galleries of Au Printemps and below, the
diagonal counter-movement of people on the escalator behind the
naked glass of the Prisunic. If you haven't had enough of the
skimpy 1920's depraved baby dolls that are today's girls, Caumartin can be useful for further female teen-ager watching. Like
the rest of the area, a shopping street, Caumartin seems to
specialize in cheaper versions of 10-inch *mini-jupes* and tubular
shirts, about the width of canneloni, that fill the windows of the
shops on Sèvres and Tronchet. Most particularly it has a branch of
Circé, a chain that will have nothing to do with footwear for
ordinary non-hip feet. Last year it was yellow plastic boots, this
year wittle baby shoes dyed in ice cream, next year maybe red,
white, and blue spats, but each season the young lemmings flock to
what Circé lures with.

If they haven't left all their money with Circé, they search
pocketbook stands, which lead a tough life trying to stock
enough conservative blacks with sturdy catches for Aunty and the
very latest plastic gem to dangle over the miniskirt. A much
younger set hangs out in the Passage off Caumartin, near Rue St.
Lazare. The mixture of goods is almost as before—bulbs, seeds,
more bags, souvenirs in the universal repellent souvenir style—
with the difference that it contains also a large collection of toys
and dolls and a chance to observe the seriousness and restraint of
French children who neither touch nor yammer to own. Years of
training to be *propre, calme* and *sage* have taught them to yearn
only with their eyes.

At the end of the passage, by way of a busy seafood place for
eating in situ or taking home, you are back very near the station.
Following Rue St. Lazare to the right a short distance, look in the
Rue de Budapest, another of those streets that hide and always
look too suddenly uncovered, a corpse of a street called Cité de
Londres (still angry about Waterloo?), the combination of modern building and old arch on Avenue du Coq and at the end of the
St. Lazare, a confection of marble, glass, mosaics and discreet gold
lettering that says "*Italiano*" even before you've seen the sign of
the Trieste-Venice banking firm that inhabits it.

NOTE: With the struggling through crowds, and listening to hawk-
ers and watching the young and the old and listening to street

singers, the Haussmann Fair shouldn't have taken more than an hour or so and there may still be time for the extraordinary house and paintings of Gustave Moreau (page 150) or the Opéra Museum (page 161) or the Cognacq-Jay Museum.

Père Lachaise Cemetery, Père Lachaise or Philippe-Auguste Métro stations. *Hours vary with season, but 8 A.M. to 5 P.M. are safe.*

In the 17th century, this country property was a Jesuit retreat one of whose priests was the confessor of Louis XIV, *le père de la Chaise*; hence the name. When the Jesuits were expelled a century later, the city took over the property and in the early 1800's redesigned it as a cemetery.

In the century and a half since then it has become a crowded bed of the famous and obscure, weighed down by a variety of stone and iron and porcelain ornaments reflecting, in each period, the tastes of their survivors. The black, stiff mourning trees have grown heavy and close. Few of them flower; the low bushes droop rather than spring. They might be stelae of blackened stone or iron except for the small birds which insist on treating them as trees, flitting from broken funerary column to tree to scarred stone head and back to an unyielding branch again. It is a large and exhausting place, probably best on an August Saturday when much of Paris is away. If it is hot, there is enough tree shade in which to shelter; if it rains the dripping trees drone a suitable dirge.

You will not want to see it all, nor can you, in one visit. The main entrance on Boulevard de Ménilmontant offers a sketchy map which will probably do unless your interest is intense. In that case you should use, in addition, the map that appears in the *Guide Vert Michelin* of Paris.

A short distance north of the main entrance lies Colette under a wide, simple marble monument. Her near neighbors are Rossini flanked by porcelain wreaths and a rotted photo, the solid, discreet family tomb of Baron Haussmann and the romantic grave of Alfred de Musset, his good-looking image accompanied by a lyre and a frail weeping-willow. In contrast to these fairly modest memorials, there is a family tomb that shows how it should really be done to prove you loved them. Heap your dead with every symbol of death, brooding angels, wreathes, weeping Niobes, dark ivy, owls, winged hourglasses and lugubrious portraits. Some liked to think of their dead surrounded by Gothic spires and lacework over the shapes of medieval vaults, others preferred the gentleness of soft female figures surrounded by roses and musical instruments, the sweet, undulant structures appearing to melt like fancy blocks of sugar in rain.

Following the Avenue du Puits one comes to the tomb of Héloïse and Abélard, brought here in 1817 from their original burial place south of Paris. If this is actually the famous pair, they resemble any medieval couple of distinction, lying side by side with clasped hands, she in what seems to be a nun's headdress, he tonsured, his feet resting on the symbol of fidelity, a small dog. They too are surrounded by the appurtenances of a Gothic tomb, with the required gargoyles and leafy finials on small towers and spiked fence, the whole as circumscribed and conventional as they were not.

Looping back along the Chemin Denon, one comes to Chopin whose proud delicate profile peers out over offerings of wax flowers and fresh flowers and then to Cherubini in the act of being wreathed by a muse. The path leads into the Chemin du Bassin and then to the flowery little square of the classic, Latin-inscribed monuments to Molière and La Fontaine, neither of whom in actuality lies here or ever did. Passing a number of the anonymous, one soon comes to the tomb of Alphonse Daudet and not too far away, the grave of Oscar Wilde. (If neither map shows it, ask one of the attendants.) The most impressive of the graves, commissioned of Jacob Epstein by "a lady," it is a large, square stone plinth, bearing on one side a male angel in low relief, the wings and legs strict, strong horizontals, the face and headdress hieratic Egyptian. On the back of the monument an evasive, short biography appears. It mentions Wilde's birth, his schooling, a number of his works, his school prizes and honors in puzzling detail and ends with the fact that he died fortified in the sacraments of the Church. The only indication of the color of his life is a foolish little poem which states that "his mourners will be outcast men and outcasts always mourn." Otherwise, it might be the biography of a religious scholar given to an occasional literary *Aussprung*, impossible to relate to the sickened lids and rouged mouth of the unbearable Lautrec portrait.

Closer to the Musulman Cemetery, obscured by the stone and

green of too many other graves, is the rather plain monument of
Sarah Bernhardt. If there is no attendant to show you the
cluttered way to it, ask one of a congress of elderly ladies sitting on
a bench on Transversale 2, the nearest big avenue. They are often
the concierges, the toilet attendants, the night office cleaners
whose Monday through Saturday A.M. dress and manners are
slatternly, at best. On Saturday and Sunday afternoons they shine.
In animated groups of four and five, dressed in their best ancient
black, a discreetly small lunch carried in a cavernous old pocketbook, they know and love the cemetery. To have survived so
many dead who, not having had their own solid practical sense
died so young, pleases them and makes them pleasing; the triumph
draws a companionable, polite old lady out of the weekday harri-
dan. She will accompany you, chirping as you trip around and over
the graves, and when you find Sarah Bernhardt, will deliver a short
lecture, full of pride and apocrypha on the actress, and then criti-
cize the tombstone. It is too straight and plain for her, *pas beau*,
lacking respect. A proper grave should have the Niobes, the
wreaths and the stone arabesques these old "eaters of death"
insist on. Nor do they like the tomb of Edith Piaf, near the
northeast corner of the cemetery, just off the meeting of Transversale 3 and the Avenue Circulaire. They don't think much of her,
either, too much of their own class and too new in death. Her
grave is *vulgaire* they say and they are right. It is a sharp, new
gray marble slab, like dozens around it. What the ladies miss is the
fact that its commonness is moving, as are the dozens of small
plants and cut flowers (the 3 and 4 francs-a-bunch varieties) and
the host of souvenirs brought by admirers from holy grottos to
heal her in her illness.

Just beyond this new shrine (and it is one, judging from the
people who come to stand for a quiet minute before it, after
they've placed their votive bunch of flowers) is the older, grimmer
"Mur des Fédérés," a shrine still to a good number of Parisians.
Here it was that the dissidents of the Commune of 1871, fighting
the government troops from among the tombstones, were rounded
up and shot—about one hundred and fifty of them—against the
cemetery wall.

There is an exit at the north, but you might want to go back to
the main entrance and, on the way, immediately off Transversale I
and southward along the Avenue of Eugène Delacroix, take a look

at another group of the renowned dead: the dark, neoclassic tomb of Delacroix and near a nexus of paths, the portentous head of Balzac, his hair neater, his face less blowsy than usual, as if he had been pared and neatened for death. Following the Avenue des Allentes to the Avenue de la Chapelle, one comes to Bizet's curly, heroic head accompanied by the inescapable lyre and the names of his operas, then, by turning right on Avenue Feuillant, to the white, secure mausoleum of the painter David and his family.

Directly south, now, lies your way out and, if it is the end of the day and if you're lucky, to a Paris curio. A dreadful ringing of bells, clamorous enough to reach every corner of the cemetery, warns people out. One thinks inevitably, "loud enough to wake the dead." At that moment a tall thin man dressed in an antique greatcoat, highwayman's hat, fine riding boots and carrying a riding crop, darts out of a clump of trees. With a supple, swift gait, leaning forward as if peering at some distant goal, he strides out of the cemetery and disappears into an alley of Ménilmontant. Bringing your astonishment and disbelief to your French friends, they assure you he is one of the local characters, a leftover of a more individualistic day when the city was full of characters.

Saturday Evening in Belleville

Following largo afternoon with the illustrious dead there should be an allegro among the obscure, ebullient living. Take the Métro a few stops northward from Père Lachaise to the Belleville station and walk a block or two along the avenues that meet here and the splinters of streets which stray from their borders. Then, if you haven't stumbled on it head for the Rue Ramponeau.* Just after dusk on a clear Saturday or when it rains a little, this is one of the most irrepressible places in Paris, as crowded and colorful as the Latin Quarter, more varied and gayer. One is never quite certain about the youth which inhabits the 5th and 6th arrondissements for nine months of the year; their style leans toward heavy silences alternating with angular discourse. There is no doubt about the eager pleasure of the quarter around the Belleville station, occu-

* Named for the owner of a pleasure garden who had talents as a song-writer and entertainer, who was a life-enhancing personality, and, furthermore, a man who sold good local wines cheaply.

pied by Tunisian Jews, glad to have escaped, to be alive and, on Saturday evening, ushering out the ceremonies and restraints of the Sabbath with a rousing farewell.

All the cars are out, rampant as dogs who desperately need exercise and relief after a shut-in day. Packed full with children and grandmas and plump aunts, they crawl along the narrow passages and at each tight intersection meet as wells of noise, all the claxons hooting, all the voices calling advice, rebuke, amusement. A hailing, kidding, augmenting chorus stands on line waiting to buy the local hero sandwiches, large rolls filled from a series of bowls—spoon-dipped if there is time for hygiene, hand-dipped if the crowd grows large and exigent—by men who move like tympanists, swiftly playing from dish to dish as they might drums. The base of the sandwich is tuna fish, then heaped with tomatoes, peppers, onions, potato, condiments and a small cloud of pepper, still another variation of the versatile *salade niçoise*. Next door, another line, abutting and mingling at times with this one, waits its turn to buy Tunisian *beignets*, deep-fried ribbons, knots, rosettes coated in thick syrup, shockingly sweet, and, judging from the number of these steamy little shops, as indispensable here as the hot dog in America. (Should you buy a sandwich or *beignets*, leave a small tip in the bowl on the counter, following the custom of the quarter.)

The restaurants (page 80), as crowded and lively as a good New York East Side delicatessen on Sunday evening, bear hand-lettered signs decorated with the Star of David and the word *Cachère* and listings of *merguez, couscous, gnaouia, mloukhia, chekchouka* in an Elizabethan range of spellings. Most conspicuously featured is *brik à l'oeuf*, a malicious little invention. It is the most challenging way to eat a fried, runny egg, delivered to you in a folded crepe, hot, buttery and frangible. If you use a knife and fork the pleasure of nibbling around the crisp edges is lost. If you bite at it carefully, you will ultimately be left holding a thin dough-cup of runny egg eager to color your shirt front. Watch the locals or take your chances as you would with a mango or a ripe peach.

On the benches of the boulevard the old women in long skirts and wrapped heads sit quietly in the noise, staring southward. Behind them waddle the glossy, smiling, fat, middle-aged women, and some young, who reflect the Tunisian taste for fleshy women which reaches an extreme expression on the island of Djerba where adolescent girls are immobilized and force-fed like the geese of Strasbourg for pâté de foie gras—also, according to a British authority, a Jewish invention. The combination of spearlike men and round women reminds one of the classic egg and dart design and to go back to still older patterns, the ovum and the sperm.

The big cafés pose again that complex question: What is a Jew? What does he look like? In Belleville, he looks like an Arab, an Italian, a gypsy, a Pole, a Marcel Proust. An old rabbinical type wearing a jaunty beret consumes a flask of wine between admonitions about *les enfants* to his old lady whose felt slippers and awkward, ugly combs link her with almost all elderly working-class Parisiennes. The children who dash around the tables often have the immense, black somber eyes of Egypto-Roman grave paintings. A lithe dark-gold girl who might be a Sahara dancing girl flashes a Star of David at her neck. A lean, swift man with thick curly hair, a dark hawk face, a touch of Negro on his mouth, speaking Italian with the gestures of Palermo, reveals a neck-chain bearing a mezuzah as he turns toward you. In a local restaurant (page 80) an amiable young waiter with a sunburst smile and ten careful words of English, who might be from Provence, works in a yarmulke.

Belleville is no place for anti-Semites. Here are the disorder, the noise, the zest, the mutual affection, the volubility and appetites they dislike, and worse, still another Phoenix flight of this terrifyingly adjustable universal bastard who refuses to be killed or even for long dampened.

NOTE: Although some of the restaurants close for August, the neighborhood stays alive. Many of the people are too poor and too new to have amassed relatives with houses in the country and, in any case, who wants to leave the color and comforting crowdedness of Belleville for a month of green, lonely quiet?

9 Make It Ten Days: The Second Sunday

Royal Cradle, Royal Grave

(To do both, one needs a car. However, you might manage to go to St. Denis another day.)

The Gare St. Lazare sits on one of the big centers of the Métro web, whose directional signs carry one into the glass and iron station so admired by Impressionist artists. It hasn't changed much, except that it lacks the indispensable magic of steam from which the trains emerged as if out of a mysterious birth passage.

The ride to St. Germain-en-Laye is less than half an hour and hardly fascinating unless this will be your first look at working-class Paris surrounding the train's progress. The end of the ride pours one into a confusion of buses, cars, wide-armed cafés, a few old houses squeezed against each other in high, narrow bundles in the medieval mode, and the thrust of a big, neoclassic church which holds the tomb of the Stuart James II, crashing into the crowded square like an ocean liner reefed on a small island. Across the square, the heavy red-brick facade of the 16th century château, resembling in color, weight and some elements of design, the Hampton Court of Henry VIII but nowhere near as noble, bereft of a Christopher Wren and a Hawksmoor to improve its changing images.

A good height commanding a wide, long view of stirrings in the city inevitably suggests a fortress, so Louis VI (the Fat) built a castle-fortress in the 12th century. The indefatigable St. Louis (Louis IX) added a lovely chapel in 1230 to house—according to the guides—fragments of the True Cross, later to be placed in his beautiful Sainte Chapelle. It was only this chapel and dungeons constructed by Charles V which remained when François I whose tastes ran to Italianate pleasure palaces decided to rebuild it entirely.

For some time thereafter, the château was a busy royal hive. It witnessed the birth and death of kings, and the games of the child Mary Stuart and her friend, the Dauphin François, whom she later married, thus becoming Queen of France for the brief rest of François' life. More than a century later, the Stuart entombed in the local church came to live, plot and die here after his flight from England. Later it was destroyed and rebuilt to the tastes of various regents, at times left in disuse, at other times military schools. The "Old" section was sold along with its park during the Revolution, and the "New" ultimately reconstructed in the style of François I by Napoleon III, and that accounts for one fresher, whiter N among the endless repetitions of F, F, F, for François, in the court and on the chimneys. It was during the time of Napoleon III that the present National Museum of French Antiquities was established.

Before visiting the château, walk past it to the terrace which affords a broad view to Paris. Because of its uniformity of height, with a few exceptions, Paris from a distance is unspectacular (closer views within the city from Notre Dame, the Eiffel Tower, the Samaritaine, Galeries Lafayette, Sacré Coeur are much more "Parisian"), but you might enjoy picking out, on a clear day, the white swellings of Sacré Coeur and the science-fiction skeleton of the Eiffel Tower. The terrace extends and extends for 2,400 meters along the edge of an extraordinarily straight ridge bordered by meticulous lines of old lime trees, a bold reshaping of nature typical of the favorite landscape artist of Louis XIV, Le Nôtre, and the tastes of his time. One enters the château through an irregular court with the usual geometric garden to the St. Louis chapel, considerably restored and as a museum, dependent on good reproductions of Gothic tombs, plaques and friezes. But the small, soaring building itself, the tracery of its rose window whose luminosity was extinguished when a later building obstructed its light, the heads in the rosettes of the ceiling ornaments are, if not overwhelming, pleasing. The guard will, incidentally, tell you that the heads in the ceiling are authentic portraits of Louis the Saint, Blanche of Castille, his mother, and his wife, Margaret of Provence. Who is a tourist, even if his French serves, to question or argue? Accept it as fact; it enhances the feeling of authentic antiquity.

The museum upstairs is a rare surprise in this castle which still looks and feels like a fortress. The objects range from the tools, artifacts and arts of Gallo-Roman times to the early medieval, all the pieces logically placed, skillfully displayed and artfully lit. Delicate ancient glass glows from the broad, even light concealed behind a backing panel; the sculptured figures are recessed in handsome wooden panels; figurines are placed on small platforms of different heights, at different depths, taking the curse off the common, deadly, row-on-row effect. Even if you don't like museums, or have had too much, walk through this one, if only for the pleasure of its intelligent taste.

On Sunday afternoons one can view from the tower (wait for a guide who waits for a sufficiently large group) into the town, into the surrounding woods and into the garden, a thousandth echo of a time (by no means dead) when a garden was an expanse of gravel surrounded by rigidly balanced, tightly reined flower beds which always look as if they've just had a close shave and haircut.

Where to eat? Have a sandwich at one of the local cafés or if you want a full meal and don't mind the cost, return to the Pavillon Henri IV on Le Nôtre's terrace. This infantophile Henri kept fourteen of his children here it is said, legitimate, illegitimate, the get of five different mothers. Here, too, and still visible, is the room in which Louis XIV was born, a distracted room of ancient elegance dripping lacey rags. You might choose to have a drink on the terrace and look at the rooms and take the 258 bus to Bougival for its Coq Hardi restaurant. That will cost and requires a reservation. If that matters, go instead to Les Tilleuls (the linden trees) whose terrace over the Seine is decorated with toy monkeys and neoclassic busts. It is neither cheap nor expensive, the food is decent, not memorable; the appeal is in the stretch of Seine which borders the terrace, as mellow and rural as when the Impressionists came here to paint the river.

The 258 bus will take you back to St. Germain-en-Laye for the train, but you might continue on in the same direction for Paris and possibly stop at Malmaison, where Napoleon and Josephine conducted whatever domestic life they could manage, now a museum of their time and objects. Or, continue on to the Pont de Neuilly for a look at the new large buildings beginning to ring

Paris and, if the descent is not blocked by cranes and derricks, on to La Grande Jatte, the island of Seurat's painting and, just south of it, the Ile de Puteaux, a colorful gathering of small boats and intense weekend athleticism. At the Pont de Neuilly you are in the city and again connected to the center by Métro and bus lines.

Basilica St. Denis, to the north, in the suburb of St. Denis, so Red, rumor has it, that church services are postponed if an important Party meeting has been scheduled for the same time. Bus 153 from Métro station Carrefour-Pleyel.

Montmartre, as mentioned, is where the Basilica of St. Denis actually began. St. Denis took his severed head in his hands and marched northward, stopping only to wash his face and continued on through what is now the area of the Marché aux Puces (a strange picture if one imagines him and his head trying to weave their way through the vast, busy plain of washcloths, towels, old costumes, unpainted furniture, overpainted furniture, antiques and "antiques" and the crush of people) to the place where the "new church" of St. Denis now stands and where he finally, totally, died. His miracle was marked by a chapel, lines of pilgrims and a village which inevitably shaped itself around the holy excitement. In the 7th century a Benedictine abbey was established by King Dagobert, not far from the chapel.

Early in the 12th century, the Abbé Suger, a powerful figure in the councils of both Louis VI and Louis VII, whose banner of red and gold became the battle flag of the early kings, began the present construction of the basilica which, for many centuries, housed the tombs of French royalty and a few of its valued assistants. These are not the only tombs built for the great. There were usually three, often widely separated; one for the heart, one for the entrails; what was left was taken to St. Denis. (See the story of Du Guesclin, page 161.) And even that is gone because, during the furies of the Revolution, it was decided that royal tombs were inappropriate to a new, egalitarian nation. The tombs were sacked; some destroyed, some saved and brought back for safety to Paris, while the skeletons were thrown into ditches and later gathered and heaped unassorted, the shanks of one century poking out of the skulls of another, in charnel boxes in the crypt.

The basilica was completed late in the 13th century, but much of it was since destroyed—by lightning, by the Revolution which ripped off its lead roof, by weather and neglect—and restored by various hands, some of them singularly inept, and finally, by the ardent medievalist, Viollet-le-Duc who left it, in the late 19th century, as one sees it now.

The earliest, unrestored sections are the ambulatory, a few remaining panels of stained glass and the romanesque vaults and pillars with carved capitals in the crypt. A few treasures remain of a wealth which must have emblazoned this imposing and foremost of basilicas: a beautiful 12th century Virgin and Child and a pair of reliquaries of a later period. The rest is tombs and tombs.

St. Louis (Louis IX), a pious man who washed the feet of the poor on Maundy Thursday, the builder of the exquisite Sainte Chapelle, a statesman and an avid pursuer of the infidel through two Crusades (the second killed him, of the plague, in Tunis), had effigies carved of his royal predecessors back to Dagobert and placed them in the basilica: rows of long, calm, remote figures, their feet resting against little dogs (to denote fidelity in women), or lions for the power of kings, or weasels, or whatever the totemic sign of a house might have been. They resemble each other in the stiff hieratic convention of early stone funerary art, except for the tombs of Frédégonde, a bloodthirsty queen of the 11th century and old Dagobert, whose monuments consist of ancient leather and inlays of enamel, much of the color rubbed away by time, leaving the velvety sheen of old metal. In the 14th century, it became the practice to make death masks of the royal dead so that the later sepulchers bear portraits, more or less, of the bodies that inhabited them.

The tombs grow more and more elaborate with the changes in styles to reach a set of apogees here, with the two tombs of Catherine de Medici and her husband, Henri II. The first is a hideously realistic rendering of the contortions of death, the figure naked except for a shroud, and already decaying. The second shows them lying fully dressed in magnificent robes wonderfully carved into the marble, appearing to be napping after a court feast, guarded by four large Virtues and the Apostles.

From here on, the guided tour (it is not permitted to enter the tomb area without the guide) descends to the crypt much like other medieval crypts. On your way out—or in—notice the plaque on the portal which tells that Jeanne d'Arc wounded at the St. Honoré Gate (the Place du Théâtre Français) came here to offer her arms in defense of St. Denis. And stop for a moment to look at the very much restored and still appealing portals which depict scenes in the life of Saint Denis, signs of the zodiac, panels of peasant life, foolish and wise virgins, and other bits of the usual, engaging medieval space-fillers.

NOTE: For those interested in architecture, St. Denis was the first gathering of the elements of style on which many Gothic cathedrals were patterned.

10 The Second Monday

Musée Cernuschi, 7 Avenue Vélasquez (8th). Villiers station or Monceau and a short walk in the Parc Monceau. *Open 10 A.M. to Noon, 2 P.M. to 5 P.M. October through March; 2 P.M. to 6 P.M., April through September. Closed Tuesdays.*

The museum sits in what was, in its time as a private house, one of the *quartiers luxueux*—Proust's aunt had a house in the area—of Paris. The splendor is dimmed, the broad boulevards of Courcelles and Malesherbes have lost their fine carriages and glamorous shops for more commonplace buses and decent, uninspired stores. Little of the change has invaded the Avenue Vélasquez, however, still one of the small, closed-off streets one enters through a handsome grillwork gate into a row of grand houses. The Musée's facade retains the style of its time and place, though its interior has been rebuilt (unlike other house-museums in Paris) to serve specifically as a museum of Chinese art.

The collection ranges through rare pottery and jades of various periods, superb silk panels, 8th century bronzes—mirrors, handles, vessels—incised with complex, rhythmic designs; funerary towers and edifices stamped with repeated designs, some of them crude, some extraordinarily sophisticated. The most beguiling collection is that of lissome Han figures, somewhat like Tanagra dancers, somewhat like Jaina Mayan women. The upper floor opens on an immense Buddha seated on a lotus leaf, not far from two large, wonderfully made bronze deer. The peak of the tasteful selections is placed apart, in a case of its own not far from the entrance, a breathtaking slender Bodhisattva, all beauty, grace and virtue.

The Musée is hardly an exhaustive collection; there are many larger ones displaying more of the incredible outpouring of

Chinese art over the centuries. But not many are so considerately lit, so reasonably arranged or so helpfully informative. Nor do they display modern mainland Chinese art as the Cernuschi does, interesting to see for itself and for the fact that it is not altogether closed off from the Western world, that it adds Futurist restlessness, the dancing symbols of Miró, the splashy dynamism and exaggerations of the Expressionists as well as poster humor, to the old, traditional modes.

NOTE: Here you might choose between lingering in the pretty Parc Monceau with its heavy trees, undefiled grass, formal plantings and sage, respectable babies, or go on to a neighboring museum.

Musée Nissim de Camondo, 63 Rue de Monceau. *Open 2 P.M. to 5 P.M. weekdays; 10 A.M. to Noon and 2 P.M. to 5 P.M. Sundays. Closed Tuesdays. (Summer closing recently changed; check.)*

The Comte Moïse de Camondo was a member of a rich family, a cultivated, public-minded one (a brother, Comte Isaac de Camondo left a sizable art collection to the Louvre) though not a very lucky one. As one enters the carriage way, past the superb gateway knockers, one sees a plaque which explains that the house and its contents are an annex to the Musée des Arts Décoratifs, given by Comte Moïse as a memorial to his son Nissim, shot down in World War I. A second plaque states that Moïse's daughter and Nissim's sister, Mrs. Leon Reinach, was taken with her son, her daughter and her husband by the Germans in 1943, and sent to Auschwitz where they were all killed.

It is a particularly somber overture to an important collection of 18th century art; lilting, ornate, decorative arts with a leaning toward the playfully sentimental. The house is a *palais* in Louis XVI style, with classic pillars, lordly salons alternating with coy nooks, with tall ceilings and large, well-proportioned windows looking on carefully restrained arabesques of garden and a park. Its silk wallpapers and carved panels enfold treasures of Sèvres and Meissen porcelain, tapestries of Aubusson, Gobelins, priceless Savonneries panels, Chinese vases, remarkably crafted French furniture, bronze objects, paintings and small sculptures—a few of them by masters—amusing screens, a dignified library and an almost square bed with a juicy nude hanging at its side.

As if to keep the bright bouquet of objects enclosed in black ribbon, the visit ends, as it began, with reminders of Nissim de Camondo, his room, his table and on it a photograph taken shortly before his death, at twenty-five.

Gustave Moreau, 14 Rue La Rochefoucauld (9th). Gare St. Lazare Métro. *Open 10 A.M. to 5 P.M. Closed Sunday, Tuesday and during August.*

Gustave Moreau, the teacher of Georges Rouault, died in 1898 in Paris where he was born. Judging from his house which stands among similar anachronisms in one of the enclaves fallen from fashion, he was popular and rich. Caught up and riding with a wave of antinaturalism, his fusion of classical and private mythology, his heavy jewel-like ornamentation, the religious strongly marked with sex, the imagination tending toward surrealism, must have appealed to his time. His work was evocative and puzzling and still is, although you may boggle at the accretion of detail which, in our sparse white on white time, is considered obscene.

The house itself is an impressive one, with a vast atelier like a Renaissance banqueting hall and large upper rooms clearly designed to show off paintings. Under the windows of the lower floor there are innumerable panels which can be drawn out of their cabinets for a survey of Moreau's skill at drawing and some of his preoccupations. In various media and with unerring draftsmanship he leads us into his world of chimeras, of griffons, bulls and great birds with nude women, of mythical beast-women and men, of exsanguinated, deathlike creatures in nightmare places.

The paintings are of strange classic courts strewn with supernaturally white, opulent women, and of improbable cities crowded with processions of grotesques and forbiddingly coupled lovers. The *Angels of Sodom* are two gray figures floating away from the black and blood-red burning city. Again and again and again the vulture chews at Prometheus. In *Fleur Mystique,* a dreamlike landscape surround a wan Virgin Mary holding a cross; she emerges as the fruit of an immense tropical plant whose roots are haloed heads and contorted bodies. The bull who carries off Europa wears a halo. Why? Why did Moreau leave so many paintings unfinished and yet work his *Jupiter and Semele* as if the large canvas were a huge ornament, building it up with layers and layers of glazing, like enamel, reworking spots of luminous color until they stud the canvas like jewels?

It is extraordinary, obsessed work, a glimpse of preoccupations we blandly label, with our unfinished knowledge, as "sick." Moreau's time was kinder. Henry James reports in his *Paris Sketches*, "I have it at heart to add that the two fantastic pictures of Gustave Moreau . . . have proved the lions of the Salon. . . . They are very remarkable, full of imagination, and if not of first-class power at least of first-class subtlety." Which shows that one era's subtlety is another's bludgeon blow, or that the young Henry James was a Puritan who refused to see what he saw.

BUS TO VINCENNES ZOO

The 86 bus (pick it up along Boulevard St. Germain) from St. Germain des Prés eastward, rolls through the no-nonsense markets of Place Maubert, neighbored by the Maubert-Mutualité Hall, the place for protest meetings, American folk-cum-social dissent concerts and foreign jazz bands. It crosses over the Pont de Sully and the wedge of park at the tip of the Ile St. Louis, surveys the facades of a few of the Ile palaces (page 119), and then enters the Marais. After the stretch of shops and atelier courts of the Faubourg St. Antoine come stands of new housing and ambitious new shops that take their architecture and lighting from the Main Streets of the questionable *Etats-Unis* and their styles from Rue Victor Hugo and the Rue de Sèvres. The approach to the zoo, a short distance beyond, is through what is left of suburb, still cluttered with red-brick houses, pulled earthward by lumpish design and inept stone ornaments, much like the worst of Victorian rows in London.

The zoo is at the near edge (Porte de Vincennes) of the large Bois de Vincennes and consists of outcroppings of many heights and shapes of artificial rock for bounding animals to bound on, for climbers to climb along, for baskers to bask on. Here and there, along the sides of the leafy paths, waterfowl paddle in little picture-ponds. In the depth of the trees, a couple of the ubiquitous welcome and welcoming cafés and stands for peanuts, candies, cake and lengths of fresh bread. The children act like children, the mothers like mothers, and the very smallest ones, grown tired and irritable, have to be carried while Grandma stuffs soothers into their petulant mouths. In other words, a zoo; neither large nor zoologically important, with the appeal of most zoos and one in which to see the French family in a native habitat.

✌ *A Pause in the Day's Occupation*

Paris is very kind to tired feet. Some of the broad boulevards still have street benches under the famous trees, most of the old churches have saved a scrap of cemetery for tiny public parks and, of course, there are the thousands on thousands of cafés, many of them open through interminable hours.

For hotel resting you might try the radio. Most stations, French or foreign, will give you the universal adolescent bleating you will find at home. "France Culture" is something quite else, a set of verbal mosaics that make an idealized self-portrait, not necessarily what you think you see, but what the intellectual Parisian thinks he sees: the 19th century stormy-haired thinker and poet; vibrant, searching, golden-tongued, with a restless, devouring interest in things of the mind and, at the same time, devoted to love, mostly as self-immolation.

In the early morning, when the air is not heavy with carefully enunciated Latin lessons, you might hear a lecture in stately detail on the difference between a puma and a jaguar, or a physics lecture surrounded by splinters of electronic music, or readings from the works of a 15th century chronicler and poet. It might be a report on recent American literature with evaluations of Saül Belleau and Jean Cheevaire, an old travel piece on Mozambique with folklorique music thrumming and ululating behind it or a description of the circumcision rites of remote African tribes described by a dry, rustling voice like the crumbling of yellowed paper. Or, you might hear a discussion of cigarette smoking and lung cancer, tactfully timed—8 A.M.—for an hour when few people can face life, much less death.

One of the favorites of the later morning hours is the long interview with a half-forgotten, elderly poet. For its length and detail it is peculiarly uninformative, probably because the questions are peculiar. The elderly gentleman's mind and creative sensibilities are explored by means of "What military figure do you most admire? Who is your favorite hero? Heroine? Writer? Painter? What are your favorite colors? Your favorite music? If you weren't a poet what would you like to have been?" And the patient old man makes polite, wordy answers to the high school yearbook questions.

The afternoon can bring a reading of Hemingway's *Old Man and the Sea* whose sparse syllables as translated into French and spoken by a member of the Comédie Française become gilded, rounded Baroque. The flesh may be that of Papa, but the voice is that of Racine.

In the late afternoon (particularly effective in the slow, sweet, sad summer twilights) comes love, rueful, lorn, tenderly clutching amorous thorns to its bosom. The tunes are often long tuneless recitatives of a hoarse, soft breathing in a minor key, the voice that oddly androgynous French voice which might be a man's high tenor or a woman's low mezzo, and always a bit rough as if passion were ripping the singer's throat.

If all this doesn't interest you and you become impatient with opera and symphonic programs that carry little music and too much program note, a mélange of information, opinion and sentimental biography ("A's life was saddened by an unrequited love which is reflected in his use of minor thirds"), you might choose to improve your French by reading one of the weekly scandal sheets which will also teach you not to envy the rich and royal mired with heavy hearts in marital confusions. Or find a tabloid that explores more personal minutiae, featuring enormous front-page headlines like, "At Eighty-Four Picasso Has All His Own Teeth." How much nearer the core of French cultural life can anyone hope to be?

11 The Second Tuesday

Musée de l'Opéra. Opéra (9th). Opéra station. *Weekdays only,*
   10 A.M. to 5 P.M.

Via "two majestuously incurvated slopes," according to a booklet that employs still another variety of Franglais, one enters that
section of the building planned as private, imperial salons, now a
large library and a small museum. It displays, among its collection of souvenirs, a brooch worn by the legendary Malibran, the
swan crown of Pavlova, the slippers and fortune-telling cards of
Nijinsky, the mantilla comb and shawl of Argentina. Under the
glow of the ornate chandeliers helped along by unobtrusive modern lighting, you can follow modes of stage design from an early
performance of Rameau's *Les Indes Galantes* to the bare gray-tan
set by Masson for *Wozzeck*, costume sketches by Derain, by
Léger and the earlier masters and portraits by painting notables
of music notables—a Delacroix sketch of a famous *danseur* and
Wagner as seen by Renoir.

Musée Jacquemart-André, 158 Boulevard Haussmann (8th).
   Miromesnil Métro station. *Open from 1 P.M. to 5 P.M. Closed*
   Monday, Friday. (Check, though.)

Like their American contemporaries the Morgans and the Fricks
of Paris were drawn irresistibly to the Italian Renaissance for its
wealth of arts and for a sense of reincarnation as a Pope Julius II
or a Lorenzo de Medici, or a Gonzaga. As in the United States, the
French industrialist was sometimes misled, surer of himself with
the objects and arts of France (Gobelins, Houdon busts, the
exquisite jeweled toys of the 18th century and earlier) and the
not-so-distant Netherlands paintings, than he was in Italian art.

He bought Hals, Rembrandt, Van der Weyden, Memling and a superb Fragonard, to hang below his painted ceilings among gilt ornaments. But a disconcerting number of "unknown," "attributed to," "school of," in the Renaissance galleries for which the museum is famous (and these are open only on weekends) reach a peak of doubtful provenance in an absurd fat lady, drawn and painted in the technique of Sicilian carts, blamed on "the school of Veronese." There are very good objects though and a number of choice paintings, other than the eccentrics, that merit your time. On the whole, the museum presents an eclectic, evocative gathering and, if you haven't been in one before, a chance to see a late 19th century Paris elaboration of the *hôtel particulier*.

Les Halles Flower Market

The afternoon flower market (best on Tuesday and Friday at about 4:30) in Les Halles is less a feast of odors—though that seems a contradiction—than of sights. Trucks rammed tight against the wall of the old church of St. Eustache and into the deep portal convert themselves into plant shops, using the street for overflow. The small botanical gardens of grouped plants: begonias of salmon, vermilion, and yellow; pink, red and white roses, leathery leaves and leaves like plumes make an almost staged strong contrast with the gray iron and walls of the market buildings and the scraped black of the church. Ivies and ferns shape dells around the mouths of trucks, myriad greens of herbal plants make the lawn of a row of *charcuteries* and *triperies*. The greens and the potted flowers meander along the streets of Mondétour, de la Grande Truanderie, into the street of the swan (du Cygne), spread along Pierre Lescot and bring you back to the central market whose outer passages accommodate the stalls of fresh flowers.

As is general in France, flowers are the concern of women, but those in Les Halles are in the main Italian women who bring the flowers in from outlying areas. They seem to work in family groups, from an imponderably old and warped though still agile grandmother down to a nubile, blondined young thing. The flowers, fresh and moist and glittering with the dew the women keep sprinkling, lie on trestled tables or in the big wicker baskets in which they are transported. Some women stand spiky rows of gladioli, white, red, and peach, as fences along the counter;

others make painstaking bouquets of concentric circles of color or
let a clump of yellow roses make its own perfect arrangement.
Large African daisies explode like fireworks. There are shy flowers
and violent, tigerish flowers, and the noise, though feminine, is not
ladylike. It is a hearty market where you can buy fresh flowers
cheaply as the day grows long—about 6 P.M.—at retail for whole
sale prices, and where, if a stiff summer breeze comes by carrying
with it the odors of the local *pissotières*, experience, willy-nilly, an
incongruous combination of sight and smell.

If you haven't walked this area before, look into shop windows,
particularly those with prepared foods—glazed ducks, fish salads
embroidered with capers and mayonnaise, pâtés of varied delicacy
or coarseness, the total salivary-gland inspirer that, if any one
thing does, means "Paris." How it's done is partially revealed in
the gleaming windows of a temple of kitchenwares on Rue
Coquillière; where some of it goes, at the cuckoo clock Alsatian
restaurant nearby and almost any other restaurant in Paris.

NOTE: At the northern end of the market you are a few minutes
away from the oldest house in Paris, number 3 Rue Volta. It was
built in the late 13th or early 14th century but its cross-beamed,
small-windowed bulk stands more sturdily than considerably
younger houses. Although the gable has been replaced by later
mansard roofs and the glass is of a more recent time, the house
and its street-floor shops (atélier-living quarters) present an
authentic medieval image. The rest of the ancient street is a row of
tenements with a distinct smell of slum that runs into the Rue au
Maire, a street built in the late 13th century and, as the name
implies, the municipal center of the priory of St. Martin des
Champs. Now the base of its old houses—none nearly as old as the
Volta house, however—is an uninterrupted row of small cafés
whose juke boxes wail in Arabic. The décor is a touch of nostalgia,
a homey tastelessness that, along with the many customers in the
limited size, make them attractive places on a cold rainy day.
(Don't search these out in the evening, there are other picturesque
slum streets where the welcome may be less warm, or possibly, less
hostile.)

12   Instead of, or in Addition to

Another Sunday Afternoon

Kremlin-Bicêtre Market, 47 bus or Métro to Kremlin-Bicêtre.

Past a great gate and a sign that insists no one with alcohol will be admitted, walking by gardens and trees and stately facades and arches one looks for a sign of the former horrors of the years when the Hospice et Fort de Bicêtre was hospital, madhouse and prison (page 95). Instead, old men on the benches under the trees, spruced up for Sunday visitors in their berets and dark suits, some alert and jovial, others lost in the fogs of senility. One group tottering briskly down a path stops to laugh at a friend who can't follow as quickly; he has forgotten where he put his belt and is losing his pants. Visitors stop for a moment to watch and smile at his stumbling progress, clutching his trousers in a bunched handful at his waist and flailing with the free arm as if it were an oar to give him speed. Then they walk on to deliver a new undershirt and a favorite cake to their own old man.

Later is the time for having a glass of cheap wine or a cheap meal in the market restaurants outside the gates; a merry-go-round or auto-bumping ride for the children, a piece of candy or a crepe from one of the many stalls. Papa may make a stop at a shooting gallery while Maman has her fortune told. Then on to shopping. The food stalls may be closed by 3:00, when the rest of the market shapes up, but the compelling odor of dried cod lingers over the piles of felt slippers and the rows of bicycles. Unlike other markets, the *puce* and *clochard* areas are not separated from the fresher, more respectable goods. Militant motorcyclists' helmets may be flanked by a dozen worn red socker shoes on one side and a minestrone of broken zippers and scarred buttons in an old copper pan—once a beauty and capable of restoration—on the other. Dusty wax flowers in a 1910 vase, somehow missed by the Left Bank collectors, guard ancient kitchen cabinets whose paint is scratched and windows broken. Old comic books lie with stamps which just may have some value; stiff new house dresses, highly enameled refrigerators and good rubber boots share space with a filthy, faded blanket and the remains of a blue-velvet drape. Fresh, fragile bright toys and gadgets are the stock of one vendor; his neighbor has one old book, a cracked school slate, a rusty gas ring and five gaping sneakers with lolling tongues to sell. An antique typewriter is enthroned on boxes of books near a stand of neat, workable machine tools. One spread of wares has fine goblets, good copper pans and attractive porcelains. One place of business is a newspaper spread on the street; on it, one corduroy jacket, one greasy pair of pants, one pair of shoes, one undershirt, one set of braces, as if a man had divested himself of all the clothing he was wearing and were lurking, nude, behind a hoarding. A few tattered old men sell each other seemingly senseless objects—a few rags, a doll's head, broken spectacle frames, burnt-out radio tubes—dragged out of black paper valises. The sales made, they join their friends to gulp harsh red wine in nests of rags and old papers. More neatly nested behind their wall of new blankets to sell, a young couple has set up a table, a tablecloth, napkins, silverware and plates on which to have the full-course dinner they brought from home.

The possibilities of finding a Sèvres piece or an old pewter wine-measure are remote. It is, though—hospice and market—an informative two hours among the gnarled, resilient, hard-working old and elderly of Paris and their attractive savage daughters in tight pants and sweaters and wildernesses of yellow-white hair; the starched, passive children, the North African vendors of incredibly ugly small rugs piled high on their shoulders; the end-of-the-line *clochards* with no energy left for the drunken jauntiness one likes to think (it saves being concerned about them) is their common trait and distinction; the bawdy *commerçants*; the tired, pale waiters, the dextrous, good-natured crepes ladies; the wives of Neapolitan masons trailing their long lines of graceful, dark goslings behind them; the gypsies that ply the markets and the railroad stations; in short, still another piece of multicolored fabric for the Paris collage.

And Yet Another Cemetery

If Père Lachaise seems too large, Montmartre Cemetery too sharply spiculed and tight, Montparnasse too open and the graves too poorly mapped, try the most prettily placed and appealing of them all, the dog cemetery at Asnières. Find the 54 bus and take it northward to its last stop. (As you ride along Avenue de Clichy, watch for number 91; if its doors are open, you may catch a glimpse of the sort of small palace that often hides behind the facades of ordinary shopping streets.) Then take any bus marked "Asnières" and get off near the edge of the Seine bridge, just as the sign for that community comes into view.

Although All Souls' Day is the favorite for grave-visiting, there are always people here on a Sunday afternoon and more children than one sees in Père Lachaise or Montparnasse. A dominant note of adoration is struck at the entrance on the upper of the two levels, in a big monument encircled by shrubs and flowers, dedicated to Barry, a Saint Bernard. On his back, a happy little girl and above him a relief of his hometown; below, the legend that "he saved the lives of forty people and was killed by the forty-first!" One would like to know why and how he was killed by a man he rescued, but there is no further information. In general, the upper level is for the aristocrats, owners and pets. The funerary urns are more numerous, the hedges deeper and better cut and, on the stones, frequent mention of prizes and lineage. A dedication that appears several times, as if for a child, is *fais petit dodo*, the gently mourning interspersed with the bitterly misanthropic: "Deceived by humans, one turns to true and faithful friends" and "Well-loved, you were too good and too intelligent to live. It was fated that you leave me alone in my sorrow, my best friend. I shall love and miss you eternally." Even for 1905 and its florid expressions, the condensed tombstone autobiography is too naked and disturbing. One turns from this cry to the dignified monument to Marquise and Tony, the dogs of a Princesse Lobanoff, standing fully life-size and in elaborate harnesses on two broad stone steps, but is soon returned to 1900's self-pity expressed in a canopied and pillared tomb for the faithful companion and only friend of an *errante et désolée* life. Going by more restrained markers, observing that male dogs have names like Laddy, Dik, Jaky, Tom, Black, obviously English, while the females stay French with fluffy names like Bonbonne, Nounouche, Bijou, Chiffon, one reaches the path to the lower level.

Here the narrow graves are like wild little gardens, some marked out by chicken wire, others by the sides of wooden boxes. A few graves are metal cribs, clearly made of broken doll beds; some are simply sticks and stones marking off a section of earth. There are none, however, without flowers though they may be dusty wax roses and apoplectic poppies stuck in a tin can. Graves continue on along the northern edge of the island, not too many yet, leaving a leafy path among shrubs and vines, a reminder and relic of a time when the Seine was fringed with tendrils of green almost anywhere.

Musée des Monuments Français, Palais de Chaillot (16th). Trocadéro station. *Open 10 A.M. to 5 P.M. Closed Tuesday.*

An adjunct of the Cluny (page 160) with murals and sculpture, almost exclusively church art, copied from the originals in divers parts of France in an astonishing display of patient skill which reproduces every blot, crack and marring erasure of time and weather. Inner rooms and niches were built to show the paintings on a long vault of ceiling, to suggest the dark mystery of an old crypt or the majesty of a cathedral entrance. Since there are few visitors and those few possibly a cluster of nuns being shown around by a priest-art connoisseur, one is quickly wrapped in a time when religious instruction, insistent, repetitious, vividly graphic, was designed to awe and frighten.

A dark, powerful angel dressed as a crusader leads to a chapel with narrow leaded windows surrounding a group of wordly saints and fine ladies much like the famous processions of Ravenna. In one dome sits a militant, fearsome Christ Triumphant; another craftsman of more naïve vision and skills saw Christ crucified with a pendulous belly marked by a large, round umbilicus, his fat, double-chinned face melting into an unkempt mass of yellow hair.

Then suddenly, among the primitives, the trace of a fine Italian hand: a figure that might have been painted by Masaccio, a drapery that suggests Giotto, a pale broad face out of a Piero della Francesca—the work of Italian painters brought to Avignon when it was the Papal seat and imported its painters from Italy.

Numerous as the saints are, the devil's minions almost crowd them out. Often as hideous as those of Bosch, sometimes as playful as the birds of Chagall, they stuff the faces of gluttons condemned to hell and stoke the fires that boil the lustful. What might be the most powerful deterrent to sin is a sadistic—someone derived a good deal of perverse pleasure out of this one—representation of the hung, disemboweled Judas, entrails, lungs and heart dangling *en plein air*, his frantic eyes staring at the demon who, with a claw clasped on its buttocks, is drawing forth Judas' soul, full-bodied, long-nosed and ripe for Hell.

In the sculpture section, Eleanor of Aquitaine lies stretched out and peaceably, as was probably not her habit, reading a missal. Not far from her, the death mask (one of the earliest made) and the story of the foolish, heroic death of Isabel of Aragon and of the adventures of the corps of Bertrand du Guesclin, the 14th century hero who freed France almost entirely of English rule. Charles V wanted him to be buried among the royal tombs in St. Denis (page 145), but Du Guesclin had asked to be interred in his native Brittany. As was the custom in the burial of kings and heroes, portions of whom were usually left in three separate places, Du Guesclin's entrails stayed in Le Puy in the Auvergne (burial 1). After several days of the northward march, the weather urged that his flesh be boiled off his bones and the cooked mass buried (burial 2). Somewhere near Dinan in Brittany the cortege was turned back by order of the king, to St. Denis. The skeleton disposed of there (burial 3), only the itinerant heart was left for Brittany (burial 4).

The upper floor sections include (copies, still) some of the warm girls of Jean Goujon, a few Houdon heads, a monstrous figure of a heroic skeleton who refuses to admit his death and the surpassingly vulgar tomb of Maurice de Saxe. The area is, however, something of a hodgepodge. You might skip it altogether and go back to examining more of the juicy versions of Hell.

Musée Cognacq-Jay, 25 Boulevard des Capucines (2nd). Opéra station. *Closed Noon to 2 P.M. and Tuesday.*

Around the corner is the Opéra, the Café de la Paix, American Express and a short distance to the west, the Madeleine; all around, the big shops and the small. Surrounded by the mercantile vigor and explosive traffic sits the house of the founder of the

Samaritaine department store, M. Cognacq and a lady named Jay, referred to on the plaque as a "devoted, cherished, lifelong companion," but not as "Madame." They filled the house at Number 25 with light, buoyant 18th century art: row on row of charming ladies doing charming things, the pleasures and pains of love prettily and bloodlessly expressed. Among these studies from skillful, now obscured hands, a number of outstanding Watteau, Fragonard, Greuze and Boucher paintings and a vigorous portrait by Vigée le Brun. Reynolds, Gainsborough and Lawrence portraits hang in conspicuous, light areas as do the Dutch works. One must peer carefully into the dark corners of the hallways to find the Canalettos and, the fillers of the dimmest places, a number of ravishing Guardis.

The rest of the collection is comprised of furnishings of the time of Louis XV, a climax of the period's silken, curved luxury appearing as a large four-poster bed whose blue damask curtains gather to a crown at the top.

The Cognacq-Jays also had a large appetite for the kind of Meissen figurines that act like too much candy on modern tastes and for playful objects of precious materials and superlative workmanship: tiny gold boxes sectioned for tinier bottles, an enameled mandolin concealing a watch, jeweled fish, jasper camels; case on case of beguiling, expensive trinkets to ramble among as a break in the inevitable day of hectic local shopping.

Les Gobelins, 42 Avenue des Gobelins, near Gobelin Métro. *Open Wednesday, Thursday, Friday, from 2 P.M. to 4 P.M.* Because time is limited and visit arrangements better geared to groups, whether you know French or not, join one of the *visites-conférences* which frequently go through. (Phone 488-05-41 to check.)

There hasn't been a Gobelin here for centuries, nor were they a family of weavers. A Jean Gobelin, a specialist in red dyes, settled here in the middle of the 15th century and prospered, along with his numerous children and grandchildren. Their children and grandchildren continued to prosper and the family was ready to retire early in the 17th century, turning its establishment over to Belgian weavers imported by Henri IV as instructors in tapestry-making. Jean Baptiste Colbert, Louis XIV's finance minister and an initiator of considerable industry, later installed the artist Le Brun to supervise the manufacture of tapestries—most of them destined for the endless spaces of Versailles—in the now-expanded set of ateliers and houses.

Lucky visitors are led by a small, alert lady who has a good knowledge of and a high passion for tapestries. Before she leads the group into the building, she delivers what the English call a potted history of tapestries: the first tapestries were Coptic; Flanders flourished in the craft during the French-English wars (clearly, the French would have taken supremacy if they hadn't been otherwise engaged) and the Flemish manufacturers grew very rich because tapestries were used as screens, hung on walls to contain their stony chill, over doors and windows to keep out drafts, as bed covers and to pad vehicles and furniture. The first French tapestries (she goes on breathlessly) were made in Fontainebleau. As early as the time of Henry IV tapestries were woven in the Faubourg St. Antoine (page 107); the choice of the location by the family of dyers was dictated by the presence of the Bièvre, a stream essential for their work, now covered. She then adds a few comments on changing styles—the large, noble style of Louis XIV diminished in Louis XV's time to rural-romantic frippery. After the destructions of the Revolution, Napoleon I, eager to revive the arts, set weavers to copying paintings, a terrible idea. Concerning techniques—only herb and earth colors were used before the 19th century; it takes about three years to weave a large panel; the design is hung behind the worker and reflected in a mirror before him, since he works on the reverse side of the tapestry.

She finishes her lecture with a zesty story about the wife of one of the Gobelin line. Marie-Madeleine de Dreux d'Aubray, later married to the Gobelin who had become Marquis de Brinvilliers (page 162), was a rich and remarkably immoral girl practically from birth. (According to historians, she boasted of having lost her virginity at seven and frequently engaging in dalliance with her brothers, all younger than she.) Her lover, a Monsieur Godin de Ste.-Croix, imprisoned in the Bastille on charges brought by the Marquise's father, learned there the art of poisoning. Once out of prison, he began to teach his skills to his mistress. As one of the ladies of charity, she was able to experiment on the sick in the Hôtel-Dieu and soon learned what, and how much of it, was most efficacious. In 1666, she managed to poison her father after ten unsuccessful attempts. Four years later she killed the oldest of her brothers, then his wife and a short time later, her youngest brother. She also tried but failed to kill her sister, a Carmelite nun who was more closely under God's eye. She then attempted to poison her husband, but here her lover put his foot down. In fear that he might have to marry her if the Marquis died, he countered each poisoning attempt with anti-measures and kept the Gobelin alive. Some years later, in 1672, Godin de Ste.-Croix died of natural causes (though many doubted that), and la Marquise made quite a fuss about getting a box from his house. She fussed too much, realized she had stirred up suspicion and fled to England. Opening the box, the police found letters written by the Marquise describing her crimes, her recipes and a number of vials of poison. Threatened with extradition, she hid in a convent in the Netherlands, but she was found and brought back to be decapitated, then burned, before a large crowd gathered on the Place de Grève, now the Place de l'Hôtel de Ville. That was not the end of her, however; she left a taste for poisoning and poison plots which ultimately enmeshed four hundred people, some of whom were imprisoned, some exiled and three dozen executed.

Having told her story of Paris high life in the 17th century, the guide leads one to a Louis XIV tapestry whose subject is the apology of a high churchman to the Sun King. The intrinsic matter, though, is the skill of the weaver: the exquisite, obsessive rendering of the airiness of plumes, the shine of ribbons, the duller shine of leather, the variety in faces and the differences in cloth textures.

To see the high craftsmanship still functioning, one goes to the ateliers of work in progress. Half-hidden by screens of heavy warp threads, like figures in a dream, the weavers work quietly and slowly, very carefully select and consider a thread from a bundle of thirty tints of the same color and then return to the precise, slow weaving, glancing up at their mirrors now and then in a gesture like prayer. The only suddenness is the faint gleam that darts occasionally from the glass tubes which divide the sections of thread on the loom. In this smooth, slow-motion world two Chagall designs, *The Creation* and *The Entry into Jerusalem* intended for Israel's Knesset, have been taking on color and substance since 1965 and will probably be on the looms until some time in 1967 or 1968. The same care given Chagall is expended on a handsome, abstract design nearby, on 18th century fruit and garland designs, on cherubs in a bosky dell. And as if to weave together various periods of the tradition, and time itself, the hallway leading out of the large atelier is hung with a tapestry portrait of Louis XIV as Alexander the Great, a display of virtuosity in rendering architectural perspectives, the complexities of a battle scene, the shine of Louis' curls.

Back of the building is the set of old courts and artisans' houses originally planned by Colbert to house his craft colony which maintained its own gardens and a school where the children were taught the community crafts. From one of the courts, one enters ateliers devoted to other kinds of weaving. There is a section for rug weaving, a different though equally demanding technique, involving double knotting and the skillful use of flat scissors to make the smooth, silky surface. The Beauvais weaving is of course, much finer, worked on horizontal looms and checked from small paintings set before the loom, from full-size drawings below the loom and hand-mirrors slipped below the chords, now and then, to make absolutely sure. At this point, where meticulous precision and skill can seem to go no further, the visit ends.

Musée Instrumental du Conservatoire National Supérieur de Musique, 14 Rue de Madrid (8th). Station Europe. *Open Thursday and Saturday, 2 P.M. to 4:30 P.M. Closed July 31 to September 1.*

Though your musical enlightenment may begin with "Chopsticks" and end with the Beatles, try an hour or two here if it is at all possible. In an odd, anonymous neighborhood, part of a scramble of old and new buildings, it has a retiring quality, a dusty, overcrowded, old-fashioned presence which make it a quite particular place. One enters through a court and from the broad new windows, and dusty old, come the sounds of a young pianist trying to capture with his two hands what Beethoven wrote in the Opus 111 for a demonic four or six. Another window yields the trills of a young voice coping with the demands of Bellini. A young Paganini doesn't quite make the fiddle gymnastics, but he keeps trying.

Guided by arrows and music students, one goes through the court and up the stairs into a world of lutes, lyres and lyre-lutes, rebecs, three-string *vièles*, five-stringed *vièles*, a psaltery, virginals and spinets of tortoiseshell and mother-of-pearl mandolins; then on to two magnificently painted harpsichords, one in "Chinese" style and the other in gold, Pompeian ornaments inside and romantic, Arcadian scenes of music-making on the outside.

Among the many guitars, there is a Venetian beauty of the 15th century, and one of the 17th century which echoes the alternating black and white of Tuscan churches, a guitar used by Paganini and ultimately given to Berlioz (it bears both great names), Django Reinhardt's guitar, a guitar made of a tortoise—legs, head, tail and all—with a projection attached to him for holding pegs and strings.

Reputedly, the collection encompasses a few Amati and Stradivari, but they are either kept apart or lost in the tight arrangements. Unlosable in any crowd, though, is the *clavecin* made in 1612 by order of Marie de Medici, every regal inch covered with small, animated paintings, and an equally ornate, painted, carved, studded, garlanded harp made for Marie Antoinette; a *clavecin* whose ivory keys, too, were incised and painted, ordered by Louis XIV for a godchild. Among the humbler instruments: a *lyronne* with 15 strings, horns like snakes, horns like hoops, portable virginals, a great variety of *vielles*, bagpipes of divers materials and sizes, flutes of glass or ivory or shell, *pochettes* (the pocket-size violins played by dancing masters), and an *octobasse*, a twelve-foot bass viol with three strings, what looks like a set of pedals and other odd attachments, tried in a performance of Gounod's *St. Cecilia Mass*. There is no mention of its use since.

Among the lovely and the peculiar, the most impressive instruments are the plainest, taking their aura from the people who used them. Here stands the piano on which Rouget de Lisle probably picked out the tune of the "Marseillaise," Bizet's piano and (one of the few instruments which has a "Do not touch" sign on it) a small clavichord that was Beethoven's. Other instruments are often played by the music students who wander in. One of the pleasures of the museum is to hear unexpectedly a young man toss off a Scarlatti sonata on one of the harpsichords while his friend picks up an old *vielle* in another corner of the room and grinds out country airs, but this instrument is inviolate. No one makes an attempt to touch it, or even go very near it; it evokes a remote terror. Few people exclaim over it, as they might over the royal harpsichords; they stand quietly for a few moments and then move on.

And still other possibilities if they match your interests more closely:

Musée de l'Homme, in the Palais de Chaillot (16th). Trocadéro station. *Open 10 A.M. to 5 P.M. (to 6 P.M. in the spring and summer months). Closed Tuesdays.*

An anthropological museum with an unusually large and interesting collection of ethnographic displays of the crafts, costumes, ornaments and ordinary objects used by the peoples of many parts of the world.

Musée Bourdelle, 16 Rue Antoine-Bourdelle (15th). Montparnasse-Bienvenue station. *Closed Tuesdays and from Noon to 2 P.M.*

A chance to explore still another *quartier* and the Rodinesque work of a highly esteemed sculptor in his day displayed in the ateliers and gardens in which Bourdelle worked and lived and, judging from the limits beyond which you may not go and a glimpse of old furnishings, still lived in by some member of the family.

Musée de l'Orangerie, at the side of the Tuileries Gardens, recently reopened with a large, imposing show of French painting of the early 20th century: Modigliani, Soutine, Renoir, Picasso, Utrillo and Cézanne, to pick out the most famous of the famous. How much of this private collection remains on permanent loan, if at all, is not yet clear. Inseparably part of the museum, though, are two oval rooms designed to hold eight of Monet's *Nymphéa* studies. The hushed, diffuse ceiling light, the large whiteness and simple arches between the rooms make of them a temple to the colorist magician and, as in a temple, voices drop, people walk slowly and gently. They stand and move musingly, held like the flowers, in the shine of water, the warm stillness of full sunlight and the cool lavender of dying day.

Musée des Arts Décoratifs, Rue de Rivoli; entrance across from the Rue de l'Echelle (1st). Palais Royal station. *Open 10 A.M. to Noon, 2 P.M. to 5 P.M. Closed Tuesdays.*

A few salons are devoted to shows of foreign art and, often, the works of established French modern painters. These are hung considerately in well-spaced, well-lit areas. The rest is an exhausting crowding, invaluable though it may be, of the decorative arts and crafts of several periods, mainly French, though foreign sections are included. It takes time and patience to find the gems among the omnivorous gatherings, but they do exist in rewarding numbers; it all depends on your degree of interest and enthusiasm.

The Grand Palais and the Petit Palais were built along with the Alexandre III bridge for the 1900 Exposition, the trio a monumental museum piece in itself. The Grand Palais includes a science museum but keeps much of its space for changing exhibitions of which every object is not always clearly visible. When it rains through the immensely high vaults of glass and the rain seeps through a lower, scrim ceiling, a particularly valuable piece of sculpture or rare Dahomey deity may stay draped in a protective shroud of plastic. The Petit Palais is either less leaky or easier to repair and the only obscurities derive from the poor lighting. If you can grope your way to them, look at some of the antiquities and a roomful of chinoiserie panels. The 19th and 20th century paintings of the **Musée des Beaux-Arts de la Ville de Paris,** enclosed by the building, are lit haphazardly, or possibly on a system of personal tastes of guards and curators. The color of the Bonnards is almost entirely lost, while a beguiling set of Vuillard panels is treated to fairly good light and and the radiance of pairs of Courbet ladies given full effulgence.

✍ *Paris in the Fall*

Fall doesn't necessarily guarantee good weather, no more than do spring or summer in northern Europe, but it is a good time to go to Paris nevertheless. Accommodations are easier, and besides that, Paris has come home. The shops and restaurants have been cleaned up and re-stocked. The children crowd the school-supplies aisles of the Supermags, the Prisunics and Monoprix, deliberating over notebooks and pencils; clothing shops warn the family to prepare Jean with pants and sweaters for the great *Rentrée,* proclaimed in ads and window signs as if it were an enemy invasion to arm against. The streets are full of energetic walkers, striding through the crisp air and swirling leaves in sturdy shoes, cheeks red, the long English schoolboy scarf wrapped around the throat once or twice, the rest of its length a toy for the wind. Fall is the time of the bivalve when *crustacés* burst into salty bloom around the big *brasseries*. In reed baskets and in white boxes woven of thin slats of wood lie mounds of red-mouthed sea urchins, little oysters, big oysters, round and smooth, bumpy and jagged oysters, things that look like sand dollars, too perfectly shaped to be nourishing. The whole gorgeous display (visible on any big Place not dedicated to monuments or luminous, expensive shops) is usually manned by red-cheeked, big-pawed *types* in heavy cotton coats, trousers and caps of a lively blue, enhancing their sea-y, folkloric fisherman look and the adroit authority with which they open the oysters and arrange the hard-shelled blobs.

Rows of hare—gray, attenuated Gothic sculptures—cling to the portals of butcher shops, flanked by pheasants whose brilliant tail feathers swing and whip in the breeze. In the windows, naked bundles of grouse, woodcock and quail lie in beds of green leaf. The Sunday morning food markets on the Carrefour de Buci, the Place Maubert, Avenue des Ternes, in every neighborhood, are now heaped high with food, correcting the more meager displays of summer. Customers run, crowd, push desperately as if starvation had been for days and returning tomorrow (in a limited sense true, since Monday is generally a closed day), yearning for the cheeses and sausages not available in their summer provinces.

Along the Faubourg St. Antoine couples examine shop after shop, searching for a new sofa and, on the side streets the do-it-yourselfers inspect coils of ball-fringe for the old chair to be recovered and consult with the shopkeeper-artisans concerning the best glue to hold down the inlays on Grandpa's old desk. The Boulevard St. Germain and the Faubourg St. Honoré bring out their fall and winter clothing in cuts and execution that sometimes make coats and suits elsewhere look like travesties. The prosperous female young nervously burrow in the shops of Sèvres, Tronchet, Victor Hugo for the latest stringy wisp or plastic geometry to wear. Their older sisters stride out in "Chelsea" suits, while Maman takes the poodles walking in her chic *tailleur*, a sober felt hat and her elderly honorable fur piece, its head clamped on its tail in the classic 1920's manner. The not so golden girls cram the big department stores and shops on Chaussée d'Antin and the leaden ladies with tricolor dyed hair rummage furiously with lightning eyes and hands through the bargains on market stalls.

The big cafés begin to immure themselves behind great glass cages. The first-run movie houses and the "art" cinemas grow longer lines for the Sunday afternoon showings. The French young take back the 5th and 6th arrondissements from the international summer young. The bookshops on Rue des Ecoles grow mountains of textbooks on law, on the sciences, on literature and the arts. Student cafés again become vivid jungles of hair and bristling sweaters, female birdcalls and deep angry masculine rumbles and always the one plain, silent bird arched over his textbook, isolated from the uproar. Around the Rue de Grenelle and the Rue des Sts. Pères, the cafés reopen to the Oriental, South American and African princelings returning to the local schools of government and management. The youngest French princelings, the crème de la crème de la crème who attend the famous Ecole Normale Supérieure, a distinction for the young about equivalent to being elected a member of the Académie for the elderly, stride the Rue d'Ulm with as much dignity as very short pants permit.

On the Place de la Contrescarpe, a new jazz café is painting its face a jazzy orange that contrasts well with the dun-color of the *clochards* lying on the street. The lady *clochard* who has been summering under a bridge is back in her safety-pinned coat and wool cap, flanked by an assortment of lumpy bundles, to take up her winter quarters on the benches near the Place des Ternes. One block from where she sits and blinks, a Faubourg St. Honoré window blazes with *sportif* fall totems devised of hunting horns, sheaves of wheat, red leaves and pheasant plumes.

The leaves on the Place des Vosges are gone, returning to it the clear, undisturbed integrity of its shape and patterns.

The Opéra begins to make its attempts at opera; the Salle Gaveau and the Salle Pleyel post large *affiches* announcing the musical delights of the coming weeks. After an interminable *relâche,* the Comédie Française begins to rehearse this year's Molière, the Théatre des Nations announces a troupe from Leningrad, the Théatre in the Palais de Chaillot prepares for Polish dancers and Chinese acrobats, while the small theaters in Montmartre and the Latin Quarter climb back on the laps of Papa Ionesco and Mama Genet.

L'Humanité holds its fair on a September weekend to gather the wandering Communist clans together, to bring them again to coherence and purpose. The site is usually a vast open area in the north, La Courneuve, bordered by endless rows of parked cars. (Best to take the Métro to La Villette-Carrefour Pleyel and then bus 153, or 155 or 177.) A 3-franc ticket buys the privilege of ambling through a fair not too unlike many others, popular entertainers, a Ferris wheel clearly marked with the name of its donor, a maker of aperitifs, an imported acrobat sponsored by another company, rows of thickly varnished, bulbous television machines; eating and eating and drinking and drinking. You might be at a big church fair if it weren't for the displays of Polish trinkets and books and records from Russia, a vehement speech that crackles through the public-address system, between broadcasts of the "Internationale" and (it appeared one year but someone may have discouraged its reappearance) construction platforms spotted with mannequins dressed in work uniforms, obviously meant for a monument to labor but the visual actuality is that of a scaffold dangling the hanged, a lugubrious sight for a chummy festival. No one seems to notice, intent on still another plateful of oysters with a glass of white wine or finding ice cream cones for the kids.

(NOTE: Late information is that the fair has moved back to its old grounds, the Bois de Vincennes. For the specific site and directions, watch *L'Humanité* and posters.)

Early in October, much of the flea market at Clignancourt and its confreres move to the Boulevard Richard Lenoir to shape the long rows of hooded stalls that make the Foire à la Ferraille (Eastertime, also). The exclusivity of metals among which sculptors and do-it-yourselfers search has been broadened to include furniture and bric-a-brac and soon the full gamut, which will make it that much more crowded, robust and entertaining.

Paris, *ça bouge,* but the loveliest aspect of autumn Paris is quiet, almost motionless. Acquire a car and make your way to St. Denis one October afternoon, timed so that the southward journey along the Seine can begin at 6:00 or 6:30. The light on the west side of the river is a deep pink-purple, the last banner of the setting sun. On the other side of the river, evening blue has already washed smoothly across the eastern sky. The coal conveyors stand like huge, black insects looming above the black tracery of leafless trees, and above them, three dark skyscrapers, isolated from each other and their surroundings, alone and mysterious in their veils of smoke. Everything is hushed, holds its breath; the only sound the sibilant whisper of auto wheels.

13   Practical Matters

The Métro

It takes a strong perverse talent to get lost in the Paris subway system, a system almost maniacally careful and repetitious, nagging like a sheep dog snapping at your sheep heels to keep you in the herd, pointed in the right direction. First off, there is a map just outside the station, or immediately inside (a few light up to indicate the path to take between where you are and where you are going) on which that particular station is circled or obliterated by the tips of countless index fingers. Find the station you need and the name of the terminal point of its line; that will be the name of the *direction* you must look for if you have to change. To get on the proper train to that juncture, look at the terminal name of the line you are entering immediately, especially important if the station is a large one where a number of lines meet. Having bought your ticket—55 centimes for second, half as much again for first class, or a *carnet* of ten at less per ticket—and having had it punched, look for the signs that lead to your first line. The platform will carry a large sign and in addition, a map to reassure you. Inside the car whose doors you must open (though they close automatically) there are other schematic maps which indicate each station on this particular line and the system of *correspondances* (connections with other lines). Having arrived at the proper change point, look for the *correspondance* sign (avoid *Sortie* unless you mean to get out into the street); but you are warned about that, too, with a sign which tells you that "beyond this point your ticket is no longer valid") and follow your *direction* relentlessly, even if it takes you through forbidding green picket fences, up and down stairs, through long tiled corridors stuttering through repetitions of the same ad, up through a glass tunnel into the street and down into the earth again, onto a moving platform and once more down the stairs to a green door which may or may not be open. Once more, check the platform sign and the list of stations in the car, making sure that you have not entered a first-class car with a second-class ticket. The rules are strict and to safeguard you from this error, the one or one and one-half first-class cars are distinctly different in color from the others, and all the cars painted with a large I or II.

It sounds more complicated than it is and a few minutes with your miniature Métro map before you venture forth should give you a good idea of how to use the extremely efficient maze. One additional piece of efficiency is that the Métro stops are close together and you can skip a change by walking the short distance between stations of different lines in the same locality as, for instance, between Sèvres-Babylone and St. Germain des Prés.

The Bus

It is almost too obvious to say walk whenever and as long as possible. Take the Métro if you must go a considerable distance quickly or if the buses have stopped running or if the taxis have gone home to eat and roost or if their moderate rate will burst an irreparable rent in a travel budget. A Métro ride is part of the required Paris course (page 172) for a number of reasons, but after initial acquaintance the route is as faceless as that of an airplane ride while the buses are efficient cheap means of nibbling at the diversities of the city.

To begin with, a busy bus stop, usually dignified by a shed, also holds a dark metal box which disgorges bits of paper with numbers on them. From the avidity with which they are ripped out of the box, it becomes clear that the limp slips are of stellar importance; they are the *priorité* numbers that create a grumbling order and justice of who's next. The god who supervises and controls is the conductor, high and powerful on his platform, yelling numbers rapidly, checking slips to banish liars and with a Jovian wave of the hand, to announce the bus *complet*. If your number doesn't make it at rush hour you have the joy of being one of the elect for the next bus and leaving a trail of the unlucky behind you. Even when there is no need, the *priorité* habit persists; everyone sees justice done by comparing numbers or peering over the shoulders of the dour elderly who won't play but keep their numbers secret and safe in the hollows of their black cotton gloves.

Inside the bus there are two maps, showing the stops this particular line makes and, in heavier markings, the division of the route into sections. Each section (and the section stop is called as "St. Philippe de Roule, Section," for instance) means a ticket, one small strip you hand back to the conductor after he has sold you the *carnet* of twenty for less than 4 francs. It is not compulsory to buy a *carnet*, simply more economical if you are going to use the buses more than once or twice.

In the older buses you can take your seat first and then figure out from the route map the number of tickets you will owe, feeling capable and native by the time the collector comes around. In the newer buses he sits behind a glass cage to be told where you are going and to tell you how many tickets you will have to pay. If he doesn't understand you and mumbles or bellows through his distorting, pockmarked plastic wall, don't flurry. Repeat your destination or show it to him on your map. He will then hold up the appropriate number of fingers, abetted, instructed, prodded and yelled at by the old ladies waiting in line who haven't the English to yell at you, so he gets it.

It will occur to the knavish that it might be possible, riding the old style buses, to hand a busy conductor two tickets for a five-ticket ride. After all, how can he remember? He will; it is his métier and heritage to be suspicious and he will have noticed you as a foreigner, in any case. Or worse still, an inspector of tickets may come on and ignorance of French or the bus system will not save you from the loud, humiliating scene in the course of which you will have to pay and/or, depending on the humors of the man and the day, be dropped into the arms of the nearest policeman to become a storm-tossed object lesson in how no one, absolutely no one, can put one over on a Frenchman.

Some time when you are at one of the large Sunday markets and searching bus legends on the informative signs at stops, you will notice a bus marked "PC" for *Petite Ceinture*, a precise description of a belt route that circles the old Portes of the city. To go from the Porte d'Orléans to the Porte d'Italie to the Porte de Charenton, past the Porte de Vincennes, up and around the Portes de la Chapelle, de Clignancourt, de Clichy and round back via the Portes of Maillot and Auteuil sounds like a journey through crenelated walls and turreted battlements, deep moats and massive portcullises, medieval banners and arquebuses pointing out of window-slits. The flat, modern truth is that almost the whole ring is superhighway and blank housing flashing its perfect, new teeth out of the dustbin of slums. It is an interesting ride for gauging the dimensions of the city and little else, unless you enjoy reflecting on the bitter disparity between romantic image and reality, or the fact that French public housing is no better than most and worse than some.

Bus incidentals: A bus marked *"Service Partiel,"* a red band through its number, means that it is not going all the way; the collector will call out the final destination as you board. Double-deckers were promised for the summer of 1966; they should be a superb means of peering into offices and hotel bedrooms.

The very sparse Sunday and holiday service may have been reduced to almost none at all by this time.

Most buses stop at about 9:30; the "night buses" stop at midnight, more or less, and the ride requires an extra ticket.

Having been instructed and warned, you might want to taste a few of the many bus-riding pleasures: The 95, which runs from the Gare Montparnasse into St. Germain des Prés skirts the glistening windows of antiques and art on Rue Bonaparte, then across the Seine, past the Louvre and the Théatre Français, up to the Opéra, past the Gare St. Lazare, over a short causeway that almost scrapes the tops of monuments in the Cemetery of Montmartre and finishes at the Porte de Montmartre, a few blocks from the flea market at the Porte de Clignancourt.

Number 82 presents other Paris faces as it leaves from the side of the Luxembourg Gardens, and enters the rectitudes of the Ecole Militaire–Champ de Mars area, almost collides with the Tour Eiffel and, having crossed the river, trundles through endless, tall rows of uncommunicative, costly houses in the 16th, to end its ride in the curious combination of modern luxury apartments and the remaining châteaux of Neuilly.

The number 30 takes its departure at the Trocadéro, fronting the Palais de Chaillot, rides through the subdued glamour of the Avenue Kléber, around the Etoile, then northward past the elderly charms of the Boulevard de Courcelles and the Parc Monceau into easygoing Batignolles; eastward now through Place Pigalle and into the proletarian color of the Boulevard de Rochechouart and taking a jog southward, rests before the return voyage at the Gare de l'Est.

The number 48 starts at the Porte de Vanves, passes near the abattoir and Sunday dog market (page 159) on Rue Brancion and shortly after, the renowned Institut Pasteur. It skirts the Luxembourg Gardens and enters St. Germain des Prés via the Art-Antiques street of Bonaparte, then trundles across the river, and into the Place du Carrousel for a glimpse of the famous alignment of the older, smaller Arc de Triomphe with the one on the Etoile, the tourist buses disgorging flat-shoed people, a flash of the Tuileries and a bevy of earthbound Maillol ladies. Then, through a tight arch of the Rue de Rivoli, past the impeccable, haunted Palais Royal (page 36) and, after a short jog on the drab end of the Rue St. Honoré and crunching a few crates left on streets at the edge of Les Halles, it enters the Place des Victoires, a tired, evocative reminder of faded vigor and glory. The bus touches briefly the street named for Etienne Marcel, the powerful 14th century merchant who, for a period in his conflict with the royal house, controlled Paris. Via the Rue du Mail and that of Montmartre the bus swings into the Faubourg Montmartre, once a tough, salacious street, surpassed now by a number of others but still hardly a monastery garden. The ticket-eating behemoth lumbers on through shopping streets of North-Africans—Jewish, Christian and Arab—pale, sharpfaced working class indigenes and takes a breather at the Gare du Nord before its return on a slightly different route through the same tonalities.

The Auto

The automobile owns Paris as it does other cities, but elsewhere there is some attempt to leave a few feet of space for the pedestrian. In London, the life-giving white bars at crossways actually function, cars come to a stop. In Rome they don't always stop, but the fine Italian eye quickly figures how fast you're going, where you'll be in three seconds and skims around you, front or back. The Parisian car may or may not stop at the metal studs, may or may not skim. It has neither the law-abiding nature of its British cousin nor the skills of its Italian relative. Watch out, everywhere. As one approaches a broad avenue or a complex of streets at a Place the very nature of the layout is warning, but there are skulking passages, cités, villas, squares that propel hidden death machines out of their seclusive depths. On avenues considered too generous for bipeds (Avenue Rapp, Bosquet, the Champs Elysées, to mention a few), the sidewalks have been sliced and while you think you are casually window-shopping or enjoying the broad walks of Paris, crippling or death zooms in behind you. Until that inevitable day when car and man fuse, sharing absolutely the same terrain and accommodating to each other's natures and limitations (as in Rome, where one looks forward to the friendship turning to intimacy and producing an extraordinary race of headlights on human legs and human heads on white-wall tires), be pathologically careful and always keep in mind the story, sworn to as true: A man knocked down by a car asks the driver, "Why did you deliberately run me over? I know you saw me." Answer: "I expected you to run; everyone else does."

One of the characteristic responses of a Paris taxi driver, too old to remember, or too young to have learned, is to ask you where your street is, which is the best way to approach it and how about the *sens uniques?* To tell him you're a stranger here yourself brings you to stalemate. So, if you are going anywhere but the deep-rutted famous paths, locate the main avenue and the nearest Métro station related to the street you want.

Once in motion, if he seems to be going in a roundabout fashion it doesn't necessarily mean that he is a crook; the world and its cities, as everyone knows, belong to the car and in accommodating to it, Paris has had to arrange its tangles of old streets in eccentric one-ways. Unless you're sure of distances and costs, or if the accumulated sum is palpably outrageous, give the driver the benefit of the doubt. A French taxi driver likes money, even as you or I, but he's middling honest, even as you or I. Also, you should be aware of the fact that baggage pays its way and that night driving is considered a daring, difficult thing and worth a supplement, legally. A reputedly legal practice is to charge an extra franc for being available at a terminal. It is the inalienable right of the Paris driver; don't fight it.

While on the subject of taxis: the general consensus is that lady taxi drivers, of whom there are a conspicuous number, are less likely to manipulate an extra franc or two out of a client. Whatever the truth of that, they are usually affable women, with an encyclopedic knowledge of the city and pleased to display it. A few of them add to these charms good looks, like the beauty with brilliant blue eyes and long red hair, in a deep blue shirt to show them both off, who drives in the Swiss Village area (page 228).

On a weekend night, especially in the high tourist season, taxis standing behind a *tête de station* in the nightclub areas—Montparnasse, Montmartre, Pigalle, Champs Elysées—will not take fares for short, non-tipsy hauls. They are waiting for the Good-time Charlies who tip like the drunken gods they are. You cannot protest, though you might beg. The driver has the right to say no, even if it is only a question of not finding it convenient to go in the direction you need.

There is—there was (one is never sure)—a booklet called "Paris, Where, What, When, How," distributed at the Gare des Invalides where the airport buses begin and end their runs to Orly. It is an intelligently arranged booklet full of information you may or may not want, and worth looking for.

Should you plan to spend any time beyond two or three days in Paris, buy one of the *Plan-Guide—Paris par Arrondissement* books. They come in a number of bindings and at least two sizes, neither cumbersome. Before you buy, examine the type in which the street names are printed; a cheaper copy can be illegible and no bargain at all. The book contains a large general map, a Métro map, lists of monuments, theaters, hospitals, churches, embassies, etc., and individual maps of each arrondissement and of several nearby suburbs. An alphabetized index to streets (as in the phone books, page 182, the first name determines the position of the listing) indicates arrondissement, position on the arrondissement map, the nearest Métro station and the streets at which your particular street begins and ends. The book also contains bus maps but is not especially helpful in telling you what bus gets you there unless you already know. Advice on that problem is best derived from the concierge of your hotel or a *monsieur l'agent* (as one is supposed to address a policeman) who may not know either. Convenient size bus maps do exist, but at this writing they are rarities and not easy to read. In your time, possibly, the Information Center at 127 Champs Elysées may have issued some or advise where they may be found. For an incredible amount of background material crammed into little space, get the *Green Guide (Michelin) to Paris.*

DO NOT DRIVE IN PARIS. The least of your problems will be parking and that can be a tough one, even in August.

Should you have to pawn the watch you bought in Switzerland, go to "Ma Tante," otherwise known as the Mont de Piété, which has a branch in the tourist belt, at 62 Rue Pierre Charron in the 8th, open on Saturday mornings.

For complex difficulties, call the American Embassy at 2 Avenue Gabriel, telephone ANJ 74-60.

Ushers are tipped everywhere; tipping is the major source of their earnings. The amount depends on the glamour of your surroundings: never less than a franc at the Opéra and downward to the dark boxes that run repetitions of Humphrey Bogart festivals. Don't make it too little, if you can help it; ushering is not a particularly lucrative métier.

Make absolutely sure that you want to see some particular exhibition. The titles, and posters especially, can be very enticing and lure you, often at the cost of 4 francs (over 80 cents) to a careless, slipshod miscellany of little information and no charm. The imposing halls of the Bibliothèque Nationale showed, in the summer of 1966, a "Paris past, present and future" with a few illuminated books from its immense collection, a few engravings borrowed from the Carnavalet Museum, a few prints available in almost any bookshop, dusty models of "future" cities and incomprehensible sketches and diagrams that might have been cities or doodles. The catalogue, equally distracted, cost the price of a book that might easily have been more informative and amusing. Museum catalogues are expensive, but often worth the price as souvenirs and reminders, although small booklets on particular sections of a vast museum, such as are published in New York and most admirably in London, hardly exist.

Similarly expensive are the programs for "events" which includes the Opéra and the Festival du Marais. A nicely designed book, full of prose concerning the vivid history and revival of the Marais, interlaced with ads, gives all the programs to be performed, at a cost of 10 francs. If you are interested in one performance, however, the title and author or composer is all you will know. No cast sheet is distributed, nothing; and you must hope to be able to find the polite words for borrowing a neighbor's program.

The government has been urging businesses to break the obdurate custom of August closing. It discourages tourism or, at least, reduces its spending and increases the inconveniences of ordinary living for those abandoned in the city. (The desperate late July rush to get laundry washed, shoes repaired, clothes cleaned, canned goods accumulated is preparation for a major siege.) A few docile places have submitted, taking their *Fermeture Annuelle* earlier or later. A few of the least ambitious, or very prosperous, stay closed throughout the summer. Therefore, if it entails going some distance, phone beforehand.

Banks give, as you know, better exchange rates than hotels but not enough to make a great difference unless you're changing a great deal of money. Most shops calculate at bank rates and should give you 20 percent on traveler's checks. One doesn't and shouldn't expect the discount in inexpensive, market purchasing or on sales in small shops, but in asking for a discount remember that you are not pleading for a favor. The discount is a tax rebate arranged between the government and the shop proprietor.

Banks are often closed Saturdays but list places on a door or window, where money can be exchanged. (The same system holds —or should—for vacationing drugstores and bakeries which post the addresses of their nearest competitors whose vacations already have been or are not yet.) American Express at 12 Rue Scribe and Thomas Cook at 2 Place de la Madeleine will cash traveler's checks and convert dollars to francs on Saturday before noon. Surprisingly, the Paris branches of American banks will not instantly cash a check; it requires cabling and waiting. Try some other way, and unless you have a great deal of time and patience never, never, ask for money to be cabled to a small-town bank in France. Communications and money may run across the ocean with breathless speed to lie mired in inexperience and indifference for weeks.

On the subject of never, never: don't ever send anything to yourself in Paris from anywhere abroad except via one of the costly shipping services. Clearly marked books or used clothing *may* get to you sent by railway express without hindrance. On the other hand, a few yards of tweed bought in London and sent on to Paris may mean a long ride to the northern edge of the city, irrational progress from desk to desk, demands for shipping papers and receipts. From personal experience: a dozen books, well-used, were shipped from London to Paris and wound up in the customs yards. Notification and an hour's hot bus ride into flat-faced emptiness. Then the search from yard to yard for the specific bureau. Inside one building, a not-too-busy gentleman answers a request for directions with "It says on your paper." Finally, a well of desks and steamy progress from one to another while papers are read, written, stamped, shuffled and heaped. Somewhere along the route, a few francs has to be paid. Now for the customs bin. A few men stand around admiring the uniform of a splendid, sworded guard in Third Empire dress uniform. No one can do anything about the quarantined books because the customs chief, himself, who handles these imposing matters, is out to lunch, at 3:00 P.M. The walls buckle in the heat or maybe it's only the sweat rolling into the eyes and distorting the vision. A few words of protest at 3:30. One man cuts the cords off the box (how you are going to retie them and get the bundle home is your problem) and he and the glorious soldier pick up a bus map of Paris (admittedly, not commonly seen) and a worn 19th century book on Paris published in England, also a Paris street directory. Two suspicious pairs of eyes. "Where are your receipts for these books?" "I have no receipts. These are old books that I've had for some time." "Well, then, how is it that maps of Paris are coming from London?" "That's where I left them on my way home from Paris some months ago." "Strange." More muttering between themselves and leafing through spy literature, this time a three-volume history of Paris streets. The heat rolls, spreads and asphyxiates. It is time to be an ugly American. "Gentlemen, I am engaged in writing a book about Paris for American and possibly other English-speaking travelers. You have a choice (giving them the existentialist either-or): give me my books now and let me return to work. Or keep them; I'll find some other place to write about." The gaping box is handed over, wounded strings trailing. The cord is ineptly tied, victim and booty accompanied by uniform (twenty-four years old, built like an oak and too frail to help tie or carry a small box of books), a stop at a sentinel's box, while a few francs cross hands and out under the close, moist sky for waiting and waiting for a taxi or a bus.

BUT the sending out of France is easy. The SNCF adjunct to the postal system, often located next to or near a post office, will ship packages cheaply and efficiently, by rail or air-freight. They will help you fill out papers, advise about how to mark your package, make sure you tuck your receipt in a safe place. It takes time, but the company is pleasant.

The encyclopedic compendium of Paris directories includes two sets that may come in handy. The volumes of listings by name stop for classified pauses. That is, it will run along alphabetically through the citizenry and then, for instance, stop for an inner alphabet of "Hotels" or "Restaurants." Sometimes, a place will appear in its category rather than under an individual alphabetical listing. The second set is alphabetized under street names. The Christian name of a man to whom a street is dedicated often determines the position in the listing; if you are looking for a number on Avenue Marcel Proust or in the Square Marie Curie, both streets, their numbers and inhabitants will appear under "M."

When you've gotten around to telephoning, notice that O and Q are mated with zero in the last dialing circle. Be careful of this. A mistake may bring you a cracked voice from the tomb that repeats and repeats exhortations to try and try again.

A re-reminder: Most museums are closed on Tuesday and many shops, some restaurants, on Monday.

One of the challenges of Paris, about as demanding as encounters with the traffic, is the "Turkish" toilet (the Turks probably call it "French") to be found—and avoided, if possible— in old cafés and in backyards of working-class restaurants. Rarely is there a light. How does one find the clay Golem footprints on which to stand, how perilously is one near to slipping into the reeking hell-hole? Similarly exasperating in its own way is the modern toilet. Theoretically the light goes on as you turn the lock.

It doesn't. Or the light does go on, but where is a traveler to hang camera, coat, pocketbook? Where is the shelf for a guidebook and maps? The damp floor will hardly do. There is no paper, either, or it is the nonabsorbent kind used by *charcuteries* for wrapping cold cuts. Don't turn on the hot water; there isn't any. The spindle of soap is worn down to bare metal; the same towel has been rotated for too many days over too many hands. Ergo, carry a good supply of Kleenex and small packaged hand cloths, travel with a friend, lover or spouse for umbrella, camera, etc., portage. Or, stop drinking wine, a silly idea.

A good way to see the city is to have expatriate friends. Having chosen Paris they enhance their exile by exploring the city, picking up gems of retiring courts and shy alleys. This holds true more generally for the person who has been in Paris five years or less; after that, like everyone else, he becomes a man of set habits and no time.

The three lodestars of St. Germain des Prés close for a full summer month—Lipp's and the Café Flore in July; the Deux Magots in August, or vice versa, arranging the matter among them.

Paris offers two ways of being confused about money. Despite the fact that signs are printed in new francs (almost 5 to the dollar) shopkeepers and much of Paris speak in old francs, 500 to the dollar. Though the change was made official some years ago, there is a glow of luxury around 10,000 francs that its current equivalent, 100 francs, lacks. Thus, it goes on and one must learn to translate quickly *"cent"* into *"one"* and *"mille"* into *"ten."* Coins are currently still a mélange of old and new francs. Newer coins are marked as "centimes" but among them you'll still find the "francs" (now worth centimes). As in learning French grammar, there are few shortcuts; one must study carefully.

The humor of all old cities is to take you a long way around to get back near your starting point, a rewarding way to walk the cities, but watch out if you're in a hurry. Unless you surely know your way, don't try for shortcuts which have the malice to lead you into unknown, unexpected neighborhoods, at considerable distances from your target.

Looking for a number in Paris streets can be quite discouraging. Normally, having found number 50 one assumes number 60 must be close. Not at all. In some areas one or two large houses absorb a whole block and one particular number can stutter through a row of *bis* so that the sense of getting nowhere adds to the ache in the feet.

Be scrupulously careful about whether the street you are looking for is a "boulevard" or "avenue" or "rue." A renowned name can have two or more stretches of Paris dedicated to it, frequently wide and costly distances apart.

Don't send a French friend chrysanthemums. They are associated in many minds with All Saints' grave offerings.

The artist looking for a Paris studio has probably found out that studio space is rare and expensive. Where it can be found, it is still unbearably *La Bohème* (with no assurance of a resident Mimi), replete with cold and inconvenience. A recent Cité des Arts has studios at modest rentals available to international artists and musicians on a quota system. The quota for the States may already have been filled for some time, but it is worth the try of writing to the American Students' Social Center at 261 Boulevard Raspail in the 14th for small studio-apartments (what the British call "self-contained") if you don't mind living in a stretch of Mussolini-modern that horrifies the river and the decayed palaces behind it. The indigenous studio might be found by watching the bulletin board of the Café Dôme on Boulevard Montparnasse. Also, the Académie de la Grande Chaumière on the street of that name, unchanged from the time it sheltered the young Giacometti and a line of predecessors, remains old-fashioned in the matter of prices, too. Five afternoon hours of sketching costs 4 francs, unless the price has been raised to 5, still under a dollar. The Entraide des Artistes, 9 and 11 Rue Berryer (8th), is an art-supply cooperative which one joins with an initiation fee of 10 francs. Profits are shared at the end of the year.

A limited French vocabulary creates, as has been suggested, many strictures including what to order in a café (you will probably have made a point of learning the names of foods, and, in any case, most good restaurants have waiters prepared to translate and explain). When you grow tired of the café, thé and bière routine, try citron pressé (fresh lemonade) or fruit extracts (jus) of ananas (pineapple), raisin (grape), abricot (what you think it is) or pomme (apple). They come in small bottles at about what they would cost at home or a bit more, depending on how luminous the café and the quarter.

If your familiar, orthodox medical treatments have proven unsatisfactory, try the homeopathic clinic on Rue Danton, off Boulevard St. Germain, or make an appointment for acupuncture, growing as popular as liver ailments, at the same address.

Like centime coins, telephone-box *jetons* (for under half a franc) come in a confusion of sizes. The small grooved coin one buys at the Métro ticket stall to use in a Métro phone will not fit the newer boxes which require a larger, flatter coin; and vice versa.

If you are in a bathless hotel (sharing a state with more than 80 percent of Paris, according to a recent survey) or consider the cost of a bath in the hotel too high, inquire about the public baths that abound in most neighborhoods, private or public, from basic to sybaritic.

Should you need to make a phone call or send a telegram late at night outside your hotel, there is such service available at 101 Rue de Grenelle, near the Mairie of the 7th.

14 Shopping

As one plods (not on Mondays) through street after street, *quartier* after *quartier*, dizzied by the multiplicity of shops, it appears increasingly odd that Napoleon, like others, called the English a nation of shopkeepers. Half the 1st arrondissement—the Rue de Rivoli, Place Vendôme, the Place de la Madeleine and the streets that run among them—is an enormous shopping center. The western section of the 2nd includes half of the Avenue de l'Opéra and its shop-filled tangents; stores stand on the southern end of the 9th. The 6th and 7th and sections of the 5th are busy with antiques, art, books, international jokes and asexual, teen-ager styles. The remotest arrondissement has its markets and shopping boulevards. Clearly, Paris has changed greatly in the last one hundred and fifty years or Napoleon wasn't noticing shops.

In an absolutely practical sense there is little reason for shopping in foreign cities. All big cities are international markets: Paris and London wear Italian shoes, Rome and London wear Paris dresses, Paris and Rome wear English cashmeres, and New York, Chicago, San Francisco, Dallas, Boston and a dozen other cities make foreign clothing and accessories easily available. It is possible to buy gloves, sweaters, shoes, et cetera, more cheaply in their native habitats—sometimes. Almost as many times, the buyer for a large department store can make a wholesale purchase that—with costs of importing, store rental, salaries and other overhead items added —keeps the price as low, or lower, than one finds abroad.

But the pleasure of saying "I bought it in Paris" is understandably irresistible and shouldn't be resisted. With it, go the different modes of display, manners of salespeople to observe and, always possible, the discovery of a rare indigenous object too expensive to export en masse or too seemingly inconsequential. It gives a trip a more luxuriant expansive quality to shop in foreign stores or, if the traveler's checks grow thin, at least to lick the windows, as the French say.

Below, a number of categories, with indications of general areas so that shopping—or window-shopping—can be combined with walks. From there on it becomes your own juggling of initial cost, customs allowances, weight-on-planes problems, how shy is your French, how much do you love your relatives or yourself. Try to keep in mind that for certain kinds of purchases—important antiques, paintings, expensive jewelry, archaeological arts and crafts—you should come well armed with knowledge and, if possible, a few addresses. Some dealers hide from the general public and see people by appointment only. In these matters, expert friends, therefore, might advise you more expertly than a guidebook can, or should.

Remember also, that bargain hunting is time-consuming and often fruitless. Paris is as expensive as New York with none or few of that city's discount houses. Usually, it is the costly object that turns out to be indisputably Parisian, but perfumes are always cheaper than they are at home, as are some cosmetics; gloves are almost always less expensive. If you are suddenly confronted with the need for inexpensive shoes, or a raincoat or a sweater, go to the shops that surround markets (Seine-Buci and Place Maubert on the Left Bank; the Niel-Bayen market in the 17th, the Cité Berryer off the Rue Royale on the Right Bank, to mention a few); the boulevards that continue from Boulevard Haussmann eastward and the Marais. Style, quality and prices begin to sink on their west to east run along the Grands Boulevards. Consequently, few real bargains.

You probably know, but as a reminder: The comparatively few department stores are like those in the States in that their divers goods are fairly priced and although their range in price may be wide, some cater to a poorer or richer clientele than others, often a question of locality. For instance, Jones on the Avenue Victor Hugo will have a quite other collection of articles, many more expensive imports, probably, than the Bazar de l'Hôtel de Ville, near Les Halles. Department stores give a 20 percent discount on traveler's checks, while discount houses which advertise in the American newspapers will give as much as 40 percent off on some items for Express checks and personal checks. Some smaller shops, especially in the Right Bank shopping areas, will accept personal checks. Where there isn't constant familiarity with tourists, you may be given only a 15 percent discount for traveler's checks, or none at all, and a personal check is not acceptable.

CAVEAT: The French government has recently cracked down on "discounts" and "reductions" offered on up-priced goods. If your purchase will be sizable, do some comparison shopping.

Women

For sociological and economic reasons not within the province of such a book as this, the "haute couture" concept is rapidly fading, to take its place in dreams of past luxury along with the *grande cocotte*. The time of opulence when a great couture house supported an expensive array of talents and exquisite manners paid for lavishly by international leaders of fashion is passing, or altogether past. French designers must turn, as has become fully evident in the United States, to working increasingly for a mass market. There are still, however, seasonal showings, such as those of autumn and winter fashions held in late July and early August for the queens and powers of fashion. The announcements in the newspapers are clearly marked "buyers only" and they mean it. Shortly thereafter lists of fashion openings appear with the legend "invitation cards generally required," usually a simple matter of phoning a few hours before.

The people who conduct you to the rows of slender, often gilt, chairs in rooms that manage to be luxurious and simple and at the same time to suggest riches and yet not distract from the display of couture, are hopeful that you will buy a creation or two after a showing but not at all exigent. The current crop of models follows the sparse lines of this year's Venus; they are smallish, thin, youngly asexual, more like beautiful grasses than girls. The favored face is exotic or antique-Etruscan, or the Spanish of old court portraits, rather than merely pretty. The eyes are drawn immense and fringed with thickets of lashes; the lipstick designs a disdainful grimace or a pre-Hellenic smile. On their spare, immature legs they quickly stride, pirouette and stride again, holding up the plastic button which defines each model as "this little number," unbuttoning, revealing as they go a blouse, a pocket, an un-expected fold of cloth. Depending on the house, you will find

subtle inventiveness in the quiet suits and coats or shockers based
on hunting costumes or the uniforms of paratroopers. One house
will load its evening dresses with Renaissance displays of sequins,
crystals and ribbons, another will permit the unadorned, creamy
silk to flow, gently restrain it and permit it again to flow into
beautifully sculptured shapes.

If you must be satisfied with a trinket or accessory from a
"name" couture, look into the boutiques where you may find large
assortments, as at Dior, or a few discreet rarities, as at Balmain or
Givenchy or Castillo, and watch for notices of sales.

The El Dorado of the Right Bank

Today, tomorrow, the next day you will walk into the Rue du
Faubourg St. Honoré, the Place Vendôme, their tangential streets
and the Champs Elysées, not quite so "dorado" as it once must
have been. You will notice that the cool plaster mannequins that
inhabit American windows are not part of the Paris scene; here the
decor is imaginative gatherings of seasonal symbols or fantasy
figures of unexpected combinations of shapes and materials.

The platinum road of the Faubourg St. Honoré and its sub-
sidiary paths is primarily the terrain of antiques, paintings and the
decoration of women. As you walk, notice the fact that absolutely
no Paris neighborhood, no matter what its concentrations, will do
without its butchers and bakers and *charcuteries*, and slip into a
court now and then to see the modest workshops that supply to
street-front glamour.

To go steadily from shop to shop on both sides of these streets
bespeaks endless leisure or mania. A casual long stroll might do it,
to find that good shops wear two basic costumes: old wobbly glass
and dark wood or a modern combination of marble, brass, light
tan wood and a pair of neat trees flanking the entrance. You may
see a window decorated with red velvet panels stuck with immense
roses and pink bows or in some other window, a life-sized figure of
paper billowed, crushed, fringed and pleated, topped by an ingenious hat made of a dyed mop. One window may have no decor
but a suit and coat that say *this* is the authoritative cut, that little
trick of fold is the only way to shape a skirt, there are no buttons
in all the world better suited for this coat; these are *the*

felicitous choice; the neckline is wide enough to embrace a scarf but not so wide as to make the shoulders too narrow. It can be enlightenment as well as pleasure.

Rue du Faubourg St. Honoré

For sets of such splendors look in at the awesomely famous Hermès and Lanvin treasuries at the meeting of the Rue du Faubourg St. Honoré and Rue Boissy d'Anglas and then, on the Faubourg itself:

Gants Aris, No. 83. Along with the superfine gloves, evening bags, costume jewelry and sweaters, look at the dolls in the window made of gloves. The middle fingers becomes the head, two others make the arms, the rest are concealed in the cuff which is arranged as a skirt; a tiny jewel, a string for belt, a little feather as a hat—*voilà*, a lively gesturing figure.

Helena Rubinstein at No. 52H, **Germaine Monteil** at No. 77 and **Lancôme** at No. 29. All display their colors, unguents, maskers, revealers, enhancers, and concealers, as if they were crown jewels.

Leda, at the corner with Avenue Marigny. To be seriously considered for a well-designed suede coat, a dashing raincoat, a fur-lined coat or just any kind of coat.

Cedric, No. 11. Shoes of pink ribbon, impermeable rain shoes of gay plaids, purple suede boots up to *here*. Clearly for the young of foot.

Rameau, No. 9. More of those beautiful creamy suedes; suits, sweaters, and coats.

Henri à la Pensée, No. 3. Recently combined with Jaeger's and the mixture a sound one of French imagination and English classicism.

Jourdan, No. 14. French shoes, fanciful and high style, for a while clustered around a full-sized 18th century carriage covered in gold velvet, which conveys some idea of pride and price. **Durer's** shoes at number 28 share the category.

L'Atelier, Cité du Retiro (in from the Faubourg St. Honoré). A large, intelligent collection of not too aggressively youngish styles made in your material or theirs, not very expensively.

Réty, No. 56. Unabashed exaggerations that frequently—not always—work: a classic trench coat in cloth of gold, lace and fur overwhelming a piece of chiffon, an aviary full of fluffy feathers tacked on anything.

Roger et Gallet, Nos. 62 and 64. If you know them for their soaps and toilet waters of a healthful, undisturbing kind, their *Boutique et Frivolités* may surprise you. Along with its classics, attractive suits and blouses, a femme fatale dress or two (satins and beads) and playful gifts.

A Fragonard, No. 66. Lush, lush dresses, coats and costumes; rich, dignified textures in deceptively simple, subtle design.

Fernande, 3 Rue d'Anjou immediately off the Faubourg. A *Rive Gauche*-ish place that drips beads, chunky, bubbly costume jewelry to hang on unusual sweaters and dresses. For the woman who, if she were a New Yorker, might shop on West 4th Street.

Amy Linker, Faubourg St. Honoré and Rue d'Anjou, one flight up. Couture clothing at not too astronomic prices.

Jean Damien, corner of Rue des Saussaies. Behind the great rubber plant that brushes across the window and a seasonal bouquet (dried pods, corn and pheasant tails), a superior collection of knits, in never-blatant materials and patterns.

Jean Hercey, corner of Rue de Miromesnil. Intricate, luxurious beadings and puffings on glowing silks for evening wear. No wayward tricks or necklines down to *there*; for ladies only.

Suzanne, 7 Rue Berryer (a modest street off the Faubourg inhabited by the ateliers of carpenters, house painters and varnishers who move their slats of wood, naked chairs and beaten-up tables onto, or near the street, for light to work by). Unassuming wool things made to measure, some hand knits. Nothing elaborate or very expensive.

Torrente, corner of Faubourg St. Honoré and Avenue Matignon. Exceedingly clever things, veering toward and from the grotesque, for the young, skinny beauty, who wants something beyond the diversions of the Rue de Sèvres, "snob" things. For the *avant* type who wears a brown crocodile jacket when others are wearing suedes, odd sweaters no one else seems to show and baggy hats to match. Surely, if a customer demands it, they would run up a coat of mail for evening wear.

Lawrence—Helena, corner with Avenue Hoche. Extravaganzas of blouses made only of beads and gold chain, suits that combine pink tweed, chiffon and gold cloth lacings, tricks with white brocade and odd fake fur. Not for the timid, although the shop holds to sanity via calmer coats.

Lola Prusac, No. 93. A very high-style boutique where anything might show up, always choice.

Sweaters Bazaar, corner of Avenue Matignon. Among the fine suits and silk dresses, woolen sweaters in superb colors and silk sweaters printed like Persian miniatures or flowers from a Redon painting.

Where the Faubourg descends to the *Rue St. Honoré*, the high tone is maintained for a while and gradually shades off. Before that happens though, there are: **Vera Borea,** at the corner of Rue St. Honoré and Rue Cambon; a couture salon upstairs, and below fur hats with scarves to match, soft, lacy, angora knits, skillful crochets in addition to cloth and silk dresses, suits, costumes of considerable distinction. **Elvine** at No. 346, shows good woolens and **Ramuz,** at No. 261, is a large place with a satisfying variety, nothing extreme.

Boulevard Malesherbes

Mettez, No. 16. Distinguished sports clothes and accessories.

Pierre, No. 39. Unusual woolens, in imaginative weaves and color combinations.

Anny Blatt, No. 29. Dignified wools, well-made, well-lined.

Elle, No. 9. Rows and rows of women's clothing, none of it startling, but the prices are moderate for the neighborhood.

While you're searching the antiques on *Rue de Miromesnil* look at the dresses, coats and accessories in the windows of **Cassy's** and **Jacqueline Delaitre.** Not too expensive for the styles and quality.

Avenue Montaigne is to women's luxuries what the Uffizi is to art: **Charles of the Ritz;** the **Christian Dior** Boutique and shoe shop; **Harry Winston** (corner of Rue Clément Marot); the **Guy Laroche** Boutique next door; the **Maggy Rouff** Boutique, edged by a baby garden at number 14; **Emilio Pucci** at number 37 Rue Jean Goujon close by. Then at Place de la Reine Astrid where the street ends, a foolish, solemn monument of France and Belgium jointly shielding a diminutive populace. Poor Astrid, the small crown on her head looks, from a short distance, like a washerwoman's topknot.

Rue La Boëtie (near the Champs Elysées)

Snob. Belle-Epoque-Drugstore style in seductress Edwardian red, arranged as two adjoining caves plastered and billowed, the ceiling of red swellings (one sees the approaches to hell in early primitive church paintings). The caves are deep enough for you to get by the eager clusters of Paris eighteen-year-olds or to stand aside and observe the universal adolescent calling and cooing over still another variation of the current spaceship or Lolita style.

La Solderie, No. 85. "Sales all the time"—a good place for occasional bargains in knits, silks, coats.

Rue Jean Mermoz

Claude Javelet, No. 15. A golden whippet used to stand in the window of this boutique, a rather precise symbol for the aristocratic collection of scarves, jewelry and women's clothing.

Marc Olivier, No. 19. A hat, a fur scarf, a hand-crocheted skirt, a three-banded necklace from a Renaissance painting.

Nobby, 69 Boulevard Haussmann. Leather and suede coats and suits, possibly less glamorous, but less expensive than those on the Faubourg St. Honoré.

Jean Lefèbure, 9 Rue du Cirque. Jewelry, evening bags, blouses, suits; quiet and confident.

NOTE: Rue du Cirque, a street of old houses behind old houses has a curious flavor. You may catch a glimpse of a court fountain, but most of the street is shut behind heavy grillwork, long, tight shutters and the Paris cliché of plump blackened ladies. The offices of the Society for the Improvement of Horse-Breeding are, not incongruously, on this crabby, disdainful street.

Adrian Page, 21 Rue Royale. A large assortment of bags and clever small leather accessories to consider in the eternal problem of "what shall we buy for Tom, Dick and Harry and Mary and Alice."

Place de la Madeleine

Gaudin, No. 20. Light-touched, imaginative bags, gloves and shoes.

Charmis, No. 7. Lace underwear, lace and gold-thread peignoirs and the curvy, be-ribboned all-in-ones French movie actresses strip down to at least twice in each film.

Michèle Colson. In the Cour Vendôme (a passage off the Place). Distinguished raincoats lined with unusual furs and non-furs.

Avenue Matignon

Lucette Hervier, near the Faubourg St. Honoré. Superb suede coats lined and unlined the specialty. Also at **Lyne Harlet,** No. 26.

Heim, No. 9. *Jeune Fille,* "Exclusively for," but she can't be a *jeune fille* who earns her pin money as a Saturday extra at Super-mag. For the golden girl the stage is set with trickly little ceiling curtains, a slight stairway surrounded by a golden railing, and charming, luxurious things to wear.

Heim, No. 15. This one is for bigger girls, with styles a shade more sedate shown behind miniature gardens; open, but partially flanked by iron grills that give an effect of hospitality and welcome to a real garden and a house beyond.

Anna Lowe, No. 35. Couture things of considerable splendor, reputedly at less than one pays at the boutiques of their "onlie begetters."

M. T. Magne, 1 Rue de Castiglione. Tasteful, well-made evening bags.

M. Soeber, 2 Place Vendôme. Fine scarves and hand-embroidered handkerchiefs. Also at **Pache** on Rue de Castiglione.

Repetto, 22 Rue de la Paix. An uncertain identity that encompasses ballet shoes, high-style patterned stockings along with classic sweaters and well-made slacks.

On shadowy Rue du Colisée, two shops worth exploring for suits, coats and dresses: **Denise Milon** at number 19 and **Fanny Seiger** at number 22.

In an area where there are specialists in children's haircutting, where every skirt fits perfectly and every bag is of genuine leather and the supermarket displays high-style sweaters, you would expect to find well-designed, well-made—not cheap—clothing. The shopping street for these as well as accessories is **Avenue Victor Hugo,** and its near annexes.

For knits, some handmade, and wool suits see **Minny,** at number 37; **Maria Pia** next door to **Prunier-Traktir;** the **Korrigan** wool boutique at 14; **Corely** at 8 and a group of similar places at 104 and 106, among them **Le Knack** which likes "Chelsea suits" and color combinations more usually seen on the Rue Tronchet and the Left Bank. For more festive wear look in past the peacock-feathers-gold-floral décor of **Selena** and next door, at **Catherine de Poorter's.** Sweaters and scarves at **Laurence,** number 101; already matched for you at **Anam,** number 15. If Paris weather chills you excessively, you can buy lightweight woolen underwear at **Sourcin,** 97, pretty-to-fierce boots at **Elyse d'Honoré,** number 14, or a bright red suit of heavy suede and a sweater at the boutique around the corner and up the hill at 7 Rue du Dôme.

There is a shop devoted to tunics, as blouses and dresses, some of them embroidered, in the Passage Jouffroy, off the Boulevard Montmartre (10th).

Men

Rue du Faubourg St. Honoré and close neighbors

Lobb, No. 47. The Paris branch of the hushed, honorable and dedicated London bootmakers.

Rambaud, No. 36. A too-quick reading may suggest the poet but the jaunty-to-suave clothing here is clearly more Chevalier-Boyer than dissolute genius. Down the street at No. 48 is **Manfield** where the mood is *sportif* in the Italian manner.

André Ghekière, No. 84. A sybarite's den of rich wools and silks as robes, ties and scarves. Not for the high-thinking, plain-living man.

Bournat, No. 105. Pleasing golden wood, polished brass and slabs of marble in the old style, to display and sell quality shirts, ties and men's wear in general.

Alexandre, 11 Rue La Boëtie. Italian, English and French skills in fine men's things, a soupçon showy.

Reboul at 24 Avenue Matignon, and a few doors on, **René Regard,** shirtmakers.

Guttierez, 29 Rue d'Anjou. Smooth, silken—with that touch of 16th century Florence.

Pierre Cardin, Faubourg St. Honoré and Rue d'Anjou. The jewel box, again, of black marble and brass-framed square windows revealing the softest of soft shoes, deep cushiony tweeds, a unique hidalgo of a hat, the finest of fine turtle-neck sweaters; for lilies of the field, male.

Doucet, 21 Rue de la Paix. Dignity, quality and discretion in a collection of ties, shirts, silk robes and sweaters.

Avenue Victor Hugo

Barclay, at No. 66, and **Jack Romoli** at 38 (also on Boulevard St. Germain at St. Guillaume). **Jacques Devillers** at 46 is a touch more outré, showing brilliant checked caps, bright red jackets and a revival of the Bernard Shaw suit of scratchy tweeds and knickers. **Holmes,** nearby, returns to the less mannered styles. **Dona-Sol** at number 22 limits itself to glorious accessories: scarves, gloves, umbrellas, leather wallets and fine leather cigar cases and flask cases, clearly for the man who cherishes himself, or his friends. **Barnett's** concentrates on sport jackets in tweed and suede. **Orson** at 27 prefers the more formal aspects of a man's attire; the suits have an ambassadorial look. **Jones,** a department store at number 39, has a big, mixed collection, embassy and the races.

For the man who can't afford a new suit the **Boutique de la Retouche** at 145 Rue de la Pompe will remake or revive the old one.

On the *Left Bank,* among the conservatives of Boulevard St. Germain and especially on Boulevard St. Michel, a recent out-cropping of men's shops, not all of them too blinding for simple Amurrican tastes.

Young men addicted to London's Soho fashions search the shops in the Rue de la Pompe–Avenue Victor Hugo area for their extravagancies and for more Dorian Gray than Mod—if that is still the word for it—to the Pierre Cardin Junior section of the "Saint Germain," at Rue Bonaparte and Rue du Four. And between the writing and reading of this book, there will undoubtedly crop up a number of newer shops which, to echo a recent ad, will show *un panorama complet de la mode masculine britannique,* with all the accessories necessary to make the *parfait* gentleman.

If the wheel of fortune has pulled you to a low point, you may find something to wear at **American Clothing,** a second-hand col-lection at 204 Boulevard St. Germain. Clothing for women, also, as well as underwear, accessories and inexpensive towels in usable shape.

Men and Women

Back to El Dorado

The sacred groves of **Hermès** and **Lanvin** if you can afford it.

Not cheap, but cheaper:

Peau de Porc, 67 Faubourg St. Honoré. Serious works in leather as map cases, travel pieces, efficient pocketbooks, mainly in pig-skin, as the name indicates. (Another on Boulevard St. Germain, near Rue du Bac.)

Unless your world stops turning if you don't have an Hermès agenda to flash at a worshiping public, you might consider those (and the fine stationery and cards they print) of **Laurent,** at 34

Faubourg St. Honoré and, on the other side of Rue Royale, **Casse-grain** at 422 Rue St. Honoré, both old houses of stately repute.

Amaryllis, 36 Faubourg St. Honoré. Should you need a He and She set of suede coats, you might try here; unmatched and separate they are good, too.

Selleries de France, 12 Faubourg St. Honoré (and at 86 Boulevard Haussmann). A place for impressive leather gifts and leather luggage which must always travel first class.

Les Trois Selliers, Boulevard Haussmann and Rue de l'Arcade. Same quality and types as Les Selleries.

Regast, 10 Rue Berryer (off the Faubourg). Women's and men's shirts made to measure, and durable, conservative ties.

Mérival, 30 Rue La Boëtie. Still more serious, well-crafted bags, baggage, accessories and gifts.

Knize, 10 Avenue Matignon. Internationally famous, as you know, for fine accessories for men and women.

Schilz, corner of Rue Caumartin and Rue Boudreau. An immense corner store high and deep with fine leather as saddles and ladies' suits, riding crops and magnificent valises.

Pascal, 28 Avenue Montaigne. Gloves, scarves, ties; Olympic, as suits the avenue.

Male and female shoes at **Berthelot,** 83 Avenue Victor Hugo.

Tedd on the Place Victor Hugo, corner of Rue Henri Poincaré. Tailors clothing for men and women, the reliable sort of thing that becomes an old friend.

Pavillon de Cuir, Rue St. Honoré at Rue de l'Echelle. Attractive leather goods at comfortable prices.

Left Bank

If you must suddenly lead an expedition into darkest Africa sartorially unprepared, **Sport et Climat** at 223 Boulevard St. Germain will supply topees, swamp boots, bush jackets and lightweight clothing.

Latreille, 62 Rue St. André des Arts. Surrounded by the zippy eccentricities of "young" art, "young" costumes, "amusing" accessories, a matter-of-fact, sensible old store which was a favorite of conservative provincials and, though they don't like navigating among the *je m'en fiche* cars and flaming youth on the string-wide sidewalks, they still shop here. The hats to go with the dresses are bought in a shop which has not yet recovered from the 20's and 30's, on Place St. André des Arts.

Children

Tit', 109 Faubourg St. Honoré. Don't let the startling contraction, meant to be cute (*petit*), numb you, although the prices may. Lovely things for doting and well-heeled grandparents.

Bellina, 7 Faubourg St. Honoré. For princelings ready to sit for a dynastic family portrait: black patent and gray suede shoes three inches long, glove-skin leather boots lined with pony fur, a Prince Albert coat for a two-year-old, and exquisite white gloves. One tries to imagine the child and evokes a miniature Huysmans.

Marina, 84 Faubourg St. Honoré. A turtleneck sweater and a contrasting V-neck to go over it for the sportsman, once he learns to walk; a red velvet dress with white lace and a flirtatious ruffle; foulard pajama pants and a piped, sashed (with fringe) smoking jacket for a Lilliputian Casanova.

Nicole France, 31 Rue Matignon. Less stagey than some and still enchanting for young children.

Mon Beau Linge, 12 Rue Lavoisier. Among the pretty, spongy things of toweling, hand-embroidered, hand-sewn clothing for very young children.

Pache, on Rue de Castiglione (above the Louis Sherry mosaic). Hand-embroidered gossamers for infants among equally delicate handkerchiefs and blouses.

Rouff, Place Vendôme at Castiglione. Hand-embroidered dresses for the most careful and decorous of little girls. And, for their exquisite mothers, table linens of airy lace and matchless embroidery.

At 7 *Rue des Canettes.* Girls' dresses that reflect the bolder styles of that neighborhood.

The Super Supermarkets

Place de la Madeleine

Past an alley of flower market thriving valiantly in the thunder of buses, one comes on the checkered canopies of **Fauchon.** First the boutique of perfumes, scarves, and household gifts of considerable distinction, a liquor section which arranges shipment, and then—the essential matter of Fauchon's—choice foods, domestic and imported, including American coffee and, if you must, varieties of popped, crisped, crunchy, health-giving American cereal and cheese-flavored popcorn. Fauchon's high art, however, appears in its presentations, as in a gallery or museum. The pâté *en croûte* in long, decorative pastry boxes; chickens dressed up in Matisse-like designs of sliced truffle; a duck whose breast is patterned with lines of pâté meeting at a high ridge of dates studded with almonds, all structures delectably, highly glazed.

Caviar and pâté come in the large economy size at Fauchon and the fruits are the goddesses of their race, and treated as goddesses. The grapes, each as large as a greengage plum, are swaddled in paper that resembles fine linen napkins, each bunch hung with a small heraldic banner of the house. In pomegranate time the fruit selected (and probably grown for Fauchon) is as large as cannon balls, but being red, appears larger. It doesn't seem likely that a boxful of avocados could be matched to within a hairsbreadth of weight and girth; Fauchon does it. One perfect cluster of blue grapes nestles in its perfect box; each apple and pear is polished and labeled. When *girolles* (yellow, lacy mushrooms) become expensive and rare, they linger here in gourmand supply.

In the *confiserie-pâtisserie* across the street, where there are coffee and cakes to match house standards, Jordan almonds are never heaped. They are wired and attached to gilded leaves to make daisies, or roses, or bunches of white grapes, or incorporated into old-fashioned sentimental pictures; reminders of the extraordinary, fussy, craftsmanship in which Paris once excelled.

The market of manna continues around the other side of the

Madeleine church. **Hédiard's** is a beguiling shop with lovely street stands of wicker filled with choice vegetables and inside, baskets and strings of small red peppers hanging over Mexican *cherimoyas,* coconuts, ginger root, rare teas and companion exotica.

A few places away (rounding back toward the front of the church) is the **Maison de la Truffe**—where, along with the truffles one selects a fine wine, a distinguished ham or a length of aristo-cratic sausage.

Then, **Caviar Kaspia** for eating small, bigger, biggest por-tions of caviar on toast or blinis in the small restaurant upstairs or for buying below, accompanied by smoked salmon or a slab of worldly pâté.

Grave penance for the rich, costly living arrives at the last food (or anti-food) shop in the high-calorie arc: health cereals, wheat germ, toothpaste and soap made of algae. To fortify the prin-ciples involved, threatening books: *The Cuisine of the Devil* shows him lurking behind the canned foods in a supermarket; *The Dance with the Devil* is banded with the legend, "Our Civil-ization, a Suicide." Stability and calm can be regained at the big, busy café in back of the church with a sandwich of salted ham, im-pure bread and the poison of a *café-crème,* doubly delicious after the terror.

Rue Royale

It starts with Maxim's and ends near Fauchon's and on the short trip between rarely lapses from the standards they set in their respective fields. Antiques, rugs, jewelry, evening bags, La-lique crystal, Italian glass in traditional shapes or a fusion of many slender cups of glass into a superb modern chandelier; **Christofle's** shows its old and new crystal and silver and at **Delvaux** (num-ber 18) a collection of some of the best in international design dis-played as rarities should be.

Toward the Madeleine, on Rue Royale, a slit of street becomes the Cité Berryer, a contrast sharp enough to seem staged. A market smell of greens, fruit, cheese and fish and cooking odors from the restaurants floats among the slapdash stalls, clings to girdles and stockings, socks and sweaters, heaped in cartons on, under, around improvised tables. Nothing at all, in mood or ma-terial, to link the short market tangent to its parent street.

Place Vendôme—Champs Elysées

It has been said before, the "historic names" on Rue de la Paix and the Place Vendôme are IBM, Coty, Schiaparelli, Cartier, Boucheron, Arden, Dunhill's, Guerlain, Caron, Charvet, Patek-Philippe, Van Cleef and Arpels, Mauboussin and on the contiguous Rue Castiglione, (a shade dimmer but still regally dressed in arcades and proud old shops), Sulka and an echo of Louis Sherry, now gone though its name still makes a mosaic pattern on the sidewalk.

Pearls, silver, gold, diamonds, perfumes and furs, exquisite gloves and ties, incomparable table linens and handkerchiefs, clothing, accessories and enchanting expensive fancies; the fairy-tale things that the prince and princess wore and were presented with as they were launched into "happily ever after." The fairest of these rare flowers is the Place itself, whose facades only were erected late in the 17th century to attract buyers and builders of houses behind them. It was originally planned by the controller of buildings under Louis XIV as a huge octagonal area to surround a statue of the Sun King, the Place to be called the Place Louis le Grand. It became a seat of court business but proved too expensive and was relinquished to rich hoi polloi—bankers and jewelers and perfumers. The Place Vendôme's smooth, satisfying shape of two seemingly unbroken arcs has chinks worth exploring. For instance, the courtyard at number 19 is attractive repetition in miniature of the Place itself. Inside number 13 (these are private courts but you may be permitted a glimpse) a cobbled walk and parked cars lead into a formal park, surrounded by a gate. Beyond the gate, white iron-work tables and chairs, a few benches and French park statuary: urns and sad stone ladies like exiled muses. At 10 Rue de la Paix is a court not so cherished, noble and sick. And as you stand at Castiglione and the Rue de Rivoli, look through the arches into a view of a healthier beauty, the westernmost section of the Louvre. After that, still another "Paris beauty" —a confiserie at Castiglione and Rue St. Honoré, terrifyingly gorgeous with its large-palace chandelier and candy boxes like royal coffins.

Inevitably, you will find yourself on the Champs Elysées. Between café stops walk into the Lido Arcade, 76 Champs Elysées. It is rather like a railroad station, full of busy people and saunterers and people hiding from the rain. A bar serves *Le Vrai* cheese-burger and hot dog. Pizza and *quiche* are sold at a set of counters where one stands to eat, Italian or Nedick's style. An open "tea-room" is for sitting with cake and coffee, while a bookshop topped by a rotating roof feeds the intellect and, upstairs, striptease (the Lido) goes on. All around, shops in several financial layers, from bargain counter to Faubourg St. Honoré with decor from *rustique* (sweaters sold among drying seedpods under a thatched roof with aged beams) to attempts at Versailles with gold silk and big chandeliers.

The movement in the arcade may be enough of itself, but there are some good shops of clothing for men and women, a number of them filled with Parisians (if this indicates anything) and a few bargain counters, mainly of sweaters, and souvenir-*objet* shops that might yield the lightweight inexpensive present every-one looks for.

Two poor cousins of this inflated passage live at number 52 (La Boëtie Passage) containing a few shops (**Dary**, a large leather-goods place may be of interest) and number 34, leading out to Rue du Colisée. The latter was once a thing of splendor, still covered with patterned bubbly glass. Now its mood is less Champs Elysées than of the Rue du Colisée, a careless street of anonymous hotels, a Chinese restaurant in an old house (recently painted red and pagoda-ed and calligraphy-ed in gold—*voilà!*—Chinese), shops of very high-heeled beaded pink satin shoes, work-shops, snack bars and a prowling look. Inside, the arcade devotes itself to inexpensive Orientalia—a Chinese restaurant, which of-fers "Eating with MUSIC. Candles Light," and an Indian shop. The Near East is suggested by a shop that resembles the spread contents of an Arab peddler's sack: quasi-Egyptian and Breughel panels, other old and not so old paintings, all printed on coarse cotton; a Lurçat tapestry on the same cotton, and sections of the Cluny Lady and Unicorn (also available on a tray for 25 francs). No one is going to love you for lugging these home, but one of your friends might enjoy the "camp" innocently inherent in them.

For some very obscure reason, the south side of the Champs Elysées except for the Drugstore and Fouquet's is usually left un-trod by tourists. Make the bold crossing for a few more sedate cafés and a number of stimulating shops. At number 71 is what might be the most resplendent *Tabac* in the world, a compendium of modern marble, brass, golden wood, glass and important doorpulls, lit by soft white lights like the geisha quarter in Kyoto. Nearby, the Renault Pub made to look like a red-plush railroad carriage of ye olde days and from the same—or similar— imagination, the asphyxiating aisles of a "Drugstore." They flank the Swedish Consulate and the serene **Maison de Suède** (number 125) with its magnificent Nordic sweaters and calm jewelry and the ghosts of neighbors who watched behind lace curtains the comings and goings at number 25, in which Merrill Lynch, Pierce, Fenner & Smith now have their Paris office. It once housed a lady who, quite young, left her tailor husband and soared and soared through jewels, titles, romantic suicides and notoriety; then sank, in the common denouement, into age and death on the Riviera.

Left Bank "Things"

The Latin Quarter, the womb of French learning, the neighborhood of Descartes, Verlaine, the Cluny, the Sorbonne, the Panthéon; a city of schools and students with streets called "l'Ecole Polytechnique" and simply "des Ecoles," has been visited in recent years by a Greenwich Village plague, persistent and contagious. Among the numerous indigenous bookshops, clothing stores, cafés and student restaurants in the section of the 5th marked off by Boulevard St. Germain, Boulevard St. Michel, Avenue Soufflot and Rue des Ecoles, there are probably several thousand modern chess sets of metal, porcelain and plastic; a ton of rural iron—horseshoes, scraps of plow, that act, reluctantly, as lamp bases; a half-ton of thin modern necklaces with free-form jangles; thousands of ceramic bead bracelets and/or enamel; mirrors framed in ceramics or glass studs; enough fat, funny stuffed dolls to people a village and hangersful of mobiles; pots and pots and pots and pots of modern pottery, and so on, with the frequent addition of batiked scarves and hand-painted blouses. Many of the "things" are attractive, even talented and caught by a casual eye in the course of a walk, amusing—for a while. If just a few will stand for the rest of the repetition:

Le Crocodile, 13 Rue de l'Ecole Polytechnique (also some old prints and small cloth rugs).

Lyane one Rue de l'Ecole Polytechnique near Rue des Ecoles.

Cadeaux, 4 Rue des Ecoles.

Emanux, 23 Rue des Ecoles (a tiny place, mainly enamel jewelry).

Kissler, 23 bis, Rue des Ecoles.

Le Parthénon, 54 Rue des Ecoles.

NOTE: Some places open only after 3 P.M., another "Village" idea.

For Young Lemmings

Rue Tronchet between the Madeleine and Boulevard Haussmann is where the Paris teen-ager dances to the piper's tunes. Although her mother might find a bag there, **La Bagagerie** (also on the Left Bank) at number 13, concentrates on the gimmicky, the fantasy in plastic: a clutch purse as long and thin as a *baguette*. Red and black plastic traveling bags, explosively shiny, to go with matching boots. (These are not, by the way, expensive and some of the extraordinary bags are very dashing.) **Marny** and **Charvy,** near Au Printemps, display clever knits and silks. **Erès** at number 4, *Après Ski*, whose quilted jackets and pants in brilliant colors get no farther than snowless, slopeless Boulevard St. Germain. **Madd** at number 20, **Miss Elle** at number 30, **Vog** at number 34 are the frenzied vortex of the young typhoon that whips down on Rue Tronchet on Thursday (no school) and Saturday P.M. There is no knowing what style the frenetic kaleidoscope of young styles will turn up the time you go, but if it's pink fake fur, athlete's shoes in white or yellow with black dots at the ankles, blinding floppy hats or plastic beehives, sweaters climbing around the ears or cut out at the navel—it will all be here and the ferreting, squealing little girls.

The Left Bank Mother Church is Rue de Sèvres and its proliferations on to Rue de Rennes, Boulevard St. Germain, Rue du Four. Across the Boulevard it splashes its synthetic radiance along St. André des Arts. The names are usually zippy, Anglo, like **Cab** (43 Rue de Rennes) or **Bus Stop** (Boulevard St. Germain), although one of the favored shops is **Dorothée** and **Dorothée Bis** at 35 and 37 Rue de Sèvres, given to window displays of large flashes of silver foil, like turned lightning, and platters of huge sequins; **Marie-Martine,** who occupies several shops at the meeting of Rue de Sèvres and Rue des Sts. Pères, is considered one of the pioneers in leading the girls away from shape and cling, or to it, in the changes of fashion. And there is **Hermia** at number 7 and **Path** (what is the logic that arrives at these names?) at number 9, both on Rue de Sèvres.

Out of a design relationship, or simple contemporaneity, these coats and dresses sometimes couple with "happenings" of architecture (or "Igloo-Dada") to produce something that calls itself **LA GAMINERIE** (Boulevard St. Germain opposite the Rhumerie café) of puffy white plaster, metal constructions stuck into undulation hollows and not much of a view of what's inside until you tunnel in.

At the edge of the spill of greens, chickens, fruits, breads, tripe, eggs, from the market at the Carrefour de Buci, where St. André des Arts begins: **Gudule,** jumpy young clothing among art constructions which light up, puzzle and horrify.

Less arty—except as the costumes represent Mondrian in plastic or pink undershirts: **Chochotte** at number 34 and, a bit beyond, **Chipie** and maybe they really know the English usage and find it *amusant.*

At 6 Rue St. Sulpice, a small, imaginative boutique of handknits, tinkly jewelry and unusual cuff links. **Fabrice,** 54 Rue Bonaparte (also at 61 Boulevard St. Michel); in a suffocation of "amusing" shops, one that really is, in its manner with enamel ornaments, beads, bits of felt and silks. At 57 Bonaparte, the **Bistrot de Tricot,** what probably was once a bistro tricked up out of recognition with old seltzer bottles, breezy signs and woodsy decor to surround English "pulls," and fanciful trinkets.

Textiles

Rue La Boëtie

Gasmey, No. 6. A large and old store specializing in varied yard goods.

Au Vieux Tisserand, No. 13. Formal silks—velvets, embroidered brocades—meant mainly for household decorative uses, though they might make spendid evening coats.

Raufast, No. 18. Luscious heavy silks and brocades for drapes and upholstery.

Several yard-goods shops, hardly for house dresses or kitchen curtains, on Rue de la Paix. Less glamorous yardage can be found on the Rue St. Honoré.

Beside the huge establishments of **Rodin,** number 36, **Max,** number 70, **Bouchara,** number 74 (with branches on the Place de la République and the Avenue des Ternes) there is **Corot,** on the other, emptier side of the Champs Elysées.

Tissroy, 97 Avenue Victor Hugo. Particularly handsome woolens.

Left Bank

Françoise Dupuy, 3 Rue de l'Université. Formal silks and brocades to cover period chairs and window-frames.

Diptyque, Rue de Pontoise and Boulevard St. Germain. Unusual modern fabrics set off the international toys for adults.

Nobilis, on both sides of the Rue Bonaparte near St. Germain des Prés, provides matching drapery material and wallpapers.

Marché St. Pierre

Up the Rue de Steinkerque from Boulevard Rochechouart, through shop after shop of yard goods manned by solicitous owners who stand outside suggesting what you'd like to see before you've quite decided, and into a sea of yard goods at the Place St. Pierre. It billows off stalls and onto the street, gathers on the shoulders of young children clinging to mamans, hangs overhead like banners. One large store keeps its varieties departmentalized, rolled and folded and seen to by (usually) an adequate staff. The more famous bargain haunt—**Dreyfus**—at the east end of the square is an oceanic turmoil of cloth, people crammed together in crowded passages and perilous stairways; confusion, disorder, customers yelling for attention, salesclerks yelling back; nervous movement where no one seems to be able to move; a light nightmare of rapacity, or fun, if you're not seriously shopping and want to "mingle with Paris life."

Miscellany—Right Bank

For costume dolls—look in at **Larcasy** on Rue de Rivoli, near Rue de Castiglione.

Aux Tortues, Rue Tronchet and Boulevard Haussmann. Frames, bridges of elephants, baby hairbrushes, chess sets, Napoleon and his court, a ball carved within a ball carved within a ball and insanely on—all in ivory.

Morabito, 1 Place Vendôme. Primarily concerned with the cream of pocketbooks in alligator and in extremes of petit point like paintings, the shop also indulges in costly, beguiling toys for ladies: embroided eyeglass cases that open like roses; velvet-backed, beaded handbag mirrors, a compact mounted by butterflies of red velvet and sequins.

Gold charms are as plentiful in Paris as everywhere else and can be found in the jewelry shops of all large shopping areas. To simplify matters, though, 19 Rue de la Paix has assembled an extraordinary number and variety, not excluding the Eiffel Tower and the famous *affiche* post, the Colonne Morris.

Raymond, 100 Faubourg St. Honoré. Longing for a bathtub with roses running around it? Or a sink thick with flowers or a million porcelain doorknobs or pink toilet paper printed in an 18th century wallpaper design? Here it is.

Peter, corner Rue Berryer and Faubourg St. Honoré. Fine knives and scissors; many-bladed penknives, versatile and murderous; small animal figures in ivory and in silver and a large collection of silver flatware. For small gifts, a pretty salt spoon, a penknife, a mushroom-shaped saltshaker or, go the whole way, with an extraordinary arrangement of antler with two shakers sunk into it.

Mandragore, 61 Rue d'Anjou. A minute museum of international crafts: straw garlic festoons on the white walls, Spanish grillwork, Polish and Russian toys of wood, china from Portugal, French enameled jewelry, none of it expensive.

Au Cytise, corner Rue d'Anjou and Rue des Mathurins. China in vases, lamps and plates staring down at a universe of lovers, shepherdesses, angels, everybody curly, be-ruffled and be-ribboned, and in high glazes.

Only if you're in the neighborhood—**Signes,** 20 Quai du Louvre; oddities of ceramics and glass embedded in plastics or papier mâché. For shrunken heads (fake), animals and objects composed of shells, shells purely themselves, and grotesque masks, push your way into **Aux Poissons Exotiques** at 30 Quai du Louvre.

Galerie Jean St. Georges, Faubourg St. Honoré and Rue Paul Cézanne. A compendium of modern furnishings, carpeting, decorative pieces and interior-planning that will give you a good idea of how prosperous present-day Paris furnishes its house.

Berthelot, 184 Faubourg St. Honoré. Established in 1852, disdainful of the modernization around it and at this time in Paris history, more suitable to the alleys of the Left Bank. It hasn't much to show—a few frames, unprepossessing little souvenirs, a few paintings, art supplies. Worth stopping at for its anachronistic self.

Dandor, 94 Boulevard Haussmann. Wild costume jewelry in Egyptian, Byzantine and Empire styles or combinations thereof. Beads made of glass, ceramics and beans, strung as necklaces and dangling from mesh shopping bags. (Gifts, possibly.)

Broderie Russe, 23 Rue La Boëtie. Established 1883. Needlework already done and, for the needlewoman, work in various patterns and degrees of complexity including the famous Unicorn tapestries (Cluny version) printed in color on canvas, ready to stitch.

Imprimerie Nationale, 20 Rue La Boëtie. Publishers and metal engravers who make and sell the seal of an arrondissement or of the Pont Neuf or the Church of St. Séverin; medallion-portraits of Schubert, Hemingway, Goethe, Chevalier or Marie Antoinette and, in smaller versions, as rings or cuff links or bracelets.

Indo-Chinese, 18 Rue La Boëtie. A shop with lovely watery silks, jewelry, temple rubbings, temple dancer figurines, ornate carved boxes.

For "decorations and gifts," shops on Avenue George V:

Robert Merceron at number 14, a bit lighter than the more stately objects at **José Pasquier,** number 7.

Medals and only medals in one or two shops in the Palais Royal.

A l'Eléphant du Congo, 32 Rue La Boëtie. "We repair ivories Religious and Profane" the sign advises. This hushed wooden anachronism of exclusivity and rare craftsmanship will sell you an exquisitely carved traveling altar, a small triptych of carved and colored saints. Or, if your drives are less spiritual, tortoiseshell comb and brush sets, also in ivory; ivory beads and bracelets or if you want to make a splash a *nécéssaire* for sewing, apparently of solid ivory with the shapes of scissors, thimble and needle-cases miraculously carved into the ivory to nest the sewing implements most precisely.

If W. H. Smith (page 277) has not satisfied your nostalgia for English things, pick up sweets and biscuits, tea, kippers and gooseberry jam from the neat counters of **The English Tea House** at 23 Rue Malesherbes, or try on a Burberry at the Paris annex on Malesherbes, number 8.

Kirby, Beard & Co., on Rue Auber, comfortably opposite American Express. A compendium of English raincoats and silver, good French and English china, Gucci bags, gloves, leather accessories; a little of everything attractively arranged.

A Portuguese peasant skirt of heavy wool, Portuguese pottery, Portuguese trinkets at **Casa o Porto,** 51 Rue Lepic—if you're in Montmartre and if the local French products won't do.

15 Rue Jean Mermoz—a pleasant old shop. Framing primarily but probably eager to sell some of the attractive old prints. Also, 21 Rue Jean Mermoz for frames and prints.

African Tourist Office, 14 Avenue Matignon. Inexpensive exotic trinkets for gifts: figures of dancers, copy of a Benin mask or an Ashanti gold weight.

On Avenue Matignon, immediately north of the Faubourg, there is a shop (institute? temple? society?) which looks on imperfect hair as diseased and immoral. It devotes itself to *Capilliculture,* sells medicaments and will give you a list of similarly dedicated hairdressers.

A bed-throw of white fox or spotted wildcat can be found on the short stretch of Avenue Matignon north of the Faubourg St. Honoré in a shop that sells, if it must, more ordinary bed-throws.

For the philatelist, the many shops in the arcades of the Palais Royal, the Thursday and weekend stalls across from Avenue Gabriel in the Champs Elysées; large number of philatelists on both sides of Avenue Drouot, near the Hôtel Drouot (page 214), and a stand or two in the Sunday markets.

Au Goût de Nos Aîeux, Avenue Matignon, near Faubourg St. Honoré. Silver, silver, silver as figures, bracelets, urns and cups; and almost next door, **Bas Reliefs,** if you want to ship back a blackamoor holding a tray or an ivory elephant standing on another elephant, etc., etc., in diminishing sizes, a shell-shaped fountain or a big stone dolphin.

Anyone for tennis? Skiing? The ballet? For looking athletic in the appropriate costume? Try **Ski** at 142 Rue de la Pompe and **Brunswick** at 82 Avenue Victor Hugo.

Not as cheap as you'll find them around Les Halles or Faubourg St. Martin, or Boulevard Sébastopol, or the markets, though they're better looking here, the cooking utensils at **Thomine & Cousin,** next to the Hôtel Alexander on Avenue Victor Hugo. But before you buy, examine the staggering connoisseur collection at **Hillerin,** 18 and 20 Rue Coquillière in Les Halles.

There doesn't seem to be very much reason to drag back home sarapes, tin chickens, Tonala clay birds, the trees of life and brilliant lighting fixtures, delightful as they are, from Mexico. However, things Mexican are admired and in vogue in Paris and if you have a hostess gift to give, see what there is at **L'Hacienda,** 65 Avenue Victor Hugo.

If a Mayan-ish stone image won't do, nor an owl painted all over with flowers, try the more seemly gifts at **Jones,** the department store that runs from 39 to 51 on Avenue Victor Hugo.

Number 3 at Place Victor Hugo takes care of your health in strong tones. Its name is frilly—**A la Petite Marquise**—but its purpose, *L'Alimentation Naturelle* is stern. It despises additives and dieting. Bread, it tells you, is the great natural food; wheat is nature's perfect creation and this perfection goes into their many kinds of bread "made with our own grain, our own butter, our own eggs" (all underlined). You can also buy their high principles in candies, salads, cakes, meats, jams, grains, non-additived, non-insecticided teas and Périgourdine specialties of cooked goose and stuffed necks of goose.

Forlane, Rue des Saules and Rue Norvins. Good ceramic caricatures. The paintings vary, too many of them "Montmartre" products.

Le Relais des Arts, 3 Rue Norvins. Fine copper figurines as caricatures, enamels, pottery and metal chess sets.

Poterie du Vieux Montmartre, 96 Rue Lepic. Pottery and ashtrays that say those clever, mildly salacious things about wine and sex.

Chambord, 12 Boulevard Malesherbes. Bright-eyed pottery; odd containers, leather frames like huge nametags and etceteras.

Marguerite Fondeur, 18 Rue d'Anjou. An immense, orderly and fascinating collection of antique buckles and buttons.

Au Bain Diane, Rue Miromesnil, near Faubourg St. Honoré. The entrance tells the story: a purple, double-curved canopy held by two green, sexy ladies lightly draped, feet gracefully crossed, one hip provocatively pushed out, like Indian goddesses and 16th century French Virgins. Inside, gilded dolphin spigots, shell soap holders and the most discreetly charming of toilet-mop holders. *En effet*, to change a lady and her bathtub into Venus and the sea.

A l'Olivier, on the Rue de Rivoli, a short distance west of the St. Paul station. Enormous Ali Baba vats stand outside and inside, vats nearer a technical age, equipped with suction devices and measuring gauges to draw off quantities of highly esteemed olive oil (hence the name) for customers who come here from distant parts of Paris. One counter holds some tins and jars of imported delicacies, not a large enough collection to act as anything but decoration for the olive oils and bottles of turtle oil, almond oil, seed oils, walnut oil, grain oils and, in recent demand as a cosmetic oil, that of the mink, on the principle that your fur can be as glossy as his, given his equipment.

Rue St. Honoré

If **Fauchon's** and its companion **Ceres** (page 200) can't still your need for Frosties, American catsup and marshmallows, try the shop at 256.

Near the American elixirs shop above there live a curious assortment. **La Jonque d'Or** (number 264) is so Frenchified that it puts beads and lace on its Chinese dresses, or cuts them in French wools, or reverses the process and uses Chinese silks for French styles; hung as usual, among lacquered screens, vases, figurines and the ubiquitous ivory chess set of furious mandarins.

Et Tout, Et Tout, whose sign says "often closed mornings," collects old belts, buttons, enormous hatpins, beads, thimbles, watchbands for a forager's heaven.

Number 3 is **l'Artisanat d'Art.** It shows stabiles and mobiles, papier mâché figures like Napoleon and Byzantine priests, ingenious fish made of bits of glass, pottery, pewter, ceramic panels, machine-embroidered panels, chunky jewelry in combinations of humor and moderation.

At **Aux Trésors d'Aladin** (about number 320) the collection becomes omnivorous, from a decorated wash basin to a Hong Kong chair with erratic stops between.

At number 414—**Le Shopping**—an alley that ends as an appealing boutique. In the cases along the way: stone figures, insane dolls, clocks made of balloon prints, Japanese calendars; a good possibility for small gifts.

At 30 Rue François Miron there is a shop called **Izraël** and its sign says *"Produits Exotiques"* not unlike signs one sees along the Rue Richer (page 56) and in Belleville (page 139). Izraël has wide-ranging curiosity or enterprise and stocks, along with the indispensable halvah and "Russian" pickles, dried chiles, ginger root, Chinese spices, strings of dried okra, long fingers of St. John's bread, Tunisian cakes, stuffed grape leaves, Greek feta, Italian pasta, curry, vats of olives, minute pickled lemons and strange non-edible little red hands with outstretched fingers that turn out to be a cluster of candles. The store is big and deep, full of heady smells; the proprietors good-natured and patient with ignorant foreigners.

Lambert, 62 Rue La Boëtie. Frames of all periods and types, to set off Fragonard or Buffet.

Léri, 64 Rue du Palais Royal. A sizable collection of old and odd-faced watches among figurines of crystal, jade and ivory; romantic, weepy watch faces, holy-picture faces, watch faces for flag-waving nationalists or Francophiles.

Au Bon Vieux Chic, 18 Quai de la Mégisserie. Antique pistols, precise models of suits of armor, shields.

To respond to a passion—and recent fashion—for chunks of semi-precious stones, or hemi-semi-demi-precious, shops on the Place des Vosges.

Behind the splendors of the antiquities at **Jansen,** 9 Rue Royale, a discriminating choice of not too costly gift items.

On Rue des Hospitalières St. Gervais, in the Marais, an Hebraica shop where you might, in the discouraged straying of modern books, old tomes, objects from Israel (including small sacks of Israeli soil, used to sprinkle on the graves of those who yearn for but can't reach burial there), find an antique candelabrum or a Saturday-night spice box, although the pickings in Paris, as elsewhere, are lean.

To judge from the delivery trucks bulging and precarious with unwieldy weights dumping heaps of assorted goods into the yards of the Hôtel Drouot, and the shapeless groupings in the big, homely rooms, no one would suspect this to be the Parke-Bernet, the Christies and Sothebys of Paris. But it is and it has housed priceless Byzantine icons, the furniture of queenly châteaux, the art collections and bijoux of the rich or profligate—and piles of sad mattresses and roomsful of scratched school desks.

Less regularly, in more lush surroundings, auctions are held at the **Musée Galliera,** near the Palais de Chaillot.

One of a number of international craft shops, **La Boutique Polonaise,** 25 Rue Drouot, offers along with Polish books and records, inexpensive dolls and crafts objects. The cheapest and most attractive are flower cutouts or boldly-colored birds often shown cheaply framed, at too many times their original cost, in decorating shops.

Where the Rue Drouot meets the Rue de Provence, **Le Grand Dépôt,** a large center for china, at somewhat less than the usual cost.

Miscellany—Left Bank

Travestis, 14 Rue des Ecoles. Two militant collies guard a slip of store crammed with Viking helmets, tinny, immense jeweled stomachers, huge studded, belligerent platelets—enough for a full season of the Ring cycle—many, many crowns and some full costumes. For whom? Your guess.

Erkilete, 13 Rue de Pontoise. This shop mounts works of art tastefully, on plastic, wood, marble, glass, depending on the aesthetic needs of the object. Even if you haven't a treasure to set off, look at other peoples' in the window and at the old instrument or African mask that might be hanging on a wall, at the solid old wine saloon next door and at the ateliers on Rue St. Victor, a splinter of the Rue des Ecoles that further divides its short run into two levels.

Petitot, 234 Boulevard St. Germain. Marks out its field as military in books, prints, lead soldiers, models, and careful depictions of uniforms, cannons and approved gun positions for 18th century soldiers.

Pomeyrol, 218 Boulevard St. Germain. Gloves in a prickly field of countless sticks and umbrellas, along with extraordinary heads and handles.

La Boutique à Boutons, 110 Rue de Rennes, boasts of 7,500 types of buttons.

Since 1826 illuminating and binding has been going on at 159 Boulevard St. Germain. Through candles, oil, gas and electricity the amount of light hasn't much increased, but the dimness goes well with the smell of age and leather and the old-fashioned sayings, illuminated and framed, in the window.

A. R. Lyon, 171 Boulevard Saint Germain. A taxidermist who arranges brilliant birds on flowered branches under bell jars and frames lovely arrangements of magnificent butterflies—if you like that sort of thing. If not, the shells, the books and postcards might interest you.

The magpie effect common to many Left Bank shops appears at **Guinnot**, 3 Rue de l'Echaudé, large and casual, and **Le Passé Composé**, 1 Rue Bourbon le Château, large, also, and more energetic, gathering old toys, old books, modern jewelry and pottery.

Darcy, 53 Rue des Sts. Pères, is a small flower shop whose young artists (a word advisedly used) will compose for you—cheaply and swiftly—highly talented floral offerings.

André Macé, 8 Rue du Fouarre. Neptune, a bishop, a gargoyle, a rosette, a fountain, all in stone, accompanied by a few stretches of old grillwork.

Becoming as rare and anachronistic as alchemists are the *herboristes*, the few left usually well-trained elderly ladies who conduct themselves with the dignified sobriety of doctors, which in a sense they are. Most of them have had to make room for the more fashionable, and profitable, health foods, but they still give space to the baskets and boxes of gums, herbs and teas, often accompanied by informative labels, that ease livers, control kidneys and make the blood run more smoothly. One such shop may still exist on 8 Boulevard St. Germain near Rue de Pontoise and another, its elixirs decoratively arranged, at 9 Rue St. Sulpice, and look for them during a walk in neighborhoods where progress hasn't stormed in too rapidly.

J. E. Bulloz, Rue Bonaparte near Rue Jacob. Dedicated to photographic reproduction and its possibilities. Culled from all sorts of art, reproductions find themselves as cards, as lamp-shields, wastebaskets, as wall-panel enlargements (a large Buddha, or a playful unicorn as big as a pony) and photo-murals derived from early engravings of the Seine.

Pierre Hautot, 36 Rue du Bac. Reproductions of many periods and points of origin, some of them already skillfully mounted.

L'Enfant Jésus, 52 Rue du Four. Flowers, fruits and what might easily be jade goddesses if they weren't artfully contrived candles.

Chunks and slabs of mineral stone as decor, weapon or jewelry at 13 Rue Jacob.

Zoo Notre-Dame, Oiseaux et Animaux, on the Quai de Monte-bello. There is no conceivable reason why you should buy an animal or even a dove with excited, curly feathers like a Monet peony, but if you're passing by, see if there is still in residence a rooster whose family once had doings with a peacock to judge from two or three radiant spots and who, maddened by the traffic on the quai, crows all day long with short intervals of staring venomously at the indifferent stones of Notre Dame.

The Seine bookstalls, barren of treasures for some time, do have large boxes full of old postcards picturing places in foreign countries and in various regions of France, and happy lovers and happy families, all with rosebud mouths and sticky expressions tinted in the colors of lollypops; thoroughly *pompier* or "camp," to use the later word.

For copper and pewter, try 14 Rue St. Sulpice, jammed with pans and tankards.

A Basque shop at 10 Rue St. Sulpice is the place to buy authentic espadrilles inexpensively.

N. Boubée et Cie. on the Place St. André des Arts. Carefully mounted skeletons, stuffed animals, microscopes, and the variety of scientific paraphernalia that is gathered under the broad designation *Naturalistes.*

Deyrolle on Rue du Bac, near Rue de l'Université, has rocks in sheets and as rough bowls cut to show the patterns of the grain, large enough for tombstones, small enough for paperweights. Also, stuffed peacocks, a stuffed deer mounting—or protecting—a stuffed doe; an ostrich and its eggs; small bewildered apes; butterflies and bugs tastefully arranged; anatomical figures and charts; books and instruments; a full and startling collection gleaned from all over the world through a long, dedicated life.

Surrounded by the African arts that are the specialty of the Rue Guénégaud, a collection of semiprecious stones worked as jewelry, at number 29.

It is not a "junk" shop and yet it is: the minute **Aventurine,** at 67 Rue du Bac, that requires its bits and pieces to have a certain *avant* air. 1930's earrings, plaster boxes into which bits of watches, buttons, and whatever is at hand have been set to make ornaments, an old flexible wooden hand, an Art Nouveau blouse and if the market is favorable, a row of middle-aged kitchen clocks. Around the corner, at 72 Rue de Grenelle, a wine and coal shop hardly large enough to hold more than four customers, displays behind a musty window, two or three things picked up in coal cellars. And that's how antique shops are sometimes born.

Claude de Muzac, corner Rue de l'Echaudé and Rue Bourbon le Château—mountings of arts objects and skillful framing.

At some point in your prowling on the Rue Laplace and its adjoining streets (page 78), you will come across **Junk** supervised by a large short-cropped lady who—in the cave of heaped, tottering, pendant, jammed, things—points to the *départements:* "kitchen" here, "iron" there. As you trip on a disarray of old locks and fireplace fenders you may land on a heap of dolls' clothing and pieces of Spanish shawl; you might, taking a narrow path through the thick dark, be smothered in an old costume or collide with the wheels of a 1900's doll carriage in the "toys" section.

Rue St. André des Arts leads a busy life and an eclectic one. One of its areas of interest is the cleverly made or cleverly found object, varied in age and size but often easily portable. At number 46, furniture, jewelry, possibly a writing box. At number 41, **Courteaux Enault**—screens, painted furniture, old bottles and prints. At number 36 beaded bags, hatpins, an old thimble, some antique jewelry. At number 32—a welter of objects, maybe a magic lantern, seals, stamps, miniature vases, candlesticks, carved wooden eggs, watch charms. At number 25, **La Rampe**—modern jewelry, crocheted hats, batiks, candle holders shining with glass studs.

Out of accumulated experience that goes back to 1643 the firm of **Carrière Frères**, 22 Rue St. Sulpice, can mold candles that look like almost anything, including precise replicas of marsh weeds, as well as good-looking variations of the basic object.

The devout, old bluestocking *Rue St. Sulpice* clutches its faded *pèlerine* about itself, trying not to notice the buses that tear through its somnolence. Buses or no, the street is reluctantly yielding, however, to the invasion of younger things shining out of the old store fronts. At number 10, **Alain Lesieutre**, Art Nouveau vases and figures. Number 6, sentimental reminders of a recent past—

photos of Sarah Bernhardt, bits of jewelry once worn by La Belle Otéro (one of the last of the great courtesans), a cast of the hand of Rachel, mournful piles of 78-records and other teary reminders of the good old days. For a deeper retreat into time, look at the designs of the ex-libris plates still printed in the shop at number 20, guaranteed to mask any old dog-eared book in dignity, and at the accumulations at number 11 and 21 that refuse to be placed in categories of time or purpose.

Appropriately placed in an old pharmacy, at 48 Rue Jacob, there is a gathering of rare books on medicine and other sciences; aged microscopes and precision instruments, models of the planetary system, and skulls meticulously marked—primitive neurology and phrenology confused—in areas of characteristics and patterns of responses.

16 Rue Jacob. Fascinating trinkets, most of them remade from Oriental ornaments: Chinese silver and jade butterflies as pins, key rings attached to coral; baubles made of clusters of coral and a specialty of long, decorative shoehorns mounted with ivory, wood and silver rams' heads and semiprecious stones.

A few doors from the house in which Alphonse Daudet died (number 41), at 31 Rue de l'Université, a shop that calls itself **Expressions** displays international modern pottery, woven bags of a few remaining semipeasant cultures, toys and toylike household ornaments. Its most attractive element, though, is the shop itself and the order of its arrangements.

Enamels as rings and necklaces are casual additions to the repertories of most Left Bank boutiques, but a place where they are treated seriously for the luster of their stained-glass colors and thoughtful shapes is a serene shop on a court (two small showcases on the street flank the opening of the court) on the street of Grégoire de Tours, a short distance from the Boulevard St. Germain.

Mortality has caught up with the seemingly immortal Raymond Duncan. His thin gray hair bound by a filet, his homespun "classic" cloaks and handmade Greek sandals and the elderly disciples who guided his careful steps through the Rue de Seine will no longer enhance the Left Bank scene. It may be, though, that the Akademia Duncan will last for a while, producing and selling the hand-loomed cloths printed with designs devised by the Master as well as the noble, primitive sandals.

If you are looking for a photograph of the "blue men" of northern Africa or a Mayan frieze in Palenque or a Paris wineshop of 1910, or almost anything capable of being photographed, try the archives of **Roger Viollet** at 6 Rue de Seine.

A. Vian's, 8 Rue Grégoire de Tours, holds an improbable collection of tired to obsolete musical instruments, and music boxes.

To see what a respected cheese shop was before the age of the supermarket, go to the *fromagerie* on Rue de Grenelle, near the Boulevard Raspail. Out of a cellar where, it is said, Madame the proprietor knows the exact time when any one of hundreds of cheeses is to be presented as ready, come cheeses that look like albacore, like big toes or stones on a dusty highway; goat triangles and sheep mounds crusted with all sorts of matter or white and expectant as snow; cheese wrapped in straw, or hung in raffia or swimming in dark juices and herbs.

La Poterie Provençale at 135 bis Boulevard Montparnasse; an interesting collection of regional craft and near the meeting of Boulevard Montparnasse with Rue de Rennes there is a shop that exploits the possibilities of cork, some of them surprising.

Galerie du Siècle, 168 Boulevard St. Germain. Modern jewelry, some of it clever, some grotesque. In the main, more thoughtful and substantial than the strands of twisted Brillo proudly displayed elsewhere, too many elsewheres.

Splendors of silver burst out of numerous shops throughout, but for the possibilities of finding small, not too imposing pieces, heaped as they might be in a big pawnshop, look over the chains, pins, porringers, key rings, cuff links, candelabra, table services at 88 Rue du Bac and the longer, higher range of silver hills at **A La Mine d'Argent,** 108 Rue du Bac and its annex across the street.

Cristal et Bronze, at the corner of Rue de Varenne and Rue du Bac, is literally that, in well-designed combinations.

La Tour de Nesle, 24 Rue Dauphine, satisfies the big eyes, small purse, longing for antiques with copies. A comforting place to anyone who knows how many spurious pieces pose as authentic.

Once upon a time, Parisians will tell you, you bought a book, almost always paperbound, and took it to one of many bookbinders to cover at no great cost. Now the "small" *relieur* shop around the corner is gone and the few binders who still exist devote their energies to fine, expensive bindings beyond the modest dignity of an ordinary book. If you are carrying around some irreplaceable, tattered favorite and don't care how much it costs to revive it, go to **Andreas,** 41 Rue Dauphine, or **Claude Delpière,** 22 Rue Bonaparte; **Devally,** 6 Rue Danton, or **Kieffer,** at 46 Rue St. André des Arts. As an imposing gift for an intellectual friend you might buy a big, boxed edition of Baudelaire's *Fleurs du Mal* bound in a paisley pattern with leaves like poisoned tongues, or the *Bestiaire* of Apollinaire illustrated with clever woodcuts.

Hélène Strich, 3 Rue de la Colombe, displays fetching ornaments and costume jewelry, outclassed however, by the enchanting dolls in beautiful period dress; collectors' items rather than toys for little girls, it would be dreadful to have these carelessly handled.

Another **Strich** shop (Rue d'Arcole) concerns itself with modern household objects which you can buy at home. The window decorations are superbly imaginative, though. One window might be of black and white geometric designs made of buttons, and the other great rays of gilt plastic shells, sand spiculed with gold penpoints, the whole sunburst studded with pearls.

The mood of junk shops is necessarily daft. 36 Rue Mouffetard (pg. 80) is dafter than most, helped by its doorway surrounded by painted panels of old mirror retrieved from a demolition heap. Inside it, in front, around and about, leather halters, iron pots, a 1925 straw hat, carriage lamps, sagging furniture, high-button shoes, buckles, lace-covered dancing pumps, anything.

At 31 Rue Monge, not far from the Mouffetard market, an ingenious shop that makes witty things; cleverly carved napkin rings, elegant puppets, figures of straw, odd shawls, felt coasters and cushions, and, in your time, possibly an entirely new cast of objects. They are not cheap, but then nothing but bread and sketching sessions are cheap in Paris.

Galleries and Graphics

Reasonably, the city that was for so long a great fount of art, has an overwhelming number of galleries. Reasonably again, the immense market attracts a few stands loaded with the spurious, the insultingly bad, the pandering to what is believed to be "tourist taste." But one man's disdained Op or Pop might be another man's Mondrian; one man's Modern can stop at Braque, another wants only what will be painted tomorrow. Consequently, the following consists of a directory, rather than recommendations, with few comments. You can treat them as points on a quest or as decorations on the dress of Paris.

RIGHT BANK

Rue du Faubourg St. Honoré

Knoedler, No. 85 bis. And who doesn't know *that* name? Or that of **Ror Volmar** at number 75. **Le Chapelin** is at number 71.

L'Elysée, No. 69. The measure of its collection can be gauged by the fact that they display a good number of Chagalls.

Galerie Jean Dufresne, No. 61. For a Derain, a Seurat or the work of confreres.

Ecole de Paris, No. 49. Behind an important-looking Empire front—bound gold fasces and all—modern French paintings.

Galerie Stiebel, No. 5 (inside the court). Modern painting, not necessarily French always.

René Drouet, No. 104. "Contemporary masters," the posters say.

Galerie Urban, No. 18. Paintings, mainly, but the pride of the house are the limited copies of plates Renoir decorated for his daughter-in-law, unless they are all gone by now.

Galerie Martin Caille, No. 34. Moderns, usually French; and at number 50, **Galerie Europe,** somewhat more adventurous.

Galerie Blumenthal, No. 159, another of the well-known.

Galerie Berri (at the corner of Rue de Berri). Painless modern.

Heim, No. 109. "Old Masters." And they just might have a Bellini hiding in the back room.

Galerie 93, No. 93. Along with—at times—modern ceramics and paintings, amusing fish and fowl and caricatures composed of bits of old ornaments and glass. Skillful, highly decorative, and not too seriously arty.

Rue La Boëtie

Galerie Paul Pétridès, No. 53.

Galerie Agora, No. 62.

Galerie Bernheim, No. 35. Rouault, Vlaminck, Van Dongen, Pascin.

Marcel Guiot Galerie, No. 7.

Jean-Paul Wick, No. 5.

Spitzer, corner of Rue La Boëtie and Rue d'Argenson. An immense collection of reproductions from Renaissance through Rouault, ancient Chinese birds and blossoms, minor Dutch masters, Renoir, Dufy. Not always as cheap as you may think a reproduction should be, but these are beautifully made.

Avenue Matignon

This street, which crosses the Faubourg St. Honoré, is an almost uninterrupted row of art galleries, a few internationally famous, of new, newish and old art.

Galerie Creuzevault, No. 9.

Galerie Matignon, No. 22.

André Weil, No. 26.

The galleries **Bernheim Jeune** at 27 Avenue Matignon and at 83 Faubourg St. Honoré.

Hervé, No. 18.

Galerie Romanet, No. 18.

Matignon north of the Faubourg St. Honoré (a short stretch) includes a cluster of galleries modern to very:

Robert Schneider

Mc Coard

Kriegel

Matignon

The well-known **Galerie Maeght** is at Avenue de Messine and Rue de Téhéran. And see what there is at the **Galerie Messine,** a smaller place at 1 Avenue de Messine. Nearby, at 47 Rue de Monceau, **Leiris,** whose growth and fame has been and is closely linked with Picasso's.

Just behind the art here, following Rue Mollien out of Place de Narvick, you'll find a large mouth-watering market (A.M.), if you want to come down to earth for a bit.

Rue de Miromesnil

D'Incelli, corner Rue de Miromesnil and Rue La Boëtie. *Avant.*

Galerie 18, some modern "Old Masters," and the **Galerie Benezit** at number 20; at number 21, **Fernand Depas.**

At number 4, **Galerie Marigny** and **Galerie Raffrey,** all contemporary to modern, or vice versa.

Katia Granoff, at Place Beauvau on the Faubourg St. Honoré. A large, well-established gallery of moderns (also on the Left Bank, 13 Quai de Conti, near the Academy).

Time off from the window-shopping: Have lunch at Le Marigny on the Place Beauvau if you can get an outside table near the classic hedge of assembled flower boxes growing heavy, bushy leaves, looking onto what's left of the still graceful Place Beauvau. Then walk down wide, dignified Avenue Marigny, past Avenue Gabriel, where the stamp collectors meet and into the park of the Champs Elysées where you might find a nun heaving a basketball at a group of school children—right out of that old Bing Crosby movie—and have your coffee at the big corner café along with the well-dressed sleek ladies of the neighborhood.

Galerie de Paris, 14 Place François Ier. Like a museum, or a château. Big shows of approved moderns.

In the gallery of the **Librairie du Globe** at 43 Rue Vivienne, exhibitions of Soviet painting.

LEFT BANK

Boulevard St. Germain

Galerie Arnaud, No. 212. Modern.

Galerie St. Germain, No. 202. Pop, Op, distortions, Dada jokes 1966 style. Belligerently avant.

Three on Rue de l'Abbaye; ranging from elderly to modern to immediately modern: **Galerie Zak, Alice Manteau** and **Delpire.**

On Rue Cardinale, number 3, **Le Point Cardinal.**

On 25 Rue de l'Echaudé, **Galerie Riquelme.**

Galerie des Jeunes, at the corner of St. André des Arts as it emerges from the Carrefour Buci, on several levels downward into medieval caves.

Outnumbered only by *antiquités,* art is almost as common a commodity on the Rue de Seine, Bonaparte, Beaux-Arts and their vicinity. A few of the many that might interest you with their displays of what is currently being done:

Galerie Jeanne Bucher, in the court of 53 Rue de Seine.

Galerie Lara Vincy, Rue de Seine and Rue Jacques Callot.

Romi, 15 Rue de Seine; primitives and some *trompe-l'oeil.*

Galerie Lambert, Rue de Seine.

Galerie Ileana Sonnabend, Rue Mazarine.

Claude Bernard, 5 Rue des Beaux Arts.

Galerie du Dragon on Rue du Dragon.

Galerie d'Ile de France, near Rue du Bac on Rue de l'Université.

Galerie Framond, 3 Rue des Sts. Pères.

Galerie Lucie Weill, 6 Rue Bonaparte.

Galerie du Passeur, 90 Rue du Bac.

Galerie Paul Facchetti. 17 Rue de Lille.

NOTE: Among the more studied forms on Rue des Beaux Arts, look at the primitive art that decorates a wineshop; inept and dashing.

Graphics

The Left Bank is where among the objects, books and paintings, generous spreads and stacks of engravings, drawings and posters live. Valued members of the last category—Lautrec posters, a Picasso poster for a Picasso exhibition, for example—are scarcer than one would like to believe, the field carefully picked over by foreign galleries or held and hidden for a rise in value. To fill the gap and follow the fashion, Belle Epoque and Pop Art stare out of the windows. Nevertheless, behind the iris and water-lily ladies and the technicolor blowups of comic-strip heroines, there are extensive varied repositories of graphics, from the meticulous, topical renderings of past centuries to little doodles, humorous or mysterious, dashed off yesterday.

Adrien Maeght, 40 Rue du Bac, an annex of the collection of "greats" in painting on the Rue de Téhéran with that reputation to maintain in art books, engravings and drawings.

Berggruen, 70 Rue de l'Université, whose standing in the field is equally respected.

The quais yield a large choice of graphics.

Marcel Adler, a huge, collection that strives to please all tastes, at the meeting of the Rue de Seine with the Quai Malaquais.

At 3 Quai Malaquais, the combination of prints and art books, largely modern.

René Bréhéret, 9 Quai Malaquais; prints and watercolors.

R. G. Michel divides itself in two, flanking a wineshop, at 17 Quai St. Michel, where it is rumored, a valued store of posters hides behind the art books and the more common graphics.

At number 17, a mixture of the Oriental and Occidental.

Gosselin, on the Quai des Grands Augustins, shows old prints and drawings.

André Rousseau, 1 Quai Voltaire; drawings and prints.

H. Berès, 23 Quai Voltaire; Japanese as well as French prints and drawings.

On the Rue Bonaparte, at number 10, more antique prints, illuminated pages, and books.

Sometimes alone, but often accompanied, graphics, as indicated, are most frequently partnered by art books. Other companions can be frames, as at 15 Rue Bonaparte.

The **Rue de Seine** is especially busy with graphics. Number 53 has among its lithographs, a dazzling set of Art Nouveau posters, their equivalents possibly attainable also at **Sources,** number 49, and at **La Nouvelle Gravure,** number 42.

Baudoin, at number 29 roams tentatively in the turn of the century though its heart lies in older prints spanning several sporting centuries: hunt scenes, soigné gentlemen riders, careful, technical drawings of guns or displays of lures out of fishing manuals.

The **Galerie Seder,** 25 Rue des Sts. Pères, offers no distractions from its graphics, (mainly modern) except the good looks of its fluent-Englished proprietress.

On the Boulevard St. Germain, at number 139, **Nicaise,** fairly new and adventurous.

Surrounded by religious articles, in a brilliant diversity of materials and styles and expressions (including a smiling wax Adonis in a smart, lightweight, turned-collar suit) and several suitably monastic old bookshops, a wide choice of antique prints at the corner of Rue St. Sulpice and Rue de Seine.

Robert Prouté, 12 Rue de Seine. A large and versatile collection including posters, watercolors, and a wide range of prints of varied styles and periods.

Drawings over the centuries at the **Galerie Lutèce** on Rue Guénégaud and at the **Bateau Lavoir,** 16 Rue de Seine.

One large repository of old prints sits in the auction, books, stamps and china gathering on the Rue Drouot, **Soccard,** at number 20.

Antiques and *Objets*, Old and New

The unique gem picked up for five francs in a flea market has almost disappeared with prosperity. As life grows safer economically and then moves onto steps of luxury, as decayed neighborhoods are infused with money and fresh paint, antique and decorations shops spring up to fill the pristine interiors. Where the young proprietors found their supplies is where you might have, in the flea markets of Paris and London. This shouldn't discourage you; for the devoted, the search is its own reward and although the markets are not necessarily profitable they provide a pleasing combination of wandering in a diversity—variously eccentric—of objects and people.

The city of warrens that comprise the Marché aux Puces off the Porte de Clignancourt Métro station (page 37) can provide, as the world knows, anything from old sheet music to an occasional rare book, an old pair of boots to a sequined 20's evening dress, old military buttons to immense armoires. Smaller flea markets spread their rusty treasures on the weekends in broken bands along the edges of the city: at the end of the Porte de Vanves market (page 19), around the Porte de Montreuil. The Place d'Aligre conducts a daily morning market, scheduled for demolition and rebuilding but that may take, like the removal of Les Halles, years. The Marché aux Puces of Bicêtre (page 157) functions on two days during the week but is best on Sundays, and the Rue de Lappe, once a street of restless men and until a few years ago the site of anything-goes dance halls, provides small household machines and tools in several stages of usability on weekday mornings.

Two *marchés* absolutely devoid of fleas or their possible bearers are the **Swiss Village** (called that because it took the place of a fair village erected early in this century) and the **Marché Ponthieu**. The former, which can be entered via the Avenue La Motte-Picquet at number 52 and is open all day except on Tuesdays and Fridays, is an attractive place, a ramble of little irregular streets called Allée de Bâle, Allée de Berne and so on, that give out the shine and gloss of well-polished furniture and glass. The range is wide—books, wooden angels, jade, Chinese porcelain, writing boxes, carafes, chests, silver, copper bowls and, at the edge of the luster, racks of unimposing men's suits. At least half the market closes in August, still a good time to go, to watch the well-dressed ladies (retired actresses, it is said) accompanied by their cigarette-holders and poodles, directing the washing of windows and the polishing of metals for the September rebirth or playing cards on an antique table and splindly, gilded chairs under the sun in a corner of an alley, or knitting and gossiping like market-women anywhere. The antiques market at 49 Rue de Ponthieu has the advantage of being much closer to the usual travelers' centers (immediately behind the Champs Elysées), is infinitely smaller and has the special charm of being embedded in an old food market: *charcuterie* abutting on 18th century screens, lettuce, radishes and green beans flanked by antique jewelry on one side and Victorian lamps on the other, and the prices, too, will be strongly contrasted. Lastly, a tiny *marché* worth a pause between Métro *correspondances* is that in the Palais Royal station.

As it is for clothing and art galleries, the Rue du Faubourg St. Honoré and its tangential streets comprise the most splendid antiques and *objets* market, dozens on dozens of costly beauties beautifully framed. It is very likely that you have already taken the slow, glittering path (and, if you've ever intended to, made your important purchases *chez* Fabre or Loo or Jansen or Seligman, *et al.* and beat Christie's out of a panel of Bayeux tapestry at the **Salle Drouot**) but you may want to do it again, and give some attention to what follows.

Rue du Faubourg St. Honoré

Lecomte-Ullmann, No. 75. An eclectic collection, maybe fans and old porcelain, a three-seater satin sofa shaped like a cookie shaped like a wheel, or an ancient seal and a Luristan figurine.

André Hurtrez, No. 43. Among a plethora of gilded contortions (Paris has almost as many as Rome), some interesting antique clocks and a few graceful or moving (they can't seem to be both at one time) saints.

Marin, No. 29. China and glass not, distinctly not, for the cereal and milk of your three-year-old.

Aux Bibelots Anciens, No. 58. A potpourri worth picking through if a collection of beads in jade, carnelian, other semi-precious stones, old china, antique pins and lockets and paintings seems promising. With differences, but au fond similar, are **Rosenthal** at number 82 and at number 86, **Popoff**, who also has ikons of value.

At Place Beauvau, **Doucet**. Antiques, furniture primarily, and especially, many beautiful chairs.

At about number 208, sits the *Mairie* of the diamond-specked arondissement. It is large, palatial and does its neighbors proud.

Delahaye, No. 131. Some pearls and jewelry, but mainly zoos and farmsful of silver animals precisely observed and rendered; many dogs of all kinds, boars and the kind of silver bird that might sit on your table at Lasserre (page 262).

Dragon Bleu, No. 140. One of those shops that defies category. It looks like a collection of necklaces and bracelets, of semiprecious stones, rings, charms, pins—of turquoise, amber, "Tibetan" stones; includes, too, figures of ivory, quartz and jade, and a good number of ivory chess sets. Whatever it is, it doesn't want you to be put off by its ambience; a sign in the window advises: "Not as expensive as you think."

Carré, No. 185. No matter what they have in your time of looking—a fine old wooden door, a mirror with a great, gilt ornament at the top, a group of silk-covered chairs or Empire chests—the objects will be choice.

Roger Imbert, No. 157. Highly reputable antiques, objects, furniture, and paintings that continue on in a courtyard. The gathering is worth time if you're searching, but you may be distracted by the court itself, especially if you haven't yet wandered in Paris courts. They are the small factories and, when the weather permits, the dining rooms of Paris. Because inner light is often limited, fur cutters in the 10th arrondissement, the scrapers, polishers, repairers, trimmers of the Faubourg St. Antoine (page 107), craftsmen around St. Séverin and St. Julien le Pauvre, small dry cleaners and laundries, will extend the shop into the court. At lunch time the workers and house painters in the area and the small shopkeepers may set up a table—tablecloth, napkins, a bottle of wine and the hot dishes a local concierge may have cooked or reheated if it's been brought from home, and a congenial time, like a scene out of an old Marcel Carné movie, fills the court.

This particular court, to get back to the Faubourg St. Honoré, is especially attractive with cascades of gray shutters and, above a stairway at one side a set of studio windows, dull now but imagine what they must have been when they shone broadly under their strong arches.

Godard-Desmarest, No. 178. 18th century furniture, clocks, vases.

Jean Royère, No. 182. What Paris can do with modern decor, the cleanliness of Scandinavian lightly touched by French habits of elaboration. It works well in attractive pottery, graceful simple chairs covered with hand-blocked cottons; delightful metal rods bent to tree shapes and bearing lights.

Number 232, once the site of the local abattoirs, gives itself to art, **Galerie Balzac,** and motorcycle repair shops while the alley at number 222 is redeemed by a Dominican church stuck, in the Roman manner, in strangling space which also holds a row of toilets and a tailor shop owned by a Dante.

Neumann—Objets, No. 240. The collection—a Lautrec drawing over primitive country furniture, jade figurines and a charming 19th century beach scene, a few small pieces of sculpture and well-designed cabinets—an eclectic one and unusual.

The immense wall on the Rue Balzac, at the Faubourg, is, in spite of its fortress presence, penetrable. It surrounds the Salomon de Rothschild Foundation whose official entrance is on Rue Berryer. The grounds (entrance at the bottom of Rue Balzac) are now a secluded public park with a view of the back of the house, romantic statues under wide trees, meandering paths and a few benches. It is quiet, subtly triste, particularly when the yellowing leaves pile up around the feet of the white figures, and a fine place for an impromptu lunch of cheese and bread and fruit to relieve the rigors of shopping.

La Demeure, 30 Rue Cambacérès. Like a small modern art gallery—polished wood, cool space—showing modern tapestries.

Rue La Boëtie

Jean Luce, No. 30. Good china, crystal, glassware, in a great variety of periods and patterns.

Baur, No. 32. Silver in flatware and patterns; solid and traditional.

At 14 Rue de Marignan, the important archaeological antiquities of **Charles Ratton,** seen by appointment only; phone Elysée 5821.

Pierre A. Bernard, 1 Rue d'Anjou. A romantic's dream of an antique shop—tight, disordered, heaped with eventful things in curious juxtapositions: lovely old goblets holding up a rare print, a bit of ancient weaving tacked to a wall next to a German angel. Judging from the people who squeeze themselves into the tight space, a popular antique haunt.

Rue de Miromesnil

The Rue de Miromesnil, especially the stretch between Faubourg St. Honoré and Boulevard Haussmann is virtually an antique *objets* market. Some specialize, some roam; all are attractive. Starting from Rue de Lisbonne (no reason why you can't reverse it, however):

Gaubert, No. 80. Persian prints, Japanese sword ornaments, Etruscan(ish?) vases, old prints, armoires, antique frames; a stimulating mélange.

Aux Armes de France, No. 46. The name leads to gay, military drums; full suits of armor as well as miniatures; toy soldiers for experts; swords, shields, flintlocks, old pistols; and for frustrated mariners, an astrolabe and a hard-brimmed sailor's hat (the kind they still wear in the Billingsgate Market in London).

Chambon, No. 44. French history as evoked in toy soldiers, emblems of the Revolution, a miniature of the beautiful Pauline Bonaparte (she of the Canova nude in the Borghese Galleries of Rome); a parchment document dated 1816, condemning rebellious troops, the spoon and fork of a man guillotined in 1793 and a finely made, gleaming model of a guillotine, maybe the same one.

Eléonore, No. 18. A mixed bag of small ivory skulls, large pieces of statuary, old paintings, Buddhas, an elaborate mantel to hold a mirror and—if it hasn't been sold (to whom, one wonders)—an oddity of a classic bust wearing a shoulder cape, under the cape a dog and a putto, dog biting putto's wing; putto, an ugly baby with a cold, properly annoyed.

Galerie Chirvan, No. 10. Persian prints, Cyrillic letters worked in pieces of old weaving, curios, rugs, Near-Eastern vases, elaborately carved boxes and small statuary with a Greek look.

Boutique Marina, No. 8. New, old; impressive, unimpressive; anything, everything. Similarly true at number 6 and, across the street, at **Piperno's** which sports, as well, a mother-of-pearl encrusted papier-mâché chair (a refugee from the incredible collection of the Victoria and Albert Museum?) and pieces of tapestry.

Céralène, 16 Avenue Montaigne. China, crystal, some silver and assorted objects and unusual, attractive handmade rugs in peasanty designs.

Au Vase Etrusque, 11 Place de la Madeleine. Many styles and varieties of china, glassware, crystal. At number 7, **Odiot,** which has been for a couple of centuries (in its recent history—one of Renoir's brothers was a designer for the firm), engaged in providing the kind of crystal, silverware and gold that makes royal wedding gifts.

312 Rue St. Honoré. A demure *antiquités*—where you may find an ancient music stand, fine lace on ivory fans, old china.

Léon Gruel, 418 Rue St. Honoré. Antique books, Spanish bridal chests, prints, paintings, old framed maps; an omniverous, stimulating collection.

Injoudjian, 26 Rue La Fayette. Deep and gloomy, dark bundles on the floor and a faint gleam of glass shelves on the walls. The bundles are a considerable number of Near Eastern rugs and the glass shelves hold antique vases and plates and a few good Persian prints.

Paule Marrot, 16 Rue de l'Arcade (Madeleine). Table linens, embroidered.

Etienne Pignatelli, western arcade of Palais Royal. In the faded royal arcades (page 36), a shop of porcelains, faience, amber, coral, jade, enamel boxes. In the course of walking in the Palais, you will find a few other shops with similar wares, including antique jewelry.

Unless they've succumbed to the *drang nach* the Left Bank, **Hindmain's** antiques should be at 14 Rue des Pyramides and **Amram's**, also a repository for a little of what is left of Judaica, at 35 Rue St. Georges.

While on the Art Nouveau walk (page 67), look in at **Le Temps Passé** at 48 Boulevard La Tour-Maubourg; not large, but it usually carries a knowing choice of old china, pewter and furniture.

The *Avenue Victor Hugo* provides in its variety, a number of antique shops: **Anika**, at number 59, old woods, wrought iron, tankards, meant for country houses. **Michel Pigniers** at number 3 and **Aignan** at 140 Rue de la Pompe (off Victor Hugo) for porcelain, silver, furniture and paintings. On the same short street, **Jacqueline Debay**, number 138 and a branch across the street with English furniture and a sizable collection of brasses. Also **Courbet, Corynna,** and a shop that sells Persian, Chinese rugs and curious, attractive runners of crude North African design.

Junk as junk or coming up in class, antiques as antiques or sliding down; odds and ends of lamp bases, simple furniture, clumsy vases which give way here and there to a superb drawing, fine old glass or a cluster of miniatures on Rue de la Tour, off the Place de Costa Rica in the 16th.

LEFT BANK

Most of whatever hasn't been encased by the Faubourg St. Honoré and environs or the Musée des Arts Décoratifs seems to have found its way across the river and massed solidly in the area bounded, with slim proliferations, by the Rue du Bac and the Boulevard St. Michel, from the river to the Vaugirard border of the Luxembourg Gardens. Although the range spreads from scrap heap to regal on almost every street, the royalty of this area are the Boulevard St. Germain, the Rue de Grenelle and the Quai Voltaire, the latter a gathering of a number of distinguished antiquarians.

Quai Voltaire

Maurice Theneday, No. 1. Antiques of the 17th and 18th centuries.

Bresset, No. 5. Furniture, wood carvings, paintings that go far back in time.

Nicolier, No. 7. Porcelains from as early as the 15th century, French and Oriental.

Camoin, No. 9. French furniture, decorative pieces and curios, mainly of the 17th and 18th centuries.

Taillemas, No. 17. Devoted to the decorative arts of the Middle Ages and the Renaissance.

Vandermeersch, No. 23. Reputedly a connoisseur's connoisseur of antique china.

Rue de Grenelle

Au Vieux St. Germain, No. 4. Brocades, choice china and glassware. At number 5, antique china.

Josette Schulman, No. 17. Archaic Oriental arts: Indian, Japanese, Chinese, Khmer. Sharing the same number, a collection of dignified antique furniture.

Maurice Ratton, No. 28. A large, well-known collection of primitive and archaic arts. At number 39, antique clocks, some with pendules strong enough to swing through the August vacation, and religious ivories.

Jean Hautinguiraut, No. 48. A one-man show of etched glass, the versatility extended to ivory and metal also. And a neighbor who works exquisite embroideries on cloths and vestments for the church.

Boulevard St. Germain

Galerie Le Corneur-Roudillon, No. 206. Primitive and archaeological antiquities—pre-Columbian, African, and Khmer—among old nautical instruments and painted furniture, in well-composed arrangements. Inside the court, a delightful satyr's head radiating trelliswork.

Maison et Jardin, No. 242. Long graceful sconces, modern Spanish rugs, an ornate metal chest, well-proportioned table lamps.

If you prefer heavier, larger decorative accessories, look at the tapestries, the big candlesticks, the red and gold chairs and the busts at No. 240.

Labatut, No. 226. Good period chairs in various coverings and large "Venetian" mirrors.

Nikolenko, No. 220. A chalet-style front leads into old paintings, Russian icons and antique furniture of various parts of Europe.

An *antiquités* at 23 Quai aux Fleurs spreads its wares on two levels behind a beguiling street sign on a corner of a fascinating, not over-touristed neighborhood.

Not very antique furniture, one hundred to one hundred fifty years old, at **Au Directoire,** 46 Rue du Bac.

Lalandre, Rue des Sts. Pères and Rue de Grenelle. Antiques luring with a grillwork ornament probably meant to hold a crown of candles and above that the legend: *"Cloue à jamais la joie au front de ta demeure."*

The Rue Guénégaud is mainly dedicated to African arts, ending at the quai with a collection of African, Oceanic, Persian, Egyptian, Indian, Byzantine, Gothic at **La Reine Margot.**

Neighboring the house in which Anatole France was born (19 Quai Malaquais) and the house in which he died, number 15: **Kamer,** archaeological and primitive arts, number 9. At number 19, **Le Veel,** rare china.

Brocéliande, 49 Quai des Grands Augustins; a mixture of household antiquities.

Rue de Beaune is an especially dense thicket. Among the many: **Epoca,** number 21, attractive modern materials and international decor. **Le Cabinet de Curiosité** at number 23; old instruments, ancient pincers, technical books of their time; many, many things, frilly to heavy, playful to serious.

An equally dense thicket is the *Rue Bonaparte.* **A la Licorne,** at number 12, is an assemblage of antique instruments, marine charts, globes, etuis, paint boxes and their contemporaries as books and prints. At number 37, gilt frames, mirrors and consoles of the 16th, 17th and 18th centuries, and at number 33, a frenzied miscellany of odd, middle-aged things.

The mixture of Rue Bonaparte continues on across the Boulevard St. Germain to meld with the religious goods of the Place St. Sulpice. Before it does, antiques, near-antiques and potpourri including late Victorian lamps, aging books, a few galleries and at number 68, **Bricus Bracum,** full of china and small crystal chandeliers, a possibility if you suspect, or can't afford, the antiques.

Rue de Furstenberg, leading to Rue Jacob, is a row of beautifully self-conscious shops with carefully painted black wood and shining irregular glass carefully revived and maintained in the old manner to show off a variety of oldish things, and the sharp contrast at *Scandiart,* some of the best of new Scandinavian design.

Rue Jacob is a minor French Portobello Road, and to judge from its shops, sometimes an annex, sporting a good number of Edwardian lamps, English boxes and fireplace brass. The rest of the street is furniture, pottery, figurines, frames and mirrors, "campy" junk and tricky junk. Among the more selective: porcelain at number 22; Chinese figurines and porcelain of various periods at number 19; **Gouspy,** near Rue des Sts. Pères who concentrates on bright fancies. On Rue de l'Université (Rue Jacob, really, after it has crossed Sts. Pères), **Berard,** number 4, porcelain and pottery; **André Payen,** at number 6, shows good small enamel pieces, apothecary jars and glass chandeliers; at number 12, attractive small antique tables and chests; at number 38, a place that calls itself **Portobello,** with the Englishness and not too antique antiquity that the name means, in silver, crystal and fruit knives; number 44 is one of those evocative clutters which make you feel there is a jewel hidden therein. Near the meeting with Rue de Poitiers, several dignified, well-decorated and arranged antique furniture places.

Back on *Rue des Sts. Pères,* a breathless collection of hunting prints and accouterments, chairs whose frames are made of animal horns, stuffed game birds, sconces of antlers, at **Air de la Chasse,** number 8. At number 7, antiquities inside the court and in an adjoining cave, modern fantasies and grotesques in ceramics. **Orient-Occident** at number 5 is a well-known source for Greek, Egyptian, Indian and Oriental antiquities, and trailing it in importance the usual *quartier* combinations of china, furniture, a shop like a pushcart of medals, beads, small bisque heads and medallions. (Look around the corner, on the Rue de Lille to see who walks in and out of the National School of Living Oriental Languages.) As you walk toward the Boulevard St. Germain see what—of the fine furniture, old globes and telescopes and tall clocks—you might want from **G. Suc.** Take a look at the old sweets shop, still hand-dipping chocolates, and its repertory of teas. Peer into the 17th century Protestant cemetery hidden behind number 30 and notice the babushka-ed, high-cheeked women who go into the Ukrainian church at the corner.

Arthus Bertrand, next door to the side end of the Deux Magots, across from St. Germain Church. Important and hushed; beautiful glass goblets set with silver, good jewelry, silver plate, finely wrought medallions; occasionally a fine piece of traditional metal sculpture, possibly a noble Assyrian steed in bronze.

Max L. Baudot, 6 Rue Bourbon le Château. Pewter, old china and glass, old prints.

African arts at 1 Rue de l'Abbaye and, adjoining it, rural antiquities.

Antiques and primitive arts at **Montbaron,** at the corner of Rue Fleurus and Boulevard Raspail.

Les Vanneries, 80 Rue Vaneau (Vaneau Métro). Isolated in the clothing area; neither large nor orderly; a potpourri of unpredictable old pieces.

Ascher, Rue de Seine at Rue des Beaux Arts; one of the leading dealers in primitive arts and antiques.

Hangers-on of "The Old Curiosity Shop" style: A clutter of old books, coins, bills, receipts, legal pronouncements, cards, photographs, engravings, and autographs at 3 Rue de l'Université. On Rue de Seine, at number 34, beads, pearled hatpins, fans, small music boxes, china and pottery ornaments; what have you—or they.

Hagnauer in the court at 10 Rue de Seine. Almost formidably imposing and poised; no "sweet little old things" picked up for a song.

Then there is the length of the Rue de Seine to consider, and the curios on a wide scale of importance and authenticity that live among its bookstores, print shops and galleries; and the old toys and games on Rue de l'Echaudé, the glass and pewter at 6 Bourbon le Château, and at the corner of that street and Rue de Buci, a market drygoods store which features towels printed like the 100 franc note, a portrait of Napoleon and the Arch of Triumph. A few steps away, on Rue Jacques Callot at number 16 there is more fine old faience and the reparation thereof. On Rue Mazarine, the neighborhood echoes reappear, with the addition of one exceptional china shop (**Clara Fandor,** number 18).

Farther southward, number 12 Rue des Ecoles (5th) pours its rural furniture, copper vats, strips of grillwork, modest chandeliers out on the sidewalk, to be watched over by a sturdy copper weather-cock. Walk, do not run, but there may be something.

Trouvailles, 9 Rue de l'Ecole Polytechnique. Not an overwhelming collection, though tasteful. Old charms and bits of jewelry, a few ancient oddities, paintings new and old, a good set of ivory beads.

Odeur du Temps, 8 Rue Laplace. Antique, rustic pottery, a 19th century christening robe, a painted cupboard. The shop is comparatively new and worth watching for additions to its gatherings.

The pattern repeats, where groceries and bakeshops and cobblers don't interfere, in most of the 6th arrondissement, some of the 7th, increasingly in the 5th and (see Walks) repetitiously, insistently, in any neighborhood of new or renewed housing. New little wonders will undoubtedly sprout up, but the above should be enough to keep you engaged and interested through an afternoon, when they are all open except possibly on Mondays. (Surely not on Sunday and almost surely not in August.)

ILE ST. LOUIS

Rue des Deux Ponts

Occasion des 2 Ponts and **Au Mortier D'Or,** two stimulating collections of aged oddities. And at number 31, nearer Pont Marie, hovering in the "junk" category with enough happy finds to warrant browsing.

At numbers 60, 88 and 90 Rue St. Louis en l'Ile, mixtures of porcelain, prints, ships models, bits of archaeology; a cave-restaurant which spends its street level on old clocks and bottles.

A few such shops on Rue Jean du Bellay, among them, **La Main Enchantée** (number 6 and near the Pont St. Louis), **La Passarelle** and, since this writing, probably a dozen others.

THE MARAIS

Just outside the *Place des Vosges,* **La Marotte** on Rue de Birague, an assortment of some of the millions of pretty old trifles Paris holds on to.

Inside the arches, at number 26, **Janette Ostier,** an Oriental gallery with particular emphasis on superb Japanese screens; at number 28, **Cugnet** who likes the stolid might of Italian and Spanish Renaissance furniture as base and stage for the many *santos* and Chinese porcelain.

A Richelieu, at number 21, prefers nautical instruments, antique scales and barometers, guns and powder bags, a venerable painted wagon wheel.

At number 18, a return to saints—big ones in stone and wood and sturdy Spanish majolica.

Books

London may have more bookshops, though it seems impossible. They are ubiquitous, remarkably numerous in some Paris quarters, sparse in others; general and confined to specialties; polyglot and monolingual; rationally arranged or stacked like Collier brothers' barricades. Publishers run bookshops and obscure print shops publish books. There are Polish, Chinese, Vietnamese, Spanish, African, Italian, American, Persian, Arabic, German, etc., etc., books available new and secondhand. Textbooks and technical books jostle student cafés; art books and rare books inhabit the showy boulevards, the "art" streets, the Left Bank quais or seclude themselves, huddling together in inconspicuous streets.

As with paintings, jewelry, primitive art, etc., a searcher should be familiar with the goals of his search. Those shops listed below are worth looking into, for their specialties, their arrangements, their customers, their owners, but there cannot be any guarantee in the case of old books as to what you may find, how much it is worth, how much you will be asked to pay.

RIGHT BANK

Rue du Faubourg St. Honoré

Lardanchet, No. 100. Among the new books, a few older, some of them beautifully bound.

René Lemoine, No. 177. Were it London, you would inevitably describe this appealing clutter of all ages and conditions of books above and around you, brushing your shoulders and stepping on your feet, "Dickensian."

Blaizot, No. 164. Roomy, dim and gloomy, the traditional atmosphere suitable to old books and manuscripts.

Pierre Chrétien, No. 178. Rare old books and special bindings.

Pierre Berès, No. 14 Avenue de Friedland, has an office in New York, as book lovers probably know. However, it might be more pleasurable to see the books, autographs, prints and pamphlets in full dimension rather than as listings in a catalogue.

Librairie Lavoisier, 11 Rue Lavoisier. Should you need a technical book in German, French, English (both varieties) it probably could be found in this vast stretch of shelves.

Legueltel, No. 17 Rue Drouot. Many new art books, and multitudes of old tomes in the happy tradition of falling stacks of books, dimness and no space to move in.

Contacts, 24 Rue du Colisée. In a surprising street: politics, art, the films, literature seriously dealt with.

On Rue de Laborde, at the eastern end of Boulevard Haussmann, one finds old and secondhand books, worth a try if you're in the neighborhood.

LEFT BANK

Présence Africaine—which explains itself, is at 25 bis, Rue des Ecoles (at Mont Ste. Geneviève).

La Maison du Livre Italien at Rue des Ecoles and Rue Thénard also has an international section and an extra educational mission. On a placard at the entrance you can learn the word for "book" in twenty languages.

At 48 Rue des Ecoles a very small shop makes room only for aviation books and magazines.

Vega Bookshop, 175 Boulevard St. Germain. A wide collection on Indian religion, a good deal of Yoga; primitive religions and the occult.

La Hune, near the Deux Magots at St. Germain des Prés has, in its diversity, books in English and curious periodicals.

Librarie du Globe, 2 Rue de Buci. German philosophy, Russian books, Russian and East European recordings. Goldwaters (and all capitalist Americans) welcome according to an ad in one of the American daily papers.

Librairie du Cygne, 17 Rue Bonaparte. General rarities, including a good number on Paris past, and lovely volumes on the practice of ancient arts and crafts.

Librairie Ancienne et Moderne, 8 Rue Bonaparte. Autographs among the antique books and prints.

Vincent, Fréal, 2 and 4 Rue des Beaux Arts. A large, authoritative shop on the arts and particularly architecture.

Marc Loliée, 40 Rue des Sts. Pères. Classically dim, with a redoubtable reputation.

The monkish quiet of Rue St. Sulpice takes its mood about equally from the broad shadow of the church, the many shops of religious articles and a number of large, sparsely lit antiquarian bookshops, almost forbiddingly sober and learned. For instance, the large **Librairie d'Argences,** the shop of **Robert Cayla** at number 28 and the venerable **Librairie Maisonneuve** where you might buy a Persian grammar or an old tome on the religions of the Near East.

Librairie du Spectacle, 37 Rue de Seine. The theater of all countries, including theater architecture, scenery and texts of plays.

Librairie Fischbacher, 33 Rue de Seine. Big, deep and multilingual. The gold lettering on its shutters mentions proudly all the included forms of literary endeavor, among them surrealism.

Occult sciences are dealt with at 42 Rue St. Jacques, off the Rue des Ecoles. Horror and "Black Guides" are supplied by a number of shops, one on the Rue de Grenelle, near the Rue du Dragon, and **La Mandragore,** Rue des Grands Augustins near St. André des Arts.

If you want to see what the mainland Chinese are publishing, some of it superb art books bound in traditional Chinese style, stop into the **Phoenix** Bookshop on Boulevard Sébastopol, south of Rue Réaumur. A smaller selection of Chinese books, Chinese cutouts, Cuban, Russian, and a considerable section of English and American books downstairs (at one time led to by a virile Cuban poster rejecting all Imperialism, U.S. primarily) are available at **La Joie de Lire,** 40 Rue St. Séverin near Boulevard St. Michel. Its unmistakable political color made it a target for Molotov cocktails during the Algerian "crisis," which hasn't affected its convictions or stock a bit. Since it stays open quite late, it serves as a way of passing an evening hour for the young intellectual and may serve you for rubbing shoulders with him and examining what the other side publishes.

Bordering the Luxembourg Gardens on the Boulevard St. Michel side, several fine old bookshops and the house where Poulenc lived (number 5).

Au Pays de Garlande, 71 Rue Galande, is a not-too-serious purveyor of old books, some not so old, appealing cards and oldish things, swathed in charm and nostalgia.

Raymond Clavreuil, 37 Rue St. André des Arts and in an annex across the street. New and old books dealing with history, mainly French.

Librairie du Pont Neuf (Left Bank of the bridge). A large, notable gatherer of old and new and, in the common practice, prints out of old books sold separately.

At 15 Quai St. Michel, less omniverous shelves of rarities.

J. Perche, 45 Rue Jacob. Another polyglot whose books speak most European and a few Oriental languages.

Calligrammes, Rue du Dragon. In spite of the Apollinaire name, German books mainly.

51 Rue Monsieur le Prince. History and arts of the Orient in books of sundry ages.

A bookshop that limits itself to tourism, maps and travel books is at 154 Boulevard St. Germain.

Club de Livre Américain at 78 Boulevard St. Michel for an immense collection of American paperbacks and a considerable number in Spanish.

Cercle Français du Livre, 28 Rue du Bac. Good art books in the diversity and enterprising collections and reprintings of historical Paris material.

Jean Journier and Cie., 22 Rue du Bac. Prints accompanied, as often, by art books.

La Danse, 14 Rue de Beaune. The name explains the specialty.

Gibert Jeune, 27 Quai St. Michel and on the Boulevard St. Michel. Bargains and crowds of students.

Music, 19 Quai des Grands Augustins. Scores, books of and about music; new, old, some especially bound.

Honoré Champion, 7 Quai de Malaquais. Pamphlets and books, many certainly out of print, on sections of Paris, the histories of Paris churches, regional French literature, poems in the patois of the Auvergne or in Provençal.

Librairie Denis at 1 and the **Librairie** at 5 on the Quai Voltaire. Old, often rare.

F. de Nobele, 35 Rue Bonaparte, calls his shop the **Librairie des Beaux Arts,** those of many countries and periods.

At 21 Rue Jacob, marine matters—sailing charts, fish, ships and by extension, foreign lands.

Librairie de l'Abbaye, Rue Bonaparte, near St. Germain des Prés. Rare books and autographs.

Librarie Bonaparte, 31 Rue Bonaparte. Books on the dance and films, but theater, mostly.

◆§ *Des Belles Choses et des Curiosités*

A few of the city's ancient enchantresses, those who have not sprayed apart like old rope into torn lace and smashed hats, dress exceedingly well and discreetly. The heel may be a bit too high for secure walking, the white plastic raincoat a touch too young, but the makeup is smooth and subtle, the practiced touch of rouge on the eyelid brings out the sheen of a fading eye. It doesn't necessarily make her look young; she does look undiscouraged.

By way of 130 Boulevard St. Germain, or immediately around the corner on the Rue de l'Ancienne-Comédie, or via 61 Rue St. André des Arts, one enters the Cour du Commerce St. André, on the contemporary face of it considerably like other Paris passages except for the presence of the hotel, rather like a country cottage, where Sainte-Beuve lived in the 1830's. Other distinctions of the passage are now almost invisible. For one thing, it runs along what was once the medieval city wall of Philippe-Auguste. For another, it was one of the most active hives of the Revolution; Danton spent much of his working time here, meeting with disciples and followers, and at number 8, Marat printed his journal *The Friend of the People*. One of their close neighbors was a German carpenter named Schmidt who devised and perfected the guillotine. His yard ran with the blood of animals on whom he practiced, guided and supervised by a Doctor Louis, the secretary of the Royal Academy of Surgeons who supplemented Schmidt's experiments with his own, first on live sheep and then on cadavers in the hospital of Bicêtre (page 157). The machine itself was named after a Doctor Guillotin who had proposed swift decapitation as a humane and egalitarian advance over earlier forms of torture and slow death that were meted out to lower-class criminals. As for Schmidt, it is reported with satisfaction that, after having become rich, he died of frequent bouts of delirium tremens.

About midway, the passage reveals, above an ironworks shop, a section of medieval tower, once part of the wall, and then opens to the Cour de Rohan which has nothing to do with the great family of the Marais (page 115) but represents an error too old to erase. It was the Paris home of the bishops of Rouen from the 14th through the 16th centuries, and is actually three minute, sequestered courts, still dressed in bits of antiquity. Leading to a printing shop in the first court is a stairway, once a ramp of the old wall. The second court shows off a Renaissance facade and an iron tripod used as a step for mounting a horse, possibly the only one left in Paris; in the third, the vestiges of an antique well.

Infinitely more appealing than its venerable pieces is the whole enchanting ensemble, inevitably suggesting stage sets and, unfortunately, used as sets by film companies which have arranged to keep you out while they're working. You may not take photographs or explore the medieval vaults, nor run up and down the wall, but to see it is to have known one of the most endearing of Paris beauties (not a word one would use for the more famous Place de la Concorde made vicious by the auto, nor the brutal waste fronting Les Invalides), sane and soothing of itself and, especially, in contrast to the funhouse flavor of its neighboring streets.

LATE NOTE: It is rumored that the Cour has been sold. See it—if you can—as fast as you can, before exclusion and changes set in.

As characteristic as the kiosks and the Eiffel Tower, though less conspicuous, and too questionable a symbol of Paris taste to be advertised, are the small "Four Graces" fountains coated in layers of green paint that appear numerously (the official number is one hundred) throughout the city. They were the gift of a Richard Wallace, born in London and enamored of Paris. In love and gratitude he offered the drinking fountains which were accepted and, at another time, his collection of paintings, invaluable *objets* and choice pieces of antique French furniture. These were turned down and now sit in a stately London house as the renowned Wallace Collection.

There is a *commerçant* in northern Paris who is lucky enough to be called Dédé Tralala.

The little twigs of malice that grow in the sagging tenements become concierges; the sweet-blossomed become motherly, gold-toothed, frizzy-haired waitresses in modest restaurants. They advise and cajole, try to indulge your eccentric whims, are genuinely crestfallen when what you want is finished and tremble with concern over the adequacy of the substitute dish. This waitress is haven and hetaera for the regular, leaving him undisturbed inside his fortress of newspaper or throwing amiable bits of conversation at him while she dashes from kitchen to tables. She may never know his name but has quickly learned his habits. If a shapeless bundle is found on a chair at closing time she knows it belongs to *le monsieur de samedi,* a careless, forgetful man, and takes charge of the package to be delivered to him on his next Saturday visit.

When her legs become too old she turns into the toilet-guarder, *jeton*-dispenser, telephone-message recorder and broadcaster, the central bureau for date-making or breaking in a large café. Knitting, mending, breaking off to call through the sound-box a name to which she adds an aristocratic ring, making suggestions about what to do about a mysteriously failed appointment, she is a vital member of a busy, important world and sitting in her booth-lined cell at the foot of the stairs, accepts tips as if she were about to turn them over to charity.

Later still, disdainful of the restraints of public assistance and afraid of being taken out of the world and shut up in an old ladies' home, she may enter the *clochard*'s domain, reduced to begging now and then, still a lady, shaky and discolored, but pleasant and tactful. Her approach will usually be to a woman whom she will ask for directions to a local church where there is a kind priest who helps the poor. That question and her appearance is all the begging she will do. It suffices.

Most of the legendary White Russian taxi drivers have used up their span of years, but there are a few left and a few of those still with ample Slavic souls. One son of Gogol, stuck with a late passenger who had only a large bill and just enough change to cover the fare, but not a tip, consoled the apologetic customer: "Don't be concerned. The next client, or the next, or the next will tip me lavishly. God will provide. Sleep well."

The huge posters proclaiming a new art exhibition not only give the city an air of artistic foment but are of themselves handsome works. More artful and charming, usually, are the smaller posters that appear in countless shops—a *triperie,* a *pharmacie,* a *maquillage* store—to advertise a neighborhood festival or a crafts or antiques show, or an exhibition culled from one set of archives or another. The lettering and design are tastefully appropriate to the matter: the Marais programs of 1965 were listed over a wonderfully grotesque ornament of a local palace; a show of primitive masterpieces was discreetly announced in a few words below a photo of a magnificent African sculpture in 1965 and a similar, equally stunning poster publicized a collection of African art in the Grand Palais in 1966. A show of documents and graphics concerning pilgrimages was designed like a page out of a *Book of Hours.* Not the highest art, but satisfying, adult and good-mannered enough to warrant more than a fast glance.

Near the end of Rue Boudreau, a step before it is lost in the Rue Auber, there is a small maze, the Square de l'Opéra-Louis Jouvet mixed up with the Place d'Edouard VII, and out of this peculiar mating, a passage of the passage (opening at number 6) with room, among other shops, for a Chinese pedicurist. The *pièce,* however, in the jumble of arches and zigzags is the octagonal inner Place built around a statue of Edward VII in a military cape, hung with medals and nobly plumed military hat, on horseback. Costume and context seem all wrong for the fat amorous bon vivant who so worried his mother.

The Gare du Nord at 11:30 at night. The dust-colored light turns undersea green as it slides along the tall palmlike pillars and holds the few somnambulistic passengers and the motionless prostitutes like insects and butterflies in a smoky gray-green gum.

15 Hotels

Unless you are a guest in a Paris household or determined to sleep on a sidewalk, you should make a reservation well ahead of time, particularly if you are coming to Paris in the late spring through summer season.

Along with the list of restaurants your friends will give you there will undoubtedly be one or two hotel names. Failing that, your travel agent should be able to give you a choice of hotels in different price categories and areas. Failing *that*, the following list of shelters, few of them known from experience other than that of friends.

The queens, as you probably know are:

Ritz, 15 Place Vendôme (1st).

George V, 31 Avenue George V (8th).

Crillon, 10 Place de la Concorde (8th).

Bristol, 112 Rue du Faubourg St. Honoré (8th).

Berkeley, Avenue Matignon and Rue de Ponthieu (8th).

Lancaster, 7 Rue de Berri (8th).

Lotti, 7 Rue Castiglione (1st).

Meurice, 228 Rue de Rivoli (1st).

Plaza-Athénée, 25 Avenue Montaigne (8th).

Prince de Galles, 33 Avenue George V (8th).

Raphaël, 17 Avenue Kléber (16th).

Royal Monceau, 35 Avenue Hoche (8th).
Figure for the above a minimum of $20 a day, for two.

The princesses, somewhat less, *environs de* $15 minimum for two:

San Régis, 12 Rue Jean Goujon (8th).

Continental, 3 Rue Castiglione (1st).

Régina, 2 Place des Pyramides (1st).

Saint James et d'Albany, 211 Rue St. Honoré (1st).

Windsor-Reynolds, 14 Rue Beaujon (8th).

Louvois, 1 Rue Lulli (2nd).

Castille, 37 Rue Cambon (1st).

And on the Left Bank:

Pont Royal, 7 Rue Montalembert (7th) and its smaller, less expensive neighbor, the **Montalembert,** at number 3.

Lutetia, 43 Boulevard Raspail (6th).

Relais Bisson, 37 Quai des Grands Augustins (6th).

Thus far, you have been moving in an area where the bathless room, though it exists at minimum rates, is rare. Below, the categories of fewer private baths down to the bathrooms and W.C.s in the hallway, baths to be arranged and paid for as extra items.

France et Choiseul, 239 Rue St. Honoré (1st).

Rond Point-Champs Elysées, 10 Rue de Ponthieu (8th).

Alexander, 102 Avenue Victor Hugo (16th).

Céramic, 34 Avenue Wagram (8th).

Family, 35 Rue Cambon (1st).

De Tamise, 4 Rue d'Alger (1st).

Oxford et Cambridge, 13 Rue d'Alger (1st).

Bois, 11 Rue du Dôme (16th).

De Calais, 5 Rue des Capucines (1st).

In this modest to moderate category are a number of the hotels that surround the railroad stations and the innumerable drabs to charmers on the Left Bank. Among the latter:

Bourgogne et Montana, 7 Rue de Bourgogne, or Aristide Briand, the new name for one section of the street (7th).

Cayré, 4 Boulevard Raspail (7th).

Pavillon, 54 Rue St. Dominique (7th).

Solférino, 91 Rue de Lille (7th).

Madison, 143 Boulevard St. Germain (6th).

Marronniers, 21 Rue Jacob (6th).

Angleterre, 44 Rue Jacob (6th).

Scandinavia, 27 Rue de Tournon (6th).

Sts. Pères, 65 Rue des Sts. Pères (6th).

Pas de Calais, 59 Rue des Sts. Pères (6th).

Saint-Simon, 14 Rue Saint-Simon, demi-pension (7th).

Trianon, 3 Rue Vaugirard, between Boulevard St. Germain and Monsieur le Prince (6th).

Le Colbert, 7 Rue de l'Hôtel Colbert (5th).

Quai Voltaire, 19 Quai Voltaire (7th).

Londres et Malaquais, 3 Rue Bonaparte (6th).

Grand Palais, 35 Boulevard de Latour-Maubourg (7th).

On the Ile St. Louis. **Hôtel de la Paix,** 29 Quai d'Anjou, and **Hôtel La Bourgogne** on the Rue St. Louis en l'Ile (4th).

Alsace, 13 Rue des Beaux Arts, Oscar Wilde's death bed may still be in use (6th).

Vieux Paris on Rue Gît-le-Coeur (5th).

D'Isly, 29 Rue Jacob (6th).

Nice et Beaux Arts, 4 bis, Rue des Beaux Arts (6th).

Bersolys, 28 Rue de Lille (7th), is reported to be, behind its self-effacing entrance a cordial, well-kept place.

Similarly, the **Stanislas,** 5 Rue Montparnasse (6th); small, clean rooms for under 15 francs (single) and free use of a shower.

Yet another **Lutèce**, at 5 Rue Jules Chaplain (6th); clean, hideous furnishings (like most in its class). The cost, with breakfast, is about 25 francs for one and includes the company, on the way to and from the Vavin Métro station, of a friendly bouquet of ladies in fluffy clouds of yellow-white hair and tight skirts.

It lacks color, but not movement, cafés and bus lines, the Ecole Militaire end of the 7th whose streets enclose a considerable number of small hotels. The Rue Chevert, for instance, has three, one of them the **Grand Hôtel du Garage et du Septième**. It *is* in the 7th, *is* situated over a *grand* four-story garage but is by no means *grand* in itself. Meticulously clean, rarely crowded, and its moderate rate (about 45 francs for two, no breakfast) entitles you to basking in the roof garden which may compensate for the "whoosh" of wheels at odd hours. Nearer the norm in the same area is the **Hôtel Duquesne**, 23 Avenue Duquesne.

There are countless others, almost as many as there are restaurants and cafés. In general, a decent hotel room can be found in the hotels of the non-tourist boulevards more cheaply than its equivalent in the glamour *quartiers* though that bespeaks already being settled and having the time to look around. If the money is dwindling, and you can't tear yourself away from Paris, and don't much care where and how you live, examine the hotels on the Rue Monge, near the Panthéon, off the Gare Montparnasse, two or three tiny places on the Rue de Lille, Rue de l'Université, and Rue de Seine; as a matter of fact, on almost any of the streets in the students' quarters. For rock bottom, before the undersides of bridges, you might check some of the places mentioned in Walks.

16   Restaurants

Yes, Virginia, there is poor food in Paris and there are unclean kitchens and you can get the gripes, dashes and nausea called in Mexico "Moctezuma's Revenge," whose French name might be "The Curse of Vercingetorix." The water is not notoriously bad, but you might be guided by the universal habit of bottled water, when water is drunk at all. As in the couture situation, the halcyon days are waning. The supply of great chefs and just good chefs is dwindling and not readily replaced by young men, who are lured to other fields where the training, earnings and status are achieved more swiftly. Consequently, *cuisine*—the slow cooking, the subtle, delicate blendings, the mating of elusive flavors—remains primarily in two categories of restaurant: the very expensive which can afford to hire well-paid chefs and the bistros lucky enough to keep one talented old retainer or those that are family affairs where Maman or Papa and somet'mes both have brought a limited but carefully studied repertory from their native province and see to it that standards are preserved.

As painstaking, patient cooking fades away, it is being replaced by *grillades*, which means hamburgers, steaks and chops in American style or Argentine style *brochettes* (meats impaled on a spit) that recall the Near East. Some of the *grillade* places make inventive sauces to go on the meats, devise Gallic variations of shish kebab, serve wines out of good cellars, keep on hand two or three delectable desserts and charge fair, moderate rates. Others scrape the beams of an old cave, hang it with copper and undistinguished old prints and ask amazing sums for what you can get at Joe's Chop House at home for half the price. There is always the possibility that tourists will want grilled meats rather than, or as a relief from, rich, mysterious sauces (a consideration that accounts in part for the numerousness of *grillade* restaurants), but why come to Paris for that? If you must, consider the fact that most classic restaurants list grilled meats, particularly hearty in the abattoir neighborhood to the north.

Many travelers, intimidated by what they think is the immutable requirement of three courses for lunch (it isn't, although some waiters act as if it were), settle for the sandwiches of ham, cheese or sausage that all cafés supply. Since fresh French bread is one of the joys of the world, it is hardly a poverty lunch but it may grow monotonous. All the main boulevards traversed by foreigners have *brasseries* with extensive lists from which you may pick one dish. Some cafés, not quite *brasseries*, expand their offerings to include salads and one or two cooked dishes. More and more *selfs* are appearing, which means variations of the cafeteria theme and one must, reluctantly, recommend the *Drugstores* for an extensive repertoire of well-presented, moderately priced dishes. Hamburgers and frankfurters are ubiquitous, as is *croque-monsieur*, once a ham and cheese sandwich dipped in batter and fried, now a carelessly grilled tasteless slab you might as well avoid.

Should you want a larger lunch, not in a cafeteria, not expensive, look for signs offering a *plat du jour* for as little as 3 francs. Have an order of *crudités* (a dish of a few forms of salad) to begin with and a quarter-liter of the house wine, your lunch should come to about a dollar. Oriental (mainly Vietnamese) restaurants, which seem to be able to do on minute profits as they do on little sleep, will give you full meals for 6, 7, 8, and up, francs. Examine the menus on Rue des Ecoles and the surrounding streets (page 78) and don't expect too much. Vietnamese cooking is, except in a few instances, a flattening of Chinese effects.

Pizza places, Oriental restaurants, *snacks*, crepes dispensaries abound on Rue Mazarine and Rue de l'Ancienne Comédie. *Couscous*, if you like the empty taste spiked by hot sauce, is ubiquitous where money is meager but for a busy concentration, no need to search, go to the Rue Geoffroy Marie, its tangents and the cafeterias on the Boulevard Montmartre, a busy row of *selfs*, which stretch Franglais to include *Le Twist*.

The inexpensive *prix fixe* menus sometimes include wine and service, sometimes neither or one; one place on the Boulevard Montparnasse gives you a paper napkin but will improve it to cloth if you pay 50 centimes more.

These inexpensive restaurants are perfectly all right, if you understand that no one can produce a magnificent meal for so little. However, avoid the bargains in and immediately near the Place du Tertre, except Mère Catherine, at the top of Montmartre. They were designed for youngsters who can't afford more, who think anything overspiced is foreign, ergo exotic, ergo good, no matter what their taste buds tell them. They don't seem to mind that the gluey sauces may mask bad food, nor that it has been mercilessly overcooked and repeatedly recooked through the afternoon and evening.

Tipping is one of those mountainous molehills that seem to threaten tourists. If your bill says *à l'appréciation de la clientèle*, the expectation is for 15 percent and a bit more if the waiters have spoiled you outrageously, as they can, and don't forget a few francs to the sommelier. Your bill may read *service non compris*; this, too, means 15 percent. Sometimes the 15 percent is added to the bill or marked *compris* which means that it has been absorbed in the price. In that case, leave a small token tip as you should—still smaller—in a café.

Other incidental intelligences before we plunge into specifics: Carry Kleenex, always—but in this context as napkins which cafés do not provide.

Crepes, like waffles, are prepared in street stalls of the big boulevards and priced at about 60 centimes for sugar coating, 80 for jam and a franc for being doused in Grand Marnier. If you prefer a more diverse group for lunch and it is not August, go to the simple *crêperie* on Rue Grégoire de Tours in the 6th or to one of a number on Rue du Montparnasse, north of the Boulevard.

Friends will have told you about the "cute" or "different" place they stumbled on during a stroll through one of the carnival streets, now gone. As in other art colonies—South Kensington, Provincetown, Greenwich Village—loony and semi-loony places are wafted into being on optimism and a gimmick and close before their existence has made a mark on anyone but the unfortunate investors.

Remember that Jewish and French waiters always know better. The French really do and are to be trusted except in the matter of medium-well or well-done steak. To a Frenchman a proper steak is raw and purple; to ask for it *à point* and expect it to be medium is a mistake. In other words, rare translates as raw, medium as rare, and a request for well-done opens a Pandora's box of difficulties. You will have to send the steak back and accept it as the chef returns it, a shade pinker but still rare. Further insistence will make your waiter impatient and scornful and may earn you an embarrassing discourse on how steak should be eaten. Continue to insist and he will bring you back a dishful of cinders. Avoid the steak and its complications if you can't eat it rare, and let the waiter guide you to a substitute.

Additional preparation for your trip, along with boning up on French phrases and practicing filling your raincoat pockets to the maximum avoidance of airlines charges, should be learning to decipher the illegible purple calligraphy of menus.

As in every large city, restaurants of diverse nationalities exist. There are still a good number of Russian restaurants, a few with sobbing balalaika music and the throaty moan of gypsy tunes, in Paris. A number of Greek places have found popularity on and around the Rue de la Huchette–Rue de la Harpe area off the Place St. Michel, and pizza (usually with a fine French dough substituted for the good old Neapolitan cardboard) and spaghetti are often their close neighbors. There are Polish restaurants, Spanish, Scandinavian, Hungarian, German as well as English pubs and even American restaurants. Those listed below are, with few exceptions, French and only a sampling of the thousands to guide you in a number of categories. The fact that any restaurant does not appear in the list has no meaning except that restaurant coverage by one person must necessarily be limited. There are hundreds of delightful, cheap, moderate and expensive others and exhaustive local guides as well as the newspapers and periodicals to tell you about them, since cooking and serving for the public is a major Paris industry and extremely well documented.

Everyone knows that chefs are notoriously temperamental, waiters have tired feet and varicosed veins, and one visit to a restaurant is not necessarily the fairest way of judging it. Try to remember the human condition if you suspect lapses. And forget your diet.

Finally, as well as firstly, in spite of the few sad notes above, Paris *is* for eating and there is usually a direct ratio between price and quality. Substitute half of a fresh *baguette* (20 to 25 centimes) for one or two meals and spend more than you can afford to for a few memorable meals, truly works of art. Maybe the feasts of Imperial Peking were better, but a really superb Paris meal can be an unequaled experience, particularly if you give it its ceremonious due. Make your reservation, and no other plans for the evening, for a little before nine (a bit early, but it gives you a chance to get

settled, to discuss your wine and dinner with the local authorities)
and then concentrate, as you wait for the nectar to be brought
forth, on the later arrivals: gaggles of enameled Parisiennes, blazing Italian matrons and the not-quite-chic glow of English ladies.
Dressed, but not overdressed, in your distinguished best, you begin
to realize that an exquisite meal is hardly a meal, in the usual sense,
at all; it is wandering among the mysteries of a unique, soon to be
vanished, craft. This knowledge, together with the vigilant,
indulgent service and the galaxies of tactful light on glossy ladies,
fills an evening much more graciously and uniquely than a rushed,
indifferent meal, followed by indifferent slapdash entertainment.

Expensive—40 Francs and Up, Up, Up

Maxim's, 3 Rue Royale (8th). Phone 265–27–94. Reserve. Closed
Sundays.

There never was, there isn't, nor will there ever be anything like
Maxim's.* Knowing that it was one of the pleasure domes where
Queen Victoria's sybarite son, Edward VII, battened and fattened,
one goes cloaked in his billowing juicy shadow—something like the
perfume of a good roast in the nostrils. The glass fronting the
street is tactfully, dimly masked by soft, shirred curtains, waiting
to rise on Chéri stroking his mistress' jewels as she finishes her
toilette. Inside, the tints and airs and curves of an extravagant
turn-of-the-century boudoir. The room, one decides, is possibly too
large for Colette's lovers, but absolutely perfect for the first act of
a Belle Epoque production of *Der Rosenkavalier*. The subtle overhead lighting is enhanced by the gentle glow of the small, pink
table lamps, the boudoir lamps accompanied by little clouds of
pink roses—the effect is to make women look, or feel, creamy and
pearly, as they were supposed to look before the 20th century
sharpened them.

Although it has been repaired from time to time, not a visible
touch of the Art Nouveau decor has been modernized. The flowing
edges of glass panels repeat the curves of broad petals; the glass
ceiling is designed in ribbonlike bands weaving through fields of
pale leaves and clusters of flowers; there are mirrors and more

* Except in Japan where a "Maxim's" has recently been opened.

mirrors and pastel murals of sweet whipped-cream nudes disporting themselves near rippling streams, rather like the famous White Rock girl but in this decor, infinitely more sensuous. Around the mirrors, the screens, across the doorways, flow great waves and coils of dark polished wood and metal bands of flower and leaf encrustations; thinning, thickening, leaping forward, retreating, and ending in great calligraphic flourishes.

At 11 o'clock, the lights are dimmed; only the small table lamps stay on and fine pinpoints of light appear in the paneling. A fiddler strikes up with something slow and throbbing from *Countess Maritza*, and is soon joined by other musicians who sob their way through the nostalgia repertoire—old Vienna, Hungarian gypsy and Gay Paree. Then, taking time out for "Happy Birthday" and "God Bless America," they go into old-fashioned dance music, a tango, a waltz, sometimes a subdued rumba or samba but never the Frug. Yours might be the particular night when an impeccably dressed, beautifully white-bearded old gentleman decides to appear with a party of handsome middle-aged ladies with whom he dances in turn, skillfully and with zest modified by dignity. Apparently, he teethed on a Maxim champagne cork and, judging from the polite friendliness of the waiters who swarm around him, rarely left this home.

The food? The wine? Maxim's is a three-star restaurant, which doesn't happen to many. Anything you order will be memorable. To help you out, the Lautrec poster-style menu sets off a list of specialties and the names of their creators. Not all the specialties are available every day, but there are enough to choose from (and keep in mind that Maxim's ordinaries are extraordinary). The *Billi By*, served hot or cold, appears as a smooth, creamy soup and turns out to be a culinary translation of Debussy. There is the famous braised sole Albert and the chicken with cucumbers "Alex Humbert" and, almost above all, the duck with fresh peaches (*caneton aux pêches fraîches*) according to Escoffier, a dish which takes you (or two of you, the whole duck must be ordered) out of the realm of cuisine and into art. For dessert, whatever dessert style of crepes, Sophie or Suzette, appears on the menu, or *soufflé glacé aux framboises*, an iced raspberry mousse buried in fresh raspberries.

Since you haven't come here to economize, you might as well start with champagne; the atmosphere begs for it and Maxim's champagne stock is renowned for its quality. Go on with the champagne or let the sommelier guide you through the rest of your choices.

All this will cost about $30 per person, plus tips, the one cloud in Eden. The menu distinctly says that service is not included and that it is *à l'appréciation de la clientèle*. However you may find a 15 percent service charge added to your bill. Check before you start acting like Santa Claus or the infamous vulgar American tourist.

Lapérouse, 51 Quai des Grands Augustins (6th). Phone DAN 68–04. Reserve. Closed summer Sundays.

What is there to say about Lapérouse? It was the subject of a long article in a popular American magazine; it is a name which inevitably appears in print and in conversation and arguments about great restaurants.

If all this acclaim has somehow avoided you: it is a series of small, low rooms whose walls, here and there decorated with what seems to be naïve aged kitchen tiling, shining as if they, like the bon vivants and gourmets they surround, had also been polished with the gloss of rich, satiny sauces. On a night when it isn't too crowded or the dinner hour grown late, you may find yourself the center of a ceremony rather like a royal accouchement: quiet bustling, attentive, breathless waiting. Then, the hush after the delivery, as you examine and enjoy what you and the kitchen have jointly brought forth. Later, the mutual congratulations and thanks which can mount, riding on the fumes of the nectars you've drunk, to avowals of eternal love and devotion.

Being realists and possibly worried about the decline of tourism in Paris, Lapérouse offers a 40-franc menu, a little over $8. It is a limited menu, but the *prix fixe* dinner here might be the supreme achievement of a lesser restaurant. However, if you must think in these terms, skip a meal or two and let yourself go to about twice that amount. Sit back and let the royal household bring you its foie gras or the *oeufs brouillés bergère* (shirred eggs with a differerence) or, if you prefer soup, the *Saint-Germain aux croûtons*. Next, either the *gratin de langoustine Lapérouse* or the *langouste Babinski*. Or the *poularde poëlée* or the steak done Lapérouse style or *Le Désir des Gourmets*. Dessert? Anything, but especially the soufflés and more especially the soufflés of raspberry or strawberries, or the combination.

Then you float out, shaking hands all the way, doing homage to the personnel as the "onlie begetters" of these culinary sonnets, and you are on the quai again. It was one of the very first built, in 1313, at the side of the monastery of the order of Saint Augustin (1293, replacing an even older religious establishment) and since grown old and weighty with ecclesiastical and royal history. Across the Seine, to your left, is the Louvre and to your right the towers of Notre Dame, across from you the bulky mass of the Palace of Justice, behind you the web of ancient streets and alleys where medieval scholars and roisterers walked. Standing in this matrix of Paris history, staring at the long, thin strip of daylight which leaves the summer sky of Paris slowly, feeling well fed and well loved, you own the Paris of the legends, the expectations have come true.

Ledoyen, Carré des Champs Elysées (8th). Reserve. Phone 265–47–82. Closed Sundays; check summer closing.

There is a distinctly *grande cocotte* quality here; one can almost see a Marguerite Gautier with a small waist and romantic cloud of hair arranging her rustling silks at the side of one of the round tables that is deep in white lace over pink; sipping out of the delicate champagne glass, tapping her mouth with one of the almost transparent lace-trimmed linen napkins, then settling back into an armchair covered with silk brocade.

The house keeps to its aristocratic, feminine self behind the trees of the eastern end of the Champs Elysées. One enters through a tunnel of lights under the 1900's cliché of glass awning, then through a blaze of chandeliers and mirrors into a large room of red and pink velvets and a genteel light breeze of piano music, clearly not the environment for hearty provincial dishes of meats too long steeped in red wine and then bedded in garlic. Ledoyen's style is the light and artful, more gourmet than gourmand. Let the scion of a great family posing as a waiter guide you through the house specialties or design your own dinner starting, possibly with the pâté or, more luxuriously, quail on a bed of pâté. The latter could be followed (although this may break some arcane rule or other) by *rouget*, two small fish decorated with a tic-tac-toe of anchovies and olives, a pastry boat of anchovy sauce on the side. Maybe, the *rouget* first and then two quail, hot, in a sauce of white grapes on rounds of toast that are very distant relatives from what usually pops out of our toasters. Finish with an omelette soufflé or the *profiterolle* inundated with chocolate sauce. Smoke a cigarette, look around you at the well-dressed women in the kindly light and not until then, begin to think about the bill. It will be high, but where, in Orange, or Evanston, or Columbus, can you buy a dish of choice quail on a platform of distinguished pâté?

Relais Gastronomique Paris-Est, first floor of the Gare de l'Est (10th). Phone 607–81–63. Closed Sundays.

Quite unlike any station restaurant one usually encounters. One makes a reservation (even for the sparse custom of an August Monday night they are due this gesture of obeisance) and enters the gold-lettered entrance immediately to the side of the station proper, where a uniformed boy delivers clients to an anteroom in which the question of reservations is again, with great politesse, reviewed. One is delivered with equal politeness into the large, dignified room hung with 1930's chandeliers to light up the dinners of traveling gourmets and indigenes. Although the tables have civilized space among them you might be able, in the intervals between your own courses, to observe the leisured progress from course to course, with appropriate wines of the gentlemen between trains, through a pâté of thrush (*grive*) or another pâté studded with pistachio nuts, followed by the lobster soufflé, then on to a *chateaubriand* or the *noisette d'agneau,* followed by cheese, then a tart of fruit in season or one of the exquisite iced mousses. During the slow, steady consumption the sommelier has been tasting, from a silver cup he wears on his chain—small sips spat out into an unseen receptacle behind a curtain—a number of bottles of wine, consumed with the same steady concentration as the food. Their dinner—and yours, possibly—ends in a virtuoso dance by the sommelier of turning glasses swiftly and gracefully in a bucket of ice, lifting them high for a quick examination in full light, a flourish of white linen dipping up the moisture in the glass and then, the final arabesque of pouring the eau-de-vie into the glasses.

The agile grace of the sommelier, the solemn profiles of the young assistants, the waiters who know how to be good hosts and, above all, the high talent of the unseen craftsmen in the kitchen are fairly expensive commodities; expect to pay but not shockingly.

Lasserre, 17 Avenue Franklin Roosevelt (8th). Phone ELY 53–43. Must reserve. Closed August and Sundays.

The "perfect" restaurant with a number of flaws. All is charm and elegance as you approach the beautifully lit entrance, prepared to spend money for an "experience." You are handed from one smiling *Bonsoir, Messieurs-Dames* to another and wafted up in a small elevator entirely padded with cut velvet. "This is going to be something" and it is. A little too much of it. The small chandeliers are lovely and would be enough. Why the extra cluster, resembling the lamps on the Alexander III bridge, rising from the floor? Must there be quite so many tables so close together, particularly for those who sit in the small alcove near the elevator? At 9:30, when the dinner hour is at its height, one has the sense of picnicking at the revolving doors of a department store on a Saturday afternoon before Christmas. The numerous, attentive, bilingual waiters have to bend, duck and ooze by each other. Instead of keeping an attentive eye on you from a polite vantage point, they keep swarming—they have to, there is no place to light. The open ceiling surrounded by trellises of flowers (sometimes they launch live white doves around the trellises, it is reported), the unique *objets* on the table, the choice wines served in lovely carafes, the pâté, the duck, the lobster confections, and the fanciful manner in which desserts are served add up to justification for the impressive prices. But, Messieurs, whoever you are, singular or plural—could it be possible to exchange the adorable little pans you give the ladies and the matches you give the gentlemen, the clever ships and fortresses which decorate your serving platters, for just a bit more unharried space. One of the important ingredients of elegance, you'll agree.

Garin, 9 Rue Lagrange (5th). Phone ODE 13–99. Closed Sundays and August.

If your preferences run to the standard fare offered in bistros that serve you "little" wines in pottery pitchers, Garin is not for you. Its cool, somewhat anonymous luster surrounds a patronage of well-padded silks who come for the inventiveness of the cuisine: an unusual confection, for instance, like the *truite soufflée*, a curious elaboration of stuffing and puffing that takes the simple fish far from its ordinary meanings. What may seem odd marriages of tastes to you—at least from the menu listings—turn out to be happy couplings, happier than the perfect, severe service. In paying the bill, incidentally, remember that you are paying for the company of *Feinschmeckers*, the choicest ingredients, and especially the talent that dreams up variations on its possibilities.

Chez Denis, 10 Rue Gustave-Faubert (17th). Phone 924–40–77. Reserve. Closed Mondays, Easter, Pentecost, from the fourth week in July to the middle of September.

Small and house-proud; the pâté is made on the premises; so are the cakes. In the spring the newest-born of baby lambs, the first sproutings of the choicest vegetables, the pick of Scotch salmon and lamprey; in the fall, princelings of partridge, pheasant, duck, ortolans, woodcocks, deer and young wild boar. In the cellar, carefully maintained aquaria for the blue iridescent lobsters of the north separated from the southern species. Beyond the lobsters, shelves on shelves of royal wines born in legendary years, and monumental cognacs. This luxurious matter is treated and served with respect and skill. If you go late and Monsieur is not too busy, you'll get some lively reminiscences, a phrase or two of justified name-dropping and, possibly, an informative verbal tour through gastronomy and viniculture.

High Moderate—30 Francs to 55

Chez les Anges, 54 Boulevard de Latour-Maubourg (7th). Phone 705–89–86. Closed Mondays.

The wines of Burgundy play a prominent role here. They are served in immense balloon glasses; they make the rich, deep sauce of the *coq au vin* (almost a test dish, since it appears on most menus) and the little bath in which eggs are poached to emerge as one of the prides of the house, *oeufs en meurette*. If a hearty wine dish on a hearty wine dish seems too much, have the delicately cooked veal. Or, better yet, let the maître d'hôtel, clearly an enthusiast as well as a connoisseur, guide you.

The English who come to Paris like it; the members of the embassies on Rue de Grenelle and Rue de Varenne not far away like it; old devotees, of course, and the people who have been shut

out of their favorites by the closed doors of August, find this a
satisfactory second best. Reserve, for lunch or dinner.

Chez Marius, 9 Rue de Bourgogne (7th). Phone 468-79-42.
Closed Saturdays and August.

A pleasing yellow room, the walls hung with numerous flower,
tree and animal paintings making the effect of a rather gay wallpaper. The headwaiter is a round, amiable man, confident in his
métier. The patron acts as host, not as inspector. He shakes hands
with old customers, makes a little conversation—only between
courses, never to interfere with the serious business of eating—and
will make suggestions or enter consultations on choice of courses,
but never insists. The emphasis is on seafood, issued as serious
works in the form of *langoustine* (crayfish) in a wine and mushroom sauce, *barbue* prepared in the style of Provence, and a renowned bouillabaisse which must be ordered in advance and for at
least two persons. But the *poulet à l'estragon* (tarragon chicken) is
a dream, too, and so are the fruits and so are the cakes. In other
words, Marius neither tries to knock your eye or your ego out; its
chosen function is to feed you well and politely and that it does in
the happiest fashion.

La Méditerranèe, 2 Place de l'Odéon (6th). Phone DAN
46-75.

The situation is delightful; the decor, mainly by Vertès, with a
helping hand, it is said, from Jean Cocteau, is Mediterranean-ish
murals, nice enough to look at and polite enough to allow being
disregarded. A more demanding part of the decor might be the
immortal Marlene Dietrich, happily rooting in a pile of mussels
or other Olympians of the performing arts.

Without *hauteur*, without cloying intimacy, the waiters treat
one like a new, pleasing acquaintance, maybe in time to be a friend.
There is rarely one serving of anything. Enjoyed the bouillabaisse?
The pot is put back on the table and large ladleful urged on you.
The mussels *marinière* keep coming back as long as you can stand
it; the *loup au fenouil* is served in a whale-sized slice. And, for the
lover of chocolate mousse who finds the minute cup it is usually
served in a source of teasing and frustration: here the big bowl is
put on the table, a huge ladleful dished out and before one is quite

through the waiter brings back the big bowl, fills the large dish again and urges one's friends to dip in, too.

La Boule d'Or, 15 Place d'Aligre (12th). Phone DID 97–70. Closed Fridays and August.

A few minutes' walk from the Place de la Bastille, in one of those secret niches of Paris which might be the marketplace of any hardworking, poor village, some of the best food at the price in Paris. It takes time, nothing is pulled out of a freezer and popped into the oven for a few minutes and no short-order cook can add a dash of this to a dash of that and produce the Boule d'Or sauces. What you will be served is the culmination of long hours of talented work to be anticipated patiently and consumed slowly.

The menu is typed and mimeographed so you don't have to grope your way through the usual beautiful, undecipherable lettering, but what to choose will be difficult. The *quiche lorraine* is a favorite but then there are the *crevettes* (shrimp) in lobster sauce, or the pâtés. Or skip those and go directly to one of the fish dishes, maybe *feuilleté d'homard,* a large, delectable pastry filled with lobster and on to a game bird (usually prepared and served for two): quail, partridge or guinea hen Normandy style, meaning a sauce of cream and Calvados on and around the bird and sections of apple which have been braised and steeped in the applejack.

The food is rich, the portions enormous, so watch your bread consumption and your planning. It may take a bit of effort, but try to have the *Mont Blanc,* a chestnut purée under a mountain of whipped cream (heavy and authentic, they don't deal in air-forced clouds here) or better still, order a lemon soufflé before you order anything else, as the menu suggests, and have that for dessert.

The waiters are gentlemen who do not try to sell you the most expensive wine on the list, the room is small, the reputation large so you must reserve, preferably a day in advance.

LATE NOTE: Since the Place d'Aligre is scheduled for destruction and improvement, the restaurant will open, in 1967, at 13 Boulevard de Latour-Maubourg, in the 7th. The rent will go up and consequently the prices, but even so—

La Chataigner, 75 Rue du Cherche Midi (6th). Phone 548–82–74. Reserve. Closed Sundays and August.

It's like the movies or stories told by travelers of the 20's and 30's of the little gem of a restaurant: obscurely situated, good-mannered, memorable. You are greeted courteously in a tiny room or invited upstairs to an equally tiny room. At the table in front of you there may be a party of six from the Japanese Embassy; to your right two people who move easily, in the habit of European diplomats, from French to Italian to Russian to German. They, the Japanese and your party—it must be small—fill the upstairs room. The linen is crisp and the roll waiting for you is an outstanding small bread, even for a country where all bread is outstanding. A large gentleman in a spotless white apron and tall chef's hat discusses the choices you might make, tells you the house *muscadet*, an inexpensive wine, is good, and leaves you to the international murmur.

Then it arrives in a neat, dignified progress: the *foie gras frais* studded with truffles and accompanied by matchless toast, lobster or turbot, or pike or other fish in season *au beurre blanc*, delicately lemony, tainted with an elusive herb sauce; the *volaille truffée*, fowl whose skin has been lifted and put back over a layer of truffles. The cheese board is versatile and the fruits in season hand-picked.

The menu is limited and so is the wine card, but if you are willing to let experts select and prepare for you a few fine dishes, and if you like the quiet of a small, sedate restaurant and are willing to pay for these virtues, the Chataigner should come high on your Paris list.

One of the names leading the list of restaurants that you *must* go to in Paris, offered along with the farewell gift of nylon clothesline and minute clothespins, will be that of **Allard**, at 41 Rue St. André des Arts (6th), once a bistro which has worked its way up to being knighted by the royal Michelin rod, to being patted on its nice red head by diverse authorities and to the prosperity of a ten-day vacation at Easter, another at Christmas and a summer closing that lasts from the third week in July to early September. A regretful minority report, because the atmosphere is lively without being forced: the kitchen has become lazy, insisting that most dishes on the menu be shared. Portions are prepared for two or three which means you must go with culinary soul mates or people whose tastes and judgments you can easily dominate. The individualistic dissident has few choices and, consequently, finds himself resenting the cost of a dish he did not much want in the first place. You will probably go anyhow and enjoy it.

La Bourgogne, 6 Avenue Bosquet (7th). Phone 705–96–78. Reserve. Closed Sundays and August.

There is something about Burgundian cuisine that makes the houses in which it is served somewhat noisier than others. It may be the deep red wine served in *ballons* or the heartiness of the wine-splashed dishes or a party of kidney-pie and Sunday-joint Englishmen maddened by French eating; or simply the acoustics which seem to make each sound bounce off the low ceiling, scrape noisily along the well-polished walls, clank along the copper. Don't try to talk; eating and drinking are quite enough, particularly if you have the capacity for both a fish and meat dish. The *mousseline de brochet Nantua,* fish ground, pounded, flavored and served as a subtle mousse, to be followed by the *steak à la moelle* (marrow), or the *boeuf bourguignon,* or one of the treatments of *poulet,* accompanied, if the season is right, by an extraordinary mushroom which looks like a black and white mourning rosette. It has an earthy flavor that suits well the sauce it is bathed in although its looks may set you back for a moment (as may, incidentally, the colors and convoluted shapes of other mushrooms used in France). They are, be assured, safe, delicious and welcome departures from the one beige model to which Americans are accustomed.

Le Baobab, 7 Rue de l'Université (7th). Phone 548–08–80. Open late every day.

It's sort of African—those pouting masks and assagais hanging on the walls and from the straw-covered ceiling. From the back comes an assault of recorded drumbeats and war shouts and plaintive calls of "Carry Me Back to Old Dahomey." The waiters are beautiful, graceful young men, inclined to clap and stomp with the music when custom grows thinner, at about midnight. But watch out for a Sporting Life type, a smooth, elegant, sinuous persuader who almost insists that you have the special specialties—easily recognized by the fact that they cost much more.

The food is varieties of coconut, salads and cakes; curries, chicken and fish; rice, odd grains and beans and one omnipresent hot sauce, only slightly varied from dish to dish. A dish to avoid:

beignets of *langouste,* fried dough surrounding an absence of *langouste* and dipped into *the* sauce. On questioning, you may be told it was all a terrible mistake; it should have been marked *beignets* of *crevettes* (tiny shrimp) and another dish is proffered—this time with the presence of a *crevette* or two. With wine and dessert (the *coupe exotique*—described as fresh tropical fruit—turns out to be a canned litchi nut, a bit of canned mango, canned pineapple) a meal comes to $8 a person—too much, unless you love African records, and African smiles, and want to do your bit for successfully emerged members of emerging countries.

Coconnas, 2 Place des Vosges (4th). Phone ARC 58–16. Reserve.

At one of the portals of the Place des Vosges (via Rue de Birague) and attractively arranged to suit the early local color. The tablemats are reproductions of old prints of the Place, the walls are hung with prints of feasting in the rich days, the lamp brackets with winged ornaments echo the decorative details of the former great houses of the Marais and the drapes are the almost inescapable red that seems to mean aristocracy or, at least, upper classness. Because there are few restaurants in the immediate area, the restaurant can afford to charge somewhat higher prices than its good but unremarkable table warrants. The assumption, correct, is that you won't mind, after trudging through the complexities of the Marais and the inexhaustible, exhausting Carnavalet (page 103). Although the house specialties, *merlan* (fish) *Coconnas* and the *poulet* surrounded by vegetables, are completely satisfactory, proximity is the great lure, and the tables in the arcades on a summer's night.

Moderate—20 to 40 Francs

La Grille, 50 Rue Montorgueil (2nd). Phone CEN 24–64. Closed Sundays and August.

They don't make them like this any more except in books of lachrymose reminiscences: the matte gleam of the curved zinc bar, waiters in black aprons held up by a T-strap arrangement, an adamant lack of decor leaving untouched the faded walls, the old pipes and rickety steps. Except for the mink stoles and good little brocade numbers that find their way into this annex of Les Halles, every thing remains sturdily bourgeois. The thoroughly reliable cuisine features a daily *plat* from the game in season, and the gamut of traditional dishes. Trust the waiters as you would your father—they may even look like him—for recommendations of wine and food offered with cordial ease.

La Rose de France, 24 Place Dauphine (1st). Phone ODE 10–12. Closed Thursdays and the first two weeks in July.

A very small restaurant with fine taste and superb manners—except when the proprietress has to get to a concert and she tells you to hurry. The kitchen wafts lovely flavors into the room so you have the advantage of partially experiencing several dishes besides the one before you. For that one, ask for the *daurade* (a fish) *aux herbes* or the *côtelettes d'agneau,* or anything whose name pleases you.

Le Santenay, 75 Avenue Niel (17th). Phone CAR 88–44. Closed Sundays and from the second week in August to the middle of September.

The cuisine is that of Burgundy and the Basque country, places that know a considerable amount about the uses of wine and things from the sea. Have the *confit d'oie* or the mussels, or any treatment of fish or wine-soaked chicken.

A Sousceyrac, 35 Rue Faidherbe (11th). Phone 700–65–30. Closed Sundays and August.

In an area you would probably never get to normally and worth seeking out if it meant a long day's march rather than the bus and Métro lines that serve streets close by. The restaurant is a family affair of brothers and mother, the family Asfaux who daily commemorate the feasts of the ancestral village. Periodically Maman and one of the brothers comes around to ask if everything goes well. The solicitude is sincere and all they require in answer is the big, replete smile on your face, surely equally sincere. Their block of foie gras is the beginning for almost every dinner, then comes the *poulet des gastronomes,* chicken layered with bits of pâté and truffle, or the duck. Free of the need to dress as if for a state occasion (although, as in churches, basic respectability is required),

basking in the amiabilities of a cordial and gifted house for just
sums, this may turn out to be one of your better Paris experiences.

La Camargue, 13 Rue du Petit Pont (5th). Phone ODE 08–03.
Closed Sundays and August; no lunches but dinner is served
quite late.

To a background of unobtrusive flamenco music that floats out
of a broad, white arc, past the wood and rush suggesting Camargue
roofs, and the hides and branding irons used in the wild, marshy
area where the gypsies of France gather for a religious festival each
spring, one eats the coarse, strong gypsy and herdsmen foods.
Though it is hardly a cuisine for regular fare, the salty, spicy dishes
and their presentation are worth a try for their singularity. A very
popular opening dish is the *assiette,* a mixed plate of cold regional delicacies and salad. The fish, *loup en cage,* is stuffed
with onions and sticks of herbs, surrounded by bread dough, baked
in a fish-shaped cage and served with a carafe of oil with which
you must douse it. Or you might choose the smoked eel or the
small rabbit (*lapereau*) tightly bundled in herbs, or the *boeuf à
la Gardienne,* prepared in a marinade of lemon, bay leaf and other
herbs.

Chez Maître Paul, 12 Rue Monsieur-le-Prince (6th). Phone 033–
74–59. Closed Thursdays and August.

If you can get into this gleaming toy cottage at all, order one of
the simple veal or chicken dishes, not as simple as all that, and
impeccably prepared and served.

La Coupole, at the meeting of Boulevard Montparnasse and
Boulevard Raspail (6th). Vavin Métro. Practically never closed.

One of the legendary trio (along with the Sélect and the Dôme)
that was club and agora to a famous generation of expatriate and
indigenous artists and writers. There is hardly a book of Paris
reminiscences that does not mention La Coupole, and its opening
party to which, seemingly, all the writers and artists of Paris were
invited and insisted on staying and drinking until the police routed
them out the next morning.

Although the personae have changed, a few of the clichés of
costume remain, borne on newer shoulders, a number of them

supremely inauthentic. Now that beards, once a symbol of "artistic" or "intellectual," cover the faces of much of the young male world, how is one to know whether the young man sitting on the vast *terrasse* in his uniform of beard, turtleneck shirt, sandals, eyes burning significantly into the distance is or is not burdened with the heavy responsibility of pushing art forward, whether or not he is a teacher of chemistry from Duluth? The girl in the tightest black tights and a mask of hair that swings occasionally away from her eyes made up to look like pits of hell, her mouth painted a ghoulish white, might be a model or a local *fille de joie,* one of a number that hang around the Rue Vavin. She is shortly joined by a blue-jeaned boy with a prominent American Adam's apple and a guitar. Accompanied by his limited skill she moves from table to table singing rueful, dull Ozark plaints in a small voice. Timidly, very timidly, in spite of her efforts at depraved looks, she holds out a leather sack for coins, the conflict between the ruffled bedroom in Connecticut and sleeping under the Pont St. Michel or (if the *flics* are not cleaning up) on the sidewalk of the Rue de la Huchette, evident in the "I'm not really doing this" look as she proffers the sack, eyes cast down. It is a generous audience, yielding coins not so much to her meager talents as to her presence as part of a varied show. The coins come from starched white Latin-American linens, the faded Russian blouses of old émigrés, the dark suits of French provincials, the silk purses of a soigné Chinese family, from the pockets of Israeli students reading hometown papers, from the wearers of short or long hair, broken shoes and discolored raincoats, from a new suede coat sitting near a closely molded, fur-trimmed red velvet dress cut for a maximum display of powdered flesh.

The variety moves restlessly between the equally ample inside and outside, the habitués veering toward the inner sections at the left and back (where, it is rumored, all sorts of odd information is gathered and divulged), the stranger guided to the right. In spite of its square red pillars and bright blocks of mural—some of it by well-known painters, in settlement of bills past and future—the *brasserie* seems a plain place, possibly because its immense size fades out its bits of decoration. The size, the hum, the movement, the waiters who are clearly old friends of many clients, create an atmosphere which strangely resembles the big boiled beef and sour cream palaces on upper Broadway in New York City.

To eat? As a *brasserie*, it gives one the privilege of one dish, but you will probably go the full course from a range which covers the provincial favorites, like *salade niçoise, choucroute alsacienne, cassoulet* and *bouillabaisse*, to international delicacies. One of the anomalies and a house specialty are the modified curries of chicken and veal served with un-Indian trimmings. If you must have total authenticity, order the *choucroute* or the turbot or the duck with olives and follow it with the local version of baked Alaska, called *omelette norvégienne*, or some such name.

One can eat more exquisitely in Paris, but there are few places that have quite the mellow, worldly atmosphere, the diversity of customers or the steady reliability of cuisine at a fair price.

La Bûcherie, 41 Rue de la Bûcherie (5th).

In spite of the crowding (one table behind a pillar may lose you to the waiter and food for a long, famished time), an engaging place to have late dinner or a snack. Right in the lazy vortex of the milling guitar-bearers, but you can escape them since the costs, though moderate, are beyond their bread-and-big-bottle-of-beer allowances. Rarely possible, but try to get a table near the fireplace in the back room or failing that, stay on for a drink at one of the fireplaces if you and your French can make a place among the clinging regulars.

Le Grand Comptoir, 4 Rue Pierre Lescot (1st). Phone GUT 56–30. Closed Sundays and July.

The front doorway proclaims it a *Café-Tabac* which it flatly is until one turns to the right at the back where it changes to a somewhat listless rococo style. There is nothing listless about the food, the service or the clientele, a mixture of St. Germain intellectual, a few American-in-Paris ladies and merchants from Les Halles, across the street. Not only the foods but the atmosphere seem to have marched across the street and pervaded the small restaurant with its noisy busyness. This is the place for sausage made of tight-coiled entrails (*andouillette*) or the spicy, fatty *saucisses de Corrèze* to begin with. Then the classic *coq au vin* or beef and lentils, or steak, followed by *clafoutis*, a wide, flat fruit tart, like a sweet pizza. And if the harried waiter drips sweat on your table, accept it as another bit of the influence of Les Halles.

Brasserie Lipp, 151 Boulevard St. Germain (6th).

A towering name in Franco-American literature, where Hemingway and Scott Fitzgerald must have had at least one of their quarrels; where one complicated system or other of French thought must have been evolved; where, still, the faces are quick and meaningful and the talk agile and swift. To be suspected of being a French intellectual you should sit outside early in the evening, but that is seldom possible; there seems to be an arcane system of priorities or maybe the habitués live in the chairs as snails in their carapaces and can't exist without them. The way out of this difficulty is to have a supper snack, at about 11:00, in the downstairs dining room or eat more lavishly upstairs. The *choucroute alsacienne,* a hill of sauerkraut sheltered by frankfurters, ham, pork and boiled potato (Lipp's specialty), accompanied by one of Lipp's famous beers, is a satisfying way of stoking up for the next day's sight-seeing or the slings and arrows of shopping. Or settle for a small steak, often surprisingly good, or cheese, or a pâté in crust served with a potato salad which bears no resemblance to the concrete in mayonnaise we Americans suffer too readily at home.

To see how a native blessing is lost on the young, go to the **Tea Caddy** at 14 Rue St. Julien le Pauvre where Paris youth expresses its awe for things British by eating tea and cakes and unprepossessing lunches in stolid, tailored surroundings.

L'Alliance, 18 Rue Vivienne (2nd). Phone 236–44–48. Closed on Sundays and most of July.

The setting is so reassuringly homely—mirrors half concealed by bucolic paintings, a stuffed duck flying out of a fringe of sausages, and stock-exchange gentlemen at lunch, their friends and their calorie-scorning wives at night—that one has immediate confidence in the food. Not misplaced, especially if you order the *bouribout,* a treatment of duck in a deep, velvety sauce with raisins, the *gratin* of lobster, or the *côte de veau sous les cendres,* served for two or more in a big dish covered with pastry crust. The house favorite for dessert is the *tatin,* but failing that, one of the fruit tarts will do, often a wedding of a liqueur and fruit, laced together with spongy, juice-filled dough. For plateful after plateful of Lyonnaise dishes, considered by many the best of French cooking, you will have difficulty passing the *Moderate* border.

Vagenende, 142 Boulevard St. Germain (6th).

A poor man's Maxim's where the big mirrors, frilly lights and graceful flow of carved wood compensate for the so-so food.

Maïtena, 208 Boulevard St. Germain (7th).

Low-ceilinged, cordially lit and hung with bottles and thises and thats which have aged decently into decor. The accent is French Basque; the simpler French classics—*sole meunière*, omelettes, scalloped veal, interspersed with sausage from the Basque country (the varieties of regional sausage are as numerous as the varieties of wines and cheeses), *salade basquaise* (a twin of *salade niçoise*), *bouillabaisse* and *paella* to straddle the two countries which share the strange Basques. The waiters are unharried gentlemen—usually—and, if you can get a terrace table on Boulevard St. Germain, there is to be enjoyed the quiet, aristocratic part of the Boulevard just before it becomes a roistering fair.

La Mamma, 6 Rue Papillon (9th). Phone 770–90–03.

The menu is Russian-Jewish, Polish-Jewish, Hungarian-Jewish and what might be called traditional-Jewish, like the gefilte fish and the *cholent* (an ingenious device for accord with Sabbath rules but hardly cuisine). The nostalgia classics—chopped liver, chopped herring, chicken soup—are always available, along with a variety of Central European dishes. But one doesn't come to Paris for this and if that were the whole story, it would not be told here. La Mamma, along with the samovars, the menus printed in peasant motifs and the recorded background music of vigorous Israeli chants, Hungarian gypsy fiddles and plaintive Yiddish airs, has dressed itself in all the trappings of the recent Paris mode of busy decorations. Behind the door on this plain street, a mixture of never-never-land Americana, Edwardian pub, Belle Epoque boudoir: green and red overstuffed chairs and couches, red drapes, red tablecloths (the toilets are red, too), brass lamps, milk glass, gallery-lit old paintings of obscure provenance and as if that weren't quite enough for the narrow space, a prayer rug, a stuffed fish and an old upright piano. The point is to be entertaining and it is, especially as linked incongruously with the neighborhood, the music, the food and the here and now heartiness of its management and patrons.

La Chaumière, 35 Rue de Beaune (7th). Phone 548–46–64. Reserve or go quite early.

It is the dining room of a number of the *quartier's* regulars, who know one another and the staff. The waitresses are easy, eager conversationalists, though fast and efficient; the *patronne* at the *caisse* sits like a goddess of Mediterranean affability, the food is solid, the wine good. Ergo, the full round sounds of voices and laughter which never seem to disturb the one or two customers who come equipped with their walls of book or newspaper, chewing and turning pages steadily through a full, stately meal.

The menu is classic bourgeois—veal, chicken, fish, steaks—carefully chosen and prepared with a largess of butter and trimmings. (The trout with almonds, for instance, is a lovely morass of sliced almonds in a depth of butter completely obscuring the fish.) The cream is served in heaps and also the strawberries and the bread, etc. The menu almost always carries three pâtés, the *terrine* being the most countrified and coarse. For a small adventure, start with a country salad of *museau*, greens mixed in a vinagrette sauce with thin slices of pigs' snout. Why not? One eats pigs' feet, *n'est-ce pas?*

La Petite Tour, 11 Rue de la Tour (16th).

Very talented in the mixing of American style Martinis served with olives big, little and littler. Equally capable with the hot *moules farcies* to launch you on a convivial meal.

Charbon de Bois, 16 Rue du Dragon (6th). Phone LIT 57–04. Open late. Closed Sundays. Reserve.

Briskly, neatly decorated in new steak house New York style. You can do it on less, but $5 to $6 will buy bread, wine, a three-course meal and good service. Since this is a place of grills, start with the *brochette de moules* (mussels) and continue with speared bits as a *brochette de gigot* (lamb) flecked with herbs and accompanied by a hot, spicy sauce. Or have the steak, or the *entrecôte* for two. In any case finish with the hot apple tart, light-years away from the wholesome mess mother used to make.

La Truite, 30 Faubourg St. Honoré (8th). Phone ANJ 12–86. Reserve. Closed Sunday and August.

Not actually on the glamour avenue, but in a section of Paris honeycomb called Cité du Retiro, a place and name suitable to the charms of this pretty country inn, in the middle of Paris. The accent is Norman, the major works are seafood, as the name implies. The *sole* and *truite* (trout) *normande,* the fowl and beef dishes, the *soufflé normand* (an imposing edifice fortified with Norman liquors) and the mellow rusticity should be enough to make you forget the nervous waiter who slaps and drops dishes on the table and forgets to pour your wine. In any case there are, at most, only two of him and you may be sitting at the table of a calmer waiter.

Brasserie Lorraine, 2 Place des Ternes (8th).

Huge, bright, brisk; tables outside, tables inside; rather like Lindy's in New York to judge from some of the clientele, and yet not, to judge from some of the others who come from the nearby "good" arrondissements, particularly for the seafood, in richest and most varied supply from the middle of September on. The Lorraine seems to bridge the gulf between *brasserie* and restaurant. It is big, it is open all day and late, it serves you coffee, a sandwich, an omelette if you like, or a full meal; it moves quickly and unaffectedly. On the other hand, the *choucroute garnie* (here done in the style of Alsace or Lorraine with no great distinction between them) is brought on a large, copper tray kept hot while your portion is being selected; the pot of mussels from which you've had a heaping plateful waits, simmering, near you should you want another heap; the sauce for the pepper-steak is prepared at your table. In other words, the care other *brasseries* don't bother with is diligently practiced here, not, understandably, on *haute* dishes, but keeping the good as good as possible.

Brasserie Bofinger, 5 Rue de la Bastille.

Quite another sort: old-fashioned, slowish, endlessly roomy, particularly at dinner when the local lunch-time regulars have returned *chez-eux* and left the rueful charm to a few wanderers.

Chez Joséphine, 177 Rue du Cherche-Midi (6th). Phone LIT 52–40. Closed Saturday evening and Sunday.

Plain and basic as the palm of your hand and one of a lamented, declining race, the talented man-and-wife bistro. The cuisine is

Landaise, rich and hearty, served lavishly. The cucumbers in cream (to start with) or the herring smothered in spices, onions and carrot rings are served in large crocks and you serve yourself to— or preferably a little beyond—the amount you think you can encompass. The *confit d'oie* (goose, served for two) heaped around with fine, crusty potato slices and watercress, the deep red-brown beef Bourguignon—for that matter, all the servings—appear larger than one can possibly eat, but one eats them. Fruit in season is about all one can absorb as dessert or the homemade sherbets (*sorbet*). For the strong in stomach and spirit, there is a *flambé'd* apple pancake bathed in lovely juices.

For a menuful of good reasons, plus the spirited good humor of hard-working Madame and Monsieur, the place is crowded to every inch of its unadorned walls and misty mirrors; reserve.

Cintra, Square de l'Opera-Louis Jouvet (9th).

A restful place peculiarly shaped to follow the eccentricities of its hidden square. Darkly paneled in a Bierstube, Olde-Englishe style, but the kitchen speaks good French.

W. H. Smith & Son, 248 Rue de Rivoli (1st).

Above the bookshop, via Tudory half-timbered, coat-of-armed, leaded-glass bits of Merrie Olde Englande; past the homey displays of Cadbury chocolate and teas, one can order *assiette Anglaise* (cold meats and potato salad), mutton chops, grilled sandwiches, tea or muffins with scones (listen to the French lady shoppers try to pronounce this and take heart about your French pronunciation), cakes and ice creams. A nod to the host country is *salade niçoise, rôti de veau* and some form of *poulet*. Although one must assume that the waitresses here speak English, go slowly and clearly; their vocabularies and frames of reference are often limited to the menu.

Tiburce, 28 Rue du Dragon (6th). Phone 548–57–89. Closed Sundays and last two weeks of August.

A small, retiring restaurant, dignified by touches of gold, touches of red and crystal. The menu is not large, but to be respected. For a light beginning, have the *champignons à la grecque*. Or the large, handsome *crêpe des fruits de mer*, and go on to *steak au volaille*, which is a breast of chicken nestled, covered and surrounded by skill and good things.

Les Marronniers, 354 Rue de Vaugirard (15th). Phone VAU 42–71. Closed Wednesdays and one summer month.

Bouquets of crayfish tails decorate the tables prettily, in season. The waitresses are profoundly interested in your tastes and the surroundings—although elegance finds its way in now and then —leave you unworried about wearing that same old suit again. Snails are taken out of their houses and served to you in a small ceramic pot. Or you might prefer, as a beginning, one of the dishes cooked with white raisins for which the house has a predilection: onions in a sauce of raisins and a touch of wine for instance. Or skip that and have the sweetbreads in a raisin sauce. If the idea doesn't attract you, take the *écrevisse* (usually a more expensive dish than a number of the others) or any of the treatments of meat, chicken and fish.

Clos des Bernardins, 14 Rue de Pontoise (5th). Phone 033–70–07. Closed Sundays.

Once in a while, the *confit d'oie* becomes a bit dry, a mistake forgotten in the excellence of the *cassoulet* or the *gigot* and the dessert soufflés. Attractive people welcome and serve in an appealing old house of whitewash and old beams hung, discreetly, with antique pans and beakers.

Louis XIV, 1 bis Place des Victoires. Phone 508–07–35. Closed August and Sundays.

An unpretentious place that clings to its old generous country manners. The herrings (masterpieces of marinating, according to aficionados) and the pickles are served in large, help-yourself vats and the butter comes to you as a sizable yellow hill rather than as the little paper-covered token too frequently seen. In the tradition also is most of the list: game birds, *coq au vin, boeuf bourguignon,* the house pâté and house wine. The open-handed portions, the tactful, knowing waiters, the quality of the dishes and the location attract a lunch-time crowd from the Stock Exchange a short distance away. The evenings are less crowded, but still there may be a run on the limited number of outdoor tables that look out on the ghost of a once-noble Place.

Chez Augusta, 98 Rue de Tocqueville (17th). Phone 924–39–97.

Not the least of its virtues is that it stays open in August. Among the others, an easy manner of not trying *too* hard and a gift with fish and grilled meats. Have the *loup en papillote* or the less aristocratic *lotte,* a meaty portion of fish served in a sauce of mushrooms, tiny shrimps and herbs and spices in cream. You'll notice, however, that many clients order the double lamb chops or the thick chunk of *chateaubriand.* If it is on the menu, order the *cassis sorbet,* a deep purple sherbet of black currants or a *mystère* cloaked in hot chocolate.

Le Voltaire, 27 Quai Voltaire (7th). Closed Mondays.

Try to go a bit earlier or later than the usual lunch and dinner hours to get an outside table from which you can look at the book-stall, its owner and customers across the road, beyond to the edge of the Louvre and the Tuileries, down a stretch of Seine bridges, and in the long summer evenings, the darkening sky splashed with a long streak of pale pink that refuses to be erased.

In addition, you get decency in the service (not always rapid, but why would you want to rush out of such a view and the presence of the foxy ghost of Voltaire who died upstairs), food, wine and price. The duck is almost superb at times and the steaks —either coated with pepper or mustard—make invigorating companions for a long evening walk later. Finish with a *tarte* of whatever fruit is in season.

L'Orée du Bois, Porte Maillot (16th-17th). Phone MAI 78–04.

At the edge of the Bois de Boulogne and at lunch time in good weather it seems to engulf a sizable portion of the park. The food is unpretentious, and the house wine, red, white and rosé, of which you may drink as much as you can decently hold, is hardly memorable. However, the leafy, treey shade, the jovial closeness of tables, the steady hum of volubility, can make you feel—after enough wine and a push of the imagination—like a character at a Renoir party.

Chiroubles, 23 Avenue Duquesne, at the side of the Hôtel Duquesne (7th). Closed Sundays and August.

Lyonnaise cooking which means slow and rich and, here, served in generous portions along with the regional wine from which the restaurant takes its name.

Procope, 13 Rue de l'Ancienne-Comédie (6th). Closed Mondays and July.

There is better and worse food in Paris but none which you will eat in such antique surroundings—the café dates from 1689—in a corner that might have been the habitual choice of Marat, Robespierre, Napoleon, Musset, Mallarmé, Verlaine or Voltaire whose table still stands on the second floor.

Ministères, 30 Rue du Bac (7th).

Almost as plain as a section of the Métro, though better lit and infinitely better smelling. The clients are often neighborhood solitaries, quietly taking course after course along with the evening paper or a book. Taciturn customers and plainness don't add up to gaiety, but they don't try for that here. The effort is careful cooking in French "home style" (definitely not suggesting what might give you pause at home) at lenient prices, and they succeed.

Au Petit Maxim's. The customary menu served in an outdoor terrace on a segment of the Boulevard St. Germain (corner of Rue de Pontoise, in the 5th) not yet touched by the posturing to the west.

A homey female welcome greets and serves you at the **Restaurant Sts. Pères** on the street of that name and the Boulevard St. Germain (6th-7th) including among its blandishments several outdoor tables, rarely free unless you go quite early. Menu and prices are less ambitious than those of the terraced neighbors that line the Boulevard.

La Ferme des Mathurins, 17 Rue Vignon, near Rue Tronchet (8th). For escape from the razzle-dazzle of the surrounding shops.

Goldenberg's or **Al-Jo** (for Albert and Joseph G), 7 Rue des Rosiers (4th). Lunch best—though open late.

The first assault as you open the door is of any Jewish delicatessen at lunch time, which welcomes you or knocks you down with its high babble, the heavy fumes of spiced meats, the clatter of dishes, the erratic stop and dash of waiters and the strong warm voice of the plump, well-corseted manageress directing the complex works. Space couldn't be tighter what with tables, chairs, bodies, a tower of Polish vodka, piles of matzos (*pain azyme*), jars of pickles and a bar of substantial size, yet a sense of swift, free movement is mysteriously achieved. Above your head are photographs of worthies of the tribe, an African in a yarmulke and a ceremonial shawl, possibly a rabbi; Maurice Schwartz, and, below him, a photo of Charles Boyer (HE'S JOOOOSH?).

The reverse side of the menu offers the classics of sandwiches and delicatessen platters in a French list with English translations, not to be altogether trusted, because, for one, the items are not properly aligned so that "hot sausages" becomes the translation of *saumon fumé*. You can make a good guess at "shapped lever and eggs" but you may be thrown by goose "gribbenes" a Frenchified spelling of the Yiddish for cracklings. The face side of the menu suggests 15 percent for service but calls it "transport." The price of dessert or fruit is decided by the "heftiness of the client" and *foie haché* (chopped liver) is fully described as *leyber eyer tzibeles*, offering the benefit of a little elementary Yiddish along with the lesson in French.

What to eat? Anything that appeals to you, the gefilte fish (*poisson farci*) is good, the soups are the sort referred to as "Jewish penicillin," and the delicatessen richly flavored if a bit different from what you are accustomed to. Possibly, you might have the frankfurters with *ratatouille*, an indigenously and famously Provençal vegetable stew. It makes a stimulating mating of cultures.

Near the Parc Monceau (14th), where the Rue Lemaignan meets the Avenue Reille, **La Cascade** very much like an Italian trattoria—a few tables nestled in greenery on trellises, convivial and crowded in favorable weather.

Auberge Franc-Comtoise, 84 Rue de Varenne (7th). Phone 468–47–33. Closed one week in July.

Often more crowded at lunch time than in the evening, because it neighbors several embassies which live in the magnificent *hôtels particuliers* on Rue de Grenelle and Rue de Varenne.

You edge past the locals in the friendly neighborhood saloon or through a door that leads directly into the restaurant decorated by someone's old aunt from the provinces, to judge from the clean, dimly lit stodginess. There is nothing stodgy about the alert service and the genuine attempt to give you a satisfactory meal at humane prices. The regional touch (the southeast) is expressed in such folk names as that for a local sausage; *"jésus de Morteau."* The rest of the menu is simpler to understand and, in any case, your hosts' good English will cut through any linguistic fog. For dessert, if there are two or more of you, have the specialty of the house, a billowy, creamy, meringuey thing, lit up with liqueur, a provincial baked Alaska.

The Auberge Franc-Comtoise is one of the few houses which considers that its modest prices cover the service. When you ask, the waiter will tell you service is *gratuit*, a civilized arrangement allowing everyone in the transaction less discomfort and more dignity. Leave a token tip; you will want to in any case.

Chez Paul, 15 Place Dauphine, Ile de la Cité (1st). Phone ODE 21–48. Closed Mondays and August.

On a lively day, the ancient Place is brightened by the table-cloths and the shine of glass and silver on the outdoor tables of several small restaurants, Paul's among them. Paul's has a remark-able unity of composition: the beamish middle-aged waitresses are plain, clean and ample; so are the long marble tables; so are the old-fashioned napkins as big as dish towels and the sturdy cus-tomers. One of the specialties of the house is *veau en papillote,* a slice of veal covered with chopped mushrooms and steamed in a paper envelope, a delightful dish if you like the damp-earth flavor of mushrooms. To begin, there are *quenelles,* two pale rolls of a type of fish mousse (the most *raffiné* version of gefilte fish) in a smooth, pinkish sauce. Finish, if they are in season, with *fraises des bois* and a last gulp of a light, white wine the house features, *Gaillac sec.*

For Corsican food, heavier handed with spices, **Chez Victor** on Rue Git-le-Coeur in the 6th.

Des Diamantaires, 60 Rue Lafayette (9th). Phone 770–78–14. Likely to be closed Friday night and Saturday until evening. Call.

The name is explicit and practical; this is where a number of the city's dealers meet and having polished off a substantial lunch and getting down to business, pull diamonds and loupes out of their pockets. Sometimes, when school is out, it is children and wives, rather than diamonds, that are brought in for approval and display. The provenance of customers and cuisine is suggested by a group of shields in the window, Greece, Turkey, Morocco among them. Except for one or two French cheeses and salads, a few French simple meat and fowl dishes, the menu wanders, as the customers may have, through Turkish pilafs, Bulgarian chopped meat, North African *couscous* and *boerek* (called *brik* elsewhere—page 140), Syrian-Lebanese-Israeli *houmous*, Greek stuffed eggplant and Italian *osso buco*.

French won't help you with this menu even though it is clearly printed. So, if you don't know Near Eastern and North African dishes place yourself in the hands of a dark volatile young waiter (the one who runs) who makes a confident stab at any and all languages. It won't be very useful but there will be the illusion—for a moment—that you understand and are understood. All communication failing, take the shish (here spelled "chiche") kebab or the chicken curry or, if you like the bland mess, *couscous*. For those people who like okra, there is *Bamias-viande*, chunks of stewed meat surrounded by dozens of the small green vegetables, only a bit gluey and quite nice. The *houmous*, to start off with, is a sesame-seed mash served with lemon which goes companionably with the crusty French bread. To finish, the possible exoticisms of rose-petal jelly (*confiture de rose*), or the homemade yoghurt (*yaourt maison*), a far cry from the substance one gets in paper containers at home.

There are small restaurants with pretty boxes of terrace on the Boulevard Beaumarchais, off the Place de la Bastille, less expensive than the same sort of restaurant on Boulevard St. Germain and frequently more careful because it has to deal with Parisians, who will not tolerate what joyous tourists, eager to like anything if it is served behind flower boxes on a sidewalk, will.

Bouteille d'Or, 9 Quai de Montebello (5th). Phone 033–52–58.

The first satisfying feature is a view of Notre Dame from the second floor, the fullness of view depending on the leafiness of the season. The second is a fixed-price-dinner that comes to about $3 for a choice of soup, a salad or pâté; chicken stewed Provençal style with tomatoes and olives or veal or fish; then cheese and fruit or cake. Wine and choices from the à la carte menu will bring the price up a little, but it will still be just for the location and quality.

Modest—to 15 Francs

La Fontaine de Mars, 129 Rue St. Dominique (7th). Closed Sundays and August.

At the side of the immense fountain of little water and the high Italianate arches which lead nowhere, a bistro with a few red-checked tablecloths outside. The menu stays in the range of inexpensive preparations of duck, *entrecôte,* chicken and veal. The astonishing square, the distinctly neighborhood clientele and the prices are the attractions.

The **Récamier** on the short street of that name, a tangent from the Rue de Sèvres (7th), rejects decor, classy accouterments and ambition. It does a few things well and is quite contented to keep serving them to the faithful locals. The star of the menu is veal in cream and mushrooms, listed as the especial specialty of the house, a dish that would bring no shame to a more showy house.

Aux Crus de Bourgogne, 3 Rue Bachaumont (2nd). Phone GUT 48–24. Closed Sundays and in August.

Among the ungainly plants and other appurtenances of a 1910 boarding-house salon, Madame appears, a square lady in a gray apron and a severe eye on the waitress. Having impressed her presence she goes back to the stove to watch the slow sauces that go on the hare or the young deer. Next to your table a factory party will be dining and wining it up, the cheeks growing rosier and the stories louder and funnier over the consumption of mounds of *ragoûts* and *poulet* while expressionless Madame makes her regular, stolid entrances like a figure on an old German clock. The company, being tickled by one of the indestructible plants, Madame's capable though naturally limited repertoire—as guardian and cook—won't necessarily lure you back night after night, but it is considerably better and more amusing than its equivalent—if there is one—at home and the total cost is negligible.

Unmoved in any way by the showiness of its new neighbors who thicken the air of the Rue du Dragon (6th) with the smoke from their grills, the **Restaurant du Dragon** plods on in its modest un-affected way, offering the simple pleasures of a few well-prepared classics served by nice, slightly frazzled ladies who manage to be attentive, though harried, even in rush hours.

Beaux Arts, corner of Rue des Beaux Arts and Rue Bonaparte (6th). Closed August.

Madame sits at the *caisse* near the entrance. Monsieur is behind the bar or checking the kitchen or shaking hands with an habitué, growing pinker and happier as the evening goes on. The murals on the wall have faded into dark brown clouds (just as well, judg-ing from the areas one can decipher) and there is, almost always, a line of students from the nearby Ecole des Beaux Arts, young expatriates carefully harboring their year's allowance and a few unattached gentlemen of the neighborhood protected from the youthful mob by periodicals. Go early or late, not too late because the best dishes give out, and have the *terrine* of chicken livers and the *duck à l'orange,* the *grenadine* of veal (large chunks of meat in a wine sauce with finely cut vegetables). It won't meet your dreams of Olympic wines and cuisine, but for a decent meal in a neighborhood bistro, with the slapdash amiability that phrase can betoken, all of it at considerably less than you'd pay at home or in other parts of Paris, you might want to take your chances on the length of the line.

Dansk Pop, 184 Rue de Rivoli (1st).

Calmly cheerful in the Scandinavian manner, a cafeteria that prepares wholesome *plats* for less than a dollar, somewhat more in the service section upstairs. Above and below, the cakes and coffee are outstanding.

When the sun is out and the trees in leaf, have a sandwich and coffee in the café at the side of the Jeu de Paume, sheltered by hedges, and if light and leaf patterns cooperate, an extension of the Impressionism inside.

An extraordinary entity in the "noble" 7th of palaces and embassies behind indomitable doors is a restaurant like a large, poor country kitchen at the end of the Rue St. Simon, near Boulevard St. Germain which serves basic lunches to local workmen and one of the regulars, a ragged newspaper vendor who settles her bill in piles of small coins carefully counted out of the pocket of her tattered apron.

La Petite Chaise, Rue de Grenelle and Rue de la Chaise (7th). Open every day.

The strongest points here are its 10-franc fixed-price meal (but, as these things go, possibly 12 when you get there) and its scorn for the universal August closing and the no-work on Sunday or Monday. This makes it a find in the neighborhood which begins to lock its doors in July and goes into a deep silence until well into September. At lunch time it becomes as crowded as a popular *boîte* on Saturday night, mainly with people who run the local galleries and antique shops; a rainy evening brings out an equally dense crowd of locals, so go early.

The days of the cheap little miracle restaurants are about over and it would be misleading to suggest that this is one of them, but the immediate neighborhood boasts few full meals and wine for about $2. The service, as it has to be, is fast, efficient and indifferent so don't order steak if you must have it precisely cooked; turning it back is a nuisance which provokes no improvement. Stay with the chicken, the veal and the stews if they are on the menu.

Le Chien Qui Fume, 32 Rue du Pont Neuf (Les Halles, 1st).

A singularly ugly little café, small and gasping with lumpish decorations. The walls are painted with broken, crooked circles to suggest stone walls and hung with lots and lots of pictures of smoking dogs, as if the idea had to be pressed again and again, like the lessons of early church murals. The house wine is what is called in New York Guinea red, both sour and watery, but the onion soup is quite good, served in vat-sized *marmites*. However, it is the Saturday night clientele and the waiter who are worth an hour of your time and the small price. Above, there is a dance hall to which the local youth (surprisingly skinny and sallow for a supposedly well-fed race) bring their girls or hope to find others. If he doesn't like the way they look or walk or talk, the tough, scarred waiter in a heavy black apron bars their way upstairs. "It's full up." "But I want to go to the toilet." "That's full up, too," and they leave, frightened by his black, threatening bulk. If you say the wine isn't very good, he tells you you don't know anything about wine. If you ask for oysters, he bellows that they are out of season and any fool knows that. Bellow back, in any language and he will soon be winking and smiling, a not uncommon Parisian response.

Bosphore, 4 Rue Ramponeau (20th). Closed August.

Only if you go to Belleville on Saturday night (see page 139), only if you avoid the dishes cooked in the Orthodox manner (slowly all Friday evening, night, and through Saturday until whatever went into the pot originally emerges as oily rags); only if you enjoy small, crowded places where food is handed back and forth from table to table, where an old beggar woman reeking of garlic is permitted to sell her few packages of chewing gum, where customers bring their well-fed and active dogs and children, where a Babel of languages is spoken at high pitch, where the waiters will bring you dish after dish to try (you don't pay if you don't like it), all of them fairly unpalatable for European-American tastes, where customers seem to sit in each other's laps and enjoy it, where old ladies who speak combinations of French, Italian and Arabic are yet Yiddishe mommas pointing out where you can sit, telling you what to eat, and toasting you in kosher wine —is this for you.

In spite of the noise and crowd, the place is fresh, clean and brightly lit and you can eat a fairly honorable dinner of *brik à l'oeuf*, or grilled fish and salad or *couscous*.

Other forms of inexpensive exotica can be eaten at a Franco-Jugoslav restaurant on the narrow Rue Prévôt off Rue St. Paul, and Franco-Polonaise on Rue François Miron, both in the Marais (4th).

Julien et Petit, 40 Rue de l'Université (7th).

Small and plain enough to appear dour on a windy, rainy night. Not to mind, as the English say; the Basquaise and Provençal specialties are reliable and inexpensive. Have the *confit d'oie* if it's on hand, as it usually is.

Guen Maï, corner of Rue de l'Abbaye and Rue Cardinale (6th).

Variously referred to as "Japanese," "vegetarian," "health," "macrobiotic." Whatever it is, the major effort is in whole grains and vegetables—mixtures of which are fried in large, crisp patties—and meeting the exigencies of slim purses.

On the Place des Abbesses (18th), a Métro-ed mesa on the hill of Montmartre, there are two unassuming restaurants, **Restaurant des Abbesses** and the **Restaurant des Carillons.** The former has outdoor tables, irresistible to young Americans. The Carillon keeps its bistro flavors indoors, dispensed by a hospitable young couple to an appreciative and hearty local clientele.

Parraudin, 157 Rue St. Jacques (5th).

The thrifty café curtains, bladelike palm plants and a gift for extracting the best possibilities of inexpensive cuts and such lowly objects as beans, for instance. Like dozens of others, happily, in many neighborhoods and like them, untouristed.

Jouanne, 9 Rue Dauphine (6th), immediately off the river, exists for the lover of tripe, done here in a number of different ways. To play it safe, a few dishes of other animal flesh, but tripe is the forte.

Foyer des Artistes et Intellectuels, Boulevard Montparnasse at Rue Montparnasse (6th).

A sign says that you must identify yourself as one of the chosen. The barriers are not usually carefully maintained but if they are and you don't qualify, you will have missed an insignificant cheap meal among some of the local elderly whose halcyon days were spent in the nearby Rotonde along with Trotsky and Rivera or in the company of Matisse when he visited the Coupole. (Go soon, if at all. There are rumors at this writing that it will soon be retired.)

Student restaurants feed their regular clientele for as little as 1 franc, 50 centimes. The same meal, in less hectic crowding will cost you about 3 francs, 50. Treat it as a sociological rather than gastronomic experience.

Worth keeping in mind: The Faubourg St. Honoré area supports a few surprisingly unpretentious places: **Tante Louise,** 41 Rue Boissy d'Anglas; **A la Poêle d'Or,** 37 Rue de Mirosmenil; **Le Mascal,** 6 Rue Jean Mermoz; **Chez José,** 181 Faubourg St. Honoré, used by local workers. Off the Rue Royale, the **Cité Berryer** holds **Chez Vania,** basic Russian dishes for about 10 francs the meal; **Moulin de Village** which serves French standard dishes and, at the meeting with Rue Boissy d'Anglas, cheaper and simpler meals at modest prices.

Recommended by glossy friends: (Keep in mind August and Sunday closings; phone.)

Moderate

Chez Galan, 36 Boulevard Henry IV (4th).

Le Roy Gourmet, 4 Place des Victoires (1st-2nd).

Troquier, at Rue Chevert and Avenue La Motte-Picquet (7th).

Le Paysan, 27 Rue de Tournon (6th).

Chez Marius, 30 Rue des Fossés St. Bernard (5th).

Chez Proust, 68 Rue des Martyrs (9th).

Les Arêtes, 165 Boulevard Montparnasse (fish) (6th).

Aux Lyonnais, 32 Rue St. Marc (2nd).

Chez Pauline, 5 Rue Villedo (1st).

Chez Nous, 40 Place du Marché St. Honoré (1st).

Le Relais de la Butte, 12 Rue Ravignan (18th).

Charlot I, 128 bis, Boulevard de Clichy (fish) (18th).

Pierre, 10 Rue de Richelieu (1st).

La Quetsch, 6 Rue des Capucines (2nd).

Brasserie Flo, 7 Cour des Petites Ecuries (10th).

Le Petit Colombier, 42 Rue des Acacias (17th).

Rech, 62 Avenue des Ternes (17th).

Le Beaujolais, 19 Quai de la Tournelle (5th).

Le Chalut, 94 Boulevard des Batignolles (17th), seafood.

Pierre, 10 Rue Richelieu (1st).

Le Boccador, 7 Rue du Boccador (8th).

Pharamond, 24 Rue de la Grande-Truanderie (1st).

Clos de Moulin, 34 bis Rue des Plantes (14th).

Au Petit Riche, 25 Rue Le Peletier (9th).

Au Petit Coq, 16 Rue de Budapest (9th).

Toki-Ona, 14 Rue Dauphine (6th), Basque.

Gratin Dauphinois, 7 Rue Chabanais (2nd).

High-Moderate

La Colombe, 4 Rue de la Colombe (4th). Candlelight and an enchanting location (page 92).

Joseph, 56 Rue Pierre Charron (8th).

La Flamberge, 12 Avenue Rapp (7th).

Raffatin and Honoré, 16 Boulevard St. Germain (5th) and a branch, **D'Chez Eux,** 2 Avenue de Lowendal (7th), gargantuan spreads of hors d'oeuvre.

Berlioz, 135 Avenue Malakoff (16th).

Lescure, 7 Rue de Mondovi (1st).

Chez Michel, 10 Rue de Belzunce (10th).

17 Entertainment

"Dancing in the streets," the garlanded phrase that evokes pictures of abandon and graceful joy, isn't quite that on the eve and night of Bastille Day, July 14th. Maybe the fact that the fall of the Bastille did not bring a just, new world dims the gaiety, or the cost of living, or the threat of another world conflagration. In any case, the *charme* and *joie* are not omnipresent. (The Francophile says "The French have a great joie de vivre in a restrained way, a joining of contradictions; they enjoy paradoxes," not the most convincing of statements but one chooses to accept it.)

The papers, French and American, list major places for dancing and fireworks displays. Assuming that Paris holds back a torrential summer shower one goes to any of the bridges just west of Notre Dame to watch and exclaim over the fireworks that soar, explode, and linger as golden threads over the river. The rest can be done like a pub crawl via Métro, if it's still running, among fete places (Place de la Bastille, Place de la Concorde, Hôtel de Ville, Place des Fêtes, Place du Commerce) or, easier, exploring local block parties.

Part of the fun is getting from place to near place, crawling through the erratic slits left by immobile cars which this night temper their braying horns to a pleasing polyphony of beeps and tootles, sometimes arranging timbres and frequencies in an impromptu band concert.

On the Left Bank the cafés are mobbed and surrounded by the Dutch, German, Scandinavian, English and American youth (the native species are often in the country with their families) who have had too much wine and look bewildered or, wallowing in the exoticism and historicity of the occasion will attempt to overturn a car or two or encourage a drunk to climb the scaffolding of a building in repair. (Which accounts for an extraordinary number of policemen in favored foreign youth enclaves like Place St. André des Arts and the contiguous Place St. Michel.)

Someone will suggest the dancing at the tip of the Ile St. Louis. It has, however, been suggested to several thousand people. As near as you can get to the dancing is the Pont St. Louis with a distant view of something that looks like maypoles under lights and the dark molecular movement of a crowd vaguely related to shreds of music floating on a sudden breeze. Back across the bridge, the Boulevard St. Germain has set up its small orchestras on un-reachable corners. The thing to do, then, is to go into side streets and look for more seclusive celebrations. The Rue Jacques Callot (page 90) lends itself by shape and mood to a good, not overly crowded (though *no* crowding would be wrong and depressing) dancing party where, it is possible, a gentleman not old enough for the "old" days, yet old enough for nostalgia of imagined days, may offer you a drink of wine from his bottle. Don't guzzle; he'll drag it away and leave you with a wet, red chin.

The Beaux Arts and its memories of wild student balls may be tempting, but the meeting of Rue Bonaparte and the river is too clogged for any fun but that generated by a good-natured subway crowd. Try the meeting of Rue Madame with the Rue du Vieux Colombier where there is often a group of African and French islands musicians making Afro-Antilles music with an insistent rhythm under slinky melodies. The young intellectual crowd waves its hips (French girls are not too good at this, but the African and islands boys compensate for the ineptness), keeps its shoulders stiff and its face disdainful in the classic Afro-Latino stance which in-sists that the top half never acknowledge what the bottom half is doing. As at all these dances, there is an unusually large fringe of eager, searching young men hoping to find or be found, trying to hide their unease under expressionless masks.

The most plain simple fun is usually to be found in the yards of fire stations, that on Vieux Colombier, for instance. The *pompiers* cover the floor of the yard with a low wooden platform and a bandstand, string up some colored lights, slap a bit of thatch over the impromptu bars and you have a dance hall. The crowd doesn't bother to look as if it were thinking of higher matters. The music can come from a three-piece orchestra or recordings that grind out scratchy *bal musette* music alternating with 1920's one-steps and polkas. These are athletic dancers, whirling in twos—

pairs of concierge ladies in paper hats, short, fat and cherry-faced—
like figures in peasant carvings. Sometimes the crowd is in the
mood for snake lines and all join in the bouncy running. Or a
group decides to do a stomp dance; it catches on and the platform
shakes and creaks under the hearty sound of several hundred feet.
No style, no attitudes, no words, no wit; a sweaty robustness is all.

The morning of the 14th, water slapped on the sleepy face and
a march to the nearest Métro *en famille* to see the parade down
the Champs Elysées, led off at the unseemly hour of 9 A.M. by
General de Gaulle. In the usual anarchy of French arrangements,
or a logic that defies American reason, some streets are closed,
some open. Some Métro stations are open, some closed. But there
has been little warning, so the lucky free can enjoy the view of the
crowded unlucky locked behind the gates of a Métro station,
clamoring to get out, like a cageful of monkeys or madmen.

The crowd is not large; many of its neighbors are home, still
asleep, or watching the parade on television with their brioche and
coffee; some of it stays away because it just doesn't care. Equipped
with ingenious periscopes made of cardboard and pocket mirrors,
children on shoulders, Paris—or a part of it—watches the handsome antique uniforms—red trousers, oddly shaped hats, plumes,
elegantly cut jackets of the leading military schools, St. Cyr and
the Polytechnique, forming colorful orderly units along the line
of march. Soon, the tall, solitary, soldierly figure in khaki of de
Gaulle appears, standing in a slow-moving open car. Flights of
planes appear, a few pointed, black and murderous; a few strange
round fat ones suspended in a square frame, rather like a simple
piece of modern sculpture. On the ground, tanks of several kinds,
big, closed and mysterious; others big, open, bristling with rockets.
The might and menace quickly displayed, the rest becomes a
mobile band concert and a fashion show of chic soldiers in the
various branches of the service: red berets, tan berets, blue berets
tastefully matched to some other part of the uniform; a flash of
gold off epaulets, the paler glow of silver off insignia. The most
dashing costume is that of the ski troops, all in white, white boots,
white berets, carrying small white skis and white gear bags, which,
unfortunately, look like laundry bags. (Someone should look into
this; it mars the *très haute couture* in soldiery and possibly keeps
it from being copied as one of the most chic of winter sports
costumes.)

Soon come the bright plumes, gleaming helmets, the black and white and red and magnificent matched horses of the Garde Républicaine, the showpiece of police who adorn the Opéra on gala nights and brighten the paths of visiting dignitaries.

And, surprisingly soon, it ends. The café tables and chairs come out; the crowd mills, gathers and disperses in wayward patterns; streets and passageways are closed and opened in their strange rhythms; people accustomed to the Métro crushes of the workday form in the same tight crushes on this holiday, and it's all over until the later attempt to get to the free July 14th performances of the Comédie Française or the Opéra Comique and more cluttered prowling and dancing, if the next day's specter of work permits.

On one of the last evenings of June the Faubourg St. Honoré puts on its choicest blandishments and pats its own silken back. The street is closed to traffic except to dowager cars and private buses that carry the royal progress of celebrities. The high skill of the window designers, spurred on by a competition, emblazens the windows with fantasy, wit, delicacy or the impact of Pop colors. The crowd dresses in its best, and small islands of it in its defiantly worst. Antique beauties totter out under the same, extravagant hat they wore in the same fashion parade thirty years ago. Against the lights of a complimenting window-display, this year's model is photographed in the apogee of this year's stylishness. Mounted gentlemen riders in red jackets and caps play hunting calls into the open doors of Hermès. On the Place Beauvau, the Garde Républicaine tootles and drums fanfares with elegant, mannered precision. A gallery in a court chooses this night for a *vernissage* of compositions devised of bits of mirror accompanied by brittle bits of music. Around the corner the music of a street band is hot, rock 'n' roll with Latin curves between its insistent beats. The dancing, where the crowd leaves room for dancing, is energetic but lacks grace and heat, singularly not abandoned for youth that necks so openly. Later, much later, when the lights are out and the last stragglers ebbing off the streets, the hunting horns, the military horns and the jazz horns stilled, come the gentler sounds of a harpsichord played by a lady in a wig and 18th century silks, surrounded by the tapestries and rugs of a fitting era, a nice gesture of rounding back in time and with that, bringing the curtain down.

What with the Marais being illuminated frequent evenings and staging a well-advertised festival, other neighborhoods are bestirring themselves. St. Germain starts early in May with as many as 100 art openings on the first evening. In late June, the Ile St. Louis shows off with a parade, folk-songs, old music, jazz, drama and films. The St. Séverin celebration, in June, shows off its old and new crafts in the *quartier* shop windows and other arrondissements are following suit. (Watch announcements and posters.)

BATEAU-MOUCHE

A night ride on the Seine with dinner, wines and old tunes, under the lights of the bridges and the mellowed ivory of the Louvre and Notre Dame framed in the dark filigree of night trees was an enchantment, a dream of "Paris." Now, to compensate for the diminished quantity and quality of the dinner and the frantic service (too fast and too slow at the wrong times) the trip which needed no embellishments has been tarted-up with "theater," as if the Square du Vert Galant at the tip of the Ile de la Cité required a clumsy duel among the Three Musketeers to point up its antiquity; or the wedge of green at the Pont de Sully on the Ile St. Louis would be empty of charm if it weren't for three ballet dancers pirouetting along the embankment. Beatniks and bottles are posed in stances of "Yo ho ho and a bottle of rum" under the Pont Neuf; farther along the quais a couple enact a pantomime out of a popular cartoon strip; around a historic bend, a ghost, who achieves his ethereal fluttering by teetering on a low tightrope. Lovers pose under romantic isolated lamp posts. (If they were the real thing— they might be—one wouldn't believe it on this route of clichés.) The most amusing part of the production is to watch the fast motorboat that rushes performers, and changes of costume from scene to scene. But don't let the foolishness—whether you find it entertaining or infuriating as still another symptom of contempt for the tourist and his tastes—distract you from the view of the back of Notre Dame; the illumination on the buttresses turns them into waxen petals of an immense flower.

With or without theatricals, the ride at night gives little, however, of the living city. For that, the day trip with a pair of sunglasses if the day is fair because the shine on the plastic boats and the dazzling reflections of the light in the water can be blinding.

As the boat passes the Ile St. Louis, it leaves the glamour behind, entering a modern composition of barges, sandpiles, cranes and construction. It soon turns back, passing the fishermen planted here by Pepin the Bald for local "Seine" color. One or two nonstationary anglers tread across the legs of sunbathers, the courageous in bikinis, the distrustful in heavy sweaters and long pants, yielding only their faces and hands to the sun. The athletic flex their tanned, oiled muscles in the swimming pools tacked on to the quais near the Louvre. The swimming skill is mediocre, the splashing overenthusiastic and the nudity, hardly disturbed by the triangles and dots of bikinis, often beautiful. The stones of the quais are littered with threadbare blankets on which couples sun themselves, eat a little, neck a little, take a spot of wine and neck a little more.

Sex as fecundity appears in the overblown statuary on the sides of the bridges, then gives place to hands-across-the-sea virtue on the Pont de Grenelle where a reduced version of the Statue of Liberty stands as a reminder of the happy days of *amitié*. Liberty leads to more sand, more coal, more small industrial plants and, around Malmaison, back to green reminders of the Seine as the Impressionists painted and *vieille vague* film-makers recreated it: stalwart young men, juicy young women, jaunty hats and graceful dresses dappled with shadows of leaves and reflections off the water.

Dufy takes over just beyond the island of the Renault plant with splashes of green, red, yellow, blue and orange awnings like pennants, near where the Seine becomes a water resort equipped with colorful houseboats, water-ski platforms and dipping, scudding sailboats.

The homeward journey starts at the turn around the auto island, waved on by the Renault workers calling and gesturing out of the factory windows. Then, with variations, what has been before except that this time you will pass closer to the Eiffel Tower and if the shy Paris sun hasn't disappeared, there will be sunbathers lying at its iron feet exemplifying yet another Paris fact: while Parisians like their monuments, they aren't awed by them—or by anything for that matter.

You might, of course, spend your day at the race tracks going by taxi, or on one of the buses which gathers enthusiasts on the Place Clichy, or get your racing kicks more lazily and cheaply by betting on the *tiercé*—the daily triple. You buy a book of tickets for 20 centimes in a local booth, trailing its long line on Sunday mornings. Punch your choices (there is a special punch at 1 franc sold for the purpose) and submit them to any café that bears the PMU sign (*pari mutuel urbain*). Keep the stubs (there is an especially designed holder available if you're a neat type) and wait or hang around and watch the PMU ticker spill the results. It's cheap, like the lottery, and brings you into café camaraderie you might not otherwise achieve.

The cheapest and most inclusive listing of Paris forms of entertainment from strip to *visites-conférences* (some in English, most in French and a good method of seeing places you might otherwise not be permitted to see, or have details pointed out that you might ordinarily miss) is *La Semaine de Paris*, dated from Wednesday through Tuesday. *Arts Loisirs* concentrates more fully on art exhibitions.

The Opéra? Renoir loathed the building, Henry James in his capacity as young reporter on Paris matters was more tactful; he used a few noncommittal phrases, summing up with a statement that the building was a representative of its times. Created in a style—or lack of style—dubbed "Napoleon III" it is an accretion of layers of ornament, sculpture, sentimentality and allegory in marble and gilt; gathered, layered and heaped to look rich and successful, borrowing from the Italian Renaissance, from Versailles, from any place that meant splendor to excess. The Chagall ceiling? No comment. The quality of performance has been mentioned elsewhere (page 24) but you may, nevertheless, want to act out the elegant legend of attending the Opéra. If the performance you choose happens to center on a star singer have your concierge get tickets from an agency; there will probably be none at the box office.

The Opéra Comique is cheaper, easier and more amusing, especially since you've paid less. The strength is, as is usual in Paris, the appeal to the eye. *The Tales of Hoffmann*, for instance, frequently fills non-aria intervals with parades of ingenious automatons and the raising and lowering of choruses in frail boxes. The singing is done in small-town Italian opera style: the singer at bat steps to front center and belts it out, (twice if you are sitting in certain sections which give back a sturdy echo), then having acknowledged his applause, relinquishes the center stage to the next singer.

For music simply as music watch the programs of the Salle Gaveau, the Salle Pleyel, and various halls and theaters where concerts are performed. The Marais Festival offers chamber operas, concerts, plays and popular entertainment, not always of paramount quality and always forgivable in the enchanting surroundings (page 110) even when the cold rains come stabbing down. Watch, also, for the concerts in, or in the courts of, various famous churches.

If your French is up to it, and the theater functioning, part of the required course is a performance of one of the classics at the Comédie Française. Language makes no difference in the displays of international entertainments at the Théatre National Populaire in the Palais de Chaillot or the groups of Czech, Polish, or American actors whom Jean-Louis Barrault imports for his theater on the Place de l'Odéon. And for years there has been at least one nonstop Ionesco festival; for a while, two, listed in *La Semaine de Paris*. You might prefer the French version of a play you saw last year in London or New York; a few are commonly available. The famous *chansonniers* are less than they were in quality and number, and unless your French is fast and colloquial, it may turn out to be a wasted evening.

Why one should want to go to the movies when the evening can be spent eating and strolling is a mysterious personal matter. If you must, try to remember that going to the cinema is the current major passion and that lines form early for each performance. The 5th arrondissement is crazy about exhaustive displays of one favorite actor or director. (You will notice that it is the director who gets top billing in French films.) The Rue Champollion, off the Rue des Ecoles, is almost exclusively a tight row of movie boxes where one can see, day after day, the works of Gérard Philippe, a run of Jean Renoir or John Ford. A house a few streets away is reviewing the frightening achievements of Luis Buñuel and around the corner, the ceaseless Humphrey Bogart worship. The best way to stay permanently immersed in old movies is to attend the *cinémathèques*, one at the Palais de Chaillot and the other on the Rue d'Ulm. On a recent day one could see *Foolish Wives*, a 1922 production of von Stroheim at 3 P.M., Eisenstein's *Que Viva*

Mexico (1930) at 6:30 and *Ivan the Terrible* (both parts) at 9:00. The latter two are extraordinarily long films; usually, there are four titles per day, each paid for nominally and separately.

The discothèques are ephemeral things, a crowded Olympus one season, a gasping void the next. As in London and New York, they are sometimes marked *privée*, a condition that can often be easily circumvented by a bit of money. There are discothèques where dancing is forbidden so, in effect, you are paying for the pleasures of seeing the Paris young hanging around while records drone on. The Paris young are in full, visible supply on all the boulevards, especially on the Left Bank, and the records can be bought and kept for the price of the entrance fee, or heard in appalling facsimile anywhere else in the world. If you still insist, ask a young employee of the hotel what and where the current favorite might be or take your chances with one of the places listed in *La Semaine de Paris*. One that has lasted for a while is **Les Zozos** at number 80 on the Quai de l'Hôtel de Ville. A newer breed is sprouting in the Marais on the Rue François Miron, the Rue de Jouy, Ste. Croix de la Bretonnerie and undoubtedly, on other streets. Also, the potentials of the Ile St. Louis one of whose cafés on the Rue des Deux Ponts calls itself a "Blues-Jazz Museum" and those of the Rue Galande, Monsieur le Prince, Mazarine, Dauphine, Grégoire de Tours, to select a few possibilities on the Left Bank.

Less limited in scope:

Galerie 55 on the Rue de Seine. Reserve if it is still popular.

L'Abbaye, 6 bis, Rue de l'Abbaye. Folk songs, mainly Anglo and French.

Djuri, 6 Rue des Canettes. Vigorous guitar and strong voice in a polyglot repertoire.

"Dancings" in public halls, usually on weekends:

Montmartre, adjoining the windmill at the meeting of Rue Lepic and Avenue Junot.

Mimi Pinson, 79 Champs Elysées.

Salle Wagram, strongly Latino in flavor; frequent dances but not constant.

The dance halls on the Rue de Lappe off the Place de la Bastille were at one time forbiddingly tough. Hardly minuet style now but no longer menacing. Not for women alone and one male escort will do, an improvement over the time when it took two large men to each woman.

Spanish? The **Catalan,** 16 Rue des Grands Augustins, inclined to overdo the heel work on the reverberating platform, but it may have changed. More relaxed flamenco, limited to voice and guitar usually, exists (if they still do) at the **Don Quixote** on the Place Montholon and at the **Barcelona,** 9 Rue Geoffrey Marie. A few Russian restaurants throb the old balalaika tunes and antique cellars on the tourist route echo with bawdy songs of a more robust time.

See, if you like, what is going on in the early hours of the morning in the jazz cafés on the Place de la Contrescarpe in the 5th or on the Rue de la Huchette and its neighbors or the large jukeboxed cafés near the Barbès-Rochechouart station to the north and the small cafés along the Boulevard Barbès. The latter belong to the North Africans who live in the angry *quartier*. You should have a good knowledge of French, leave your women back at the hotel and know what you are about. Otherwise stay in the well-lit gaud of the Place Blanche and the Place Pigalle a short distance to the west.

Cupcakes Variés

The Paris entertainment is, as every one knows, sex—in generous supply, dragging tons of breasts, real and fake, in a diversity limited only by the limitations of the human body. As you make your selection remember that the best seats in large places come with the dinner and a half-bottle of champagne at the equivalent of $11 or $12 and that whisky comes very high.

All over the world, the male homosexual has, like a slow-growing plant, burst into conspicuous bloom in recent years, while the female homosexual has, more or less, remained anaerobic, sequestered in her own harems. Except in Paris which maintains, at least in the world of inverts, a true if scrambled equality of the sexes. For the price of a half-bottle of champagne (about $8), **Elle et Lui,** 31 Rue Vavin, returns entertainment and/or stimulation for couples who like it their way although devotees of the plainer varieties of sex are welcomed, too. At the bar, *la patronne* stands sleek and strong, hair perfectly cropped, makeup subtle and delicate, dressed in an impeccable dinner jacket, watching, watching, only the sharp eye moving in the indomitable face. The champagne is brought to the hand-size table by close-cropped, dinner-jacketed boy-girls, aloof and good-looking. (The job doesn't necessarily designate them as Lesbians—it's a job—but insiders are more likely to get it.)

A typical show, starting at about 11 P.M. and then again at about 1 A.M., may begin with a beautiful girl in black pants and chains, twisting, turning, struggling out of pants and chain down to a jeweled triangle. An "Oriental" dancer then shakes her soft breasts behind sequined veils and soon gives way to a stocky, jovial "boy" in a neat suit who sings several songs in a hearty tenor voice, fingers snapping, feet tapping, as sunny and wholesome as wheat and apples. A dreamy waltz soon launches a tall blonde making high-school drama-club gestures of high-life and ennui. Her face, streaked with white lipstick, as white as her pyramid of stiff curls, is as uncommunicative as an eggshell. The prop phone next to the prop chaise longue rings; her lover is coming. The white lipstick stretches to a smile. Languidly she strips out of her coat and dress and is ready. The phone rings again. A pout; the lover isn't coming. She gets back on the chaise and begins to stroke herself, suggesting, in time, a ladylike climax. The phone rings again. She says—you've guessed it—"*Trop tard.*"

The operatic tradition of assigning both the roles of Orpheus and Eurydice to women's voices is treated literally here; they are women and lovers. Eurydice, with long blond hair and a dead-white face wears a gauzy Isadora Duncan-ish costume. Orpheus, considerably taller, hair bobbed short, is in a sort of classic battle tunic which permits her breasts to peep through the leather strips. Stroking, caressing, Orpheus undresses Eurydice, but the mounting passion doesn't convincingly mount—the acting is not of the highest quality—and you know some culmination point has been reached when Orpheus kneels in front of the nude Eurydice and the spotlight disappears. The last and interminable act is that of Miss Insatiable of 1966, more or less naked under her red cloak and long, disheveled hair. Mouth working, begging, sucking, skinny legs and arms beckoning, starved-looking and *vicieuse*, she congratulates the women in the audience on their men, pleads with other men—in words and contortions—to come to her, examines one clearly homosexual man (possibly hired for the act), discards him with a quip and continues on frenetically, repetitiously, until it is her time to get off the stage.

General dancing follows. The couples on the floor are quite attractive, the "men" in beautifully cut suits, silk shirts with museum-piece cuff links and antique rings on well-kept hands; the women in simple dresses achieved at a price. Most of the couples dance well and decorously, only the smile, the eye-to-eye look betraying intensity. A few couples, usually younger, choose to be more defiantly, more conspicuously what they are: a tall, graceful creature—a Diana, an androgynous Apollo?—kissing, as they dance, the shoulders of an older, tormented kohl-eyed girl.

It makes an instructive evening for the price of your half-bottle: sadism, auto-eroticism, nymphomania, female homosexuality burlesqued, female homosexuality elegant and female homosexuality in the spitting-in-your-heterosexual-eye style.

Carrousel, 29 Rue Vavin.

Next door to Elle et Lui and possibly an even more crowded *boîte* (literally a box and in this context, small, crammed and airless) whose entertainment is more catholic—male, female, a bit of both in one pot, strippers, singers and an audience of a like mélange. The price of entertainment is covered by the usual minimal half-bottle at the usual price, but in striving to meet all tastes for a "big" show, Carrousel becomes careless in its program planning and its choice of entertainers. Worth trying, though, if Elle et Lui wasn't quite enough or too crowded.

For Men Who Like Girls

Crazy Horse Saloon, 12 Avenue George V.

Don't use the bathroom first, it is discouraging. In Italian, German, French and English, the signs one finds in "joke" stores along with rubber turds: "Don't use the toilet while the train is in the station" and "Never say I'll do it to-morrow; do it now" and so on. Don't leave, the show is infinitely more worldly and clever than the toilets. In the fleshly crowding (particularly on weekends) that Paris seems to want, perhaps needs—knees companionably pressed into foreign haunches, bottles on the floor because tables waste customer space—comes *le strip* surrounded by pantomimists, yokel humor and music; in short, what is left of vaudeville. The star of the show is the unseen wit who devises the lights and slides that screen, pattern, shade or spot the girls, sometimes to enhance an erotic effect, sometimes to make a comment. One recent show opened with a delectable girl lying against a changing set of color photos of New York City; playing on her nudity, reflections of American dollar bills in increasing denominations. Another girl, sitting on a slowly revolving stool, strokes down her long black gloves and gently, with dedication, rolls down her long black stockings (apparently still the most titillating props of stripping, used repeatedly and everywhere) while the lights and patterns that play on her gather, as a finale of flash, on the big, glittering diamond of her G-string. A girl in a helmet, boots, broad belt and a whip strides back and forth looking vigorous and cruel against a background of German symbols. A slow, narcissistic bather becomes more suggestive and prettier viewed in silhouette.

The specifics of the show change, but the matter remains basically the same. The girls are lovely, the staging inventive, the price not too high for the show (unless you insist on drinking frequent shots of imported whisky) and the audience usually an interesting mixture of international tourists and the nouveau riche of the French provinces, and here and there, a middle-aged French couple: worn, beautifully dressed, he somberly watching the show, she watching his face with equal concentration. What this means —is this a way of keeping him from wandering, or simply offering him distraction or hoping to stimulate an appetite that thirty years of marriage has dulled—is anyone's guess, but it is not an uncommon sight to see even younger French couples at strip shows. It may be, simply, the current chic thing to do.

Concert Mayol, 10 Rue de l'Echiquier (10th). Métro Strasbourg St. Denis. Matinées and evenings. Check infrequent closing times.

According to the program (for which you have paid too much, to which you had to add a tip, because the hay-haired dragon who sells them won't let you by until you have fully understood and responded to her hobnailed hint that service is not included, and which you won't be able to bring back to the United States if your customs inspector decides that pictures of naked girls, no matter how unluscious, is pornography), the Mayol and its devoted directors, of a line of martyrs who dedicated themselves to their art "until the last breath," whose demises "threw the whole entertainment world into a state of consternation," are hoping to make of the Mayol a favorite establishment "not only for the spectators of the Capital, but also for all of those for whom Paris is the World Center of refinement and good taste." This undoubtedly means you. See for yourself.

The hall, once a music hall which showed off Yvette Guilbert, Raimu, Lucienne Boyer and Fernandel, still has considerable charm, of a kind the English call "a bit tatty." It is a long narrow house, quite small, with mirror-backed loges at the side; the center ceiling ornaments are innocent white tulips on a blue-green ground. A bit below the ornaments are portraits of the stars, heads and breasts framed in a lyricism of leaves and roses.

The audience, most of it working-class men and some women, pays its $2 to $5 for front seats in the loges where the girls can touch you, if they choose, and places itself, having tipped the usher, on its half-green, half-pinkish-red seats. Recorded *bal musette* music fills the hall as you admire the small pink lights along the top of the loges and decide that the outer stage curtain has the shine, color and consistency of a rayon petticoat you saw hanging in one of the Sunday markets. The orchestra gathers: a drummer, a saxophonist, a horn player, a bass-fiddle player and a lady piano player who seems to be the leader of the orchestra. The petticoat rises and reveals a red velvet curtain which parts on a screen that shows (with sound) pictures of the various directors, the credits for music, costumes, scenery, etc. Then, the musicians strike up and the naked parade begins with a bevy of girls singing in near-unison as they saunter around the stage in short, transparent nightgowns and narrow G-strings. One delightful creature with long skinny legs, scrawny arms, an unkempt mop of yellow something, once hair, and a completely blank face wanders among her peers, quite lost and she stays in this vague underwater mood, possibly her only one, throughout the show. One begins to wait for her with affection and yearns to see what she will do with the exigencies of a solo strip, but the management is too smart for that; she never does. Nor does a plump little girl who might be your son's high-school date, obviously hired in the desperate need to fill a stage cheaply.

The girls work hard. They sing: in chorus, alone, in duets and in trios with a couple of crisp juveniles and one who hasn't been crisp for thirty years. They dance, a few of them using the ballet steps they may still be studying, the rest kicking and stepping in the deathless, basic routines of vaudeville. They act as straight men for the not very funny clowns, and they dress and undress in all sorts of costumes, or half-costumes, or bits of costumes. As fertility goddesses from the various provinces of France, carrying fish or fruit or flowers, they wear regional headdresses and a big bow low on their backs. This costume, with feathers supplanting the bow, does for a big Brazilian number and the few other numbers clearly designed (if one can call it that) to offer more flesh, and a breathing spell to the two or three strippers. The immutable end of an act—bare breasts and a bow or G-string—has sundry beginnings. They come out in raincoats and umbrellas, soon they are nude; they emerge as medieval ladies, soon they are nude; they are Maid Marions, again soon naked; it is spring and they are all be-ruffled and be-rosed one moment, naked the next. Or, they come on with nothing and leave with nothing.

The strippers have the satisfactions and the few francs more that come with solo work, but their hearts, and in a curious way, their bodies, aren't always in it. Undressing out of black velvet and pearls in front of a three-way mirror and, back to the audience, making unmistakable gestures with her legs, hips and hands, one of the girls manages to suggest what she is suggesting. A little girl in a madras shirt, tights and rain boots makes quite a production out of that, with the delighted cooperation of one of the loge gentlemen who helps her pull off one of the boots. One act that requires some skill is a classic and still a favorite: a girl's right arm and leg, in Mandarin costume and surmounted by a Mandarin's head, makes love to the left half of her body in the guise of a Thai princess or dancing girl or some such piece of "Oriental" exotica. This manages to get a round of applause from the small, torpid audience.

There is a star, of course, no better a dancer than the others, but she is exceedingly pretty and has the loveliest body. She knows how to belt out a song in a gravelly hard voice, she wears her ridiculous costumes of gold-mesh tights, flashing jewels on the belly, flapping lamé below the knee as if they were haute couture. She's lovely, tough, confident, a magnetic girl and a professional, fun to watch and listen to the rare times she's on.

During the intermission, not to break the spell, the audience in its sagging "good" coat and its stupefied slightly worried face, spends another dollar to fill the time downstairs at the "Palais Mauresque with its lovely nude dancers." Then it returns for more of the same upstairs, never shouting "take it off," never dashing to the front of the loges, never reaching up to the runways—unless specifically invited to. They must be enthusiasts, otherwise why spend all that money? And if they are, why don't they show or sound it? Or is this the only thing a number of dull, middle-aged men in Paris can think of doing with their afternoons?

The Moulin Rouge, reputedly on the place where the famous old one stood, is immense and thus can afford you broad acres of girls in feathers as tall as trees embellishing niches around the stage. Considerate of all tastes, the management includes a few Apollos dressed only in golden lids and lamé loincloths who try hard to force their immobile faces into some expression of interest in a nude female partner. For the opera lover, there is the last act of Carmen—Bizet jazzed, crippled, bumped and stripped. As a grand finale, a huge tank of water is raised from below the stage; one Apollo and one Circe dive into it and as gracefully as they can, try to make love—sort of—underwater.

The places described above give only a notion of the diversity surrounding the same basic matter. If you haven't had enough and your tastes urge you toward the homosexual hinterlands still, try Le Monocle at 60 Boulevard Edgar-Quinet in Montparnasse, advertised as a cabaret féminin. The other side of the coin will face you at Madame Arthur, 75 bis, Rue des Martyrs in Montmartre; at Le Fiacre, 4 Rue du Cherche-Midi, and La Montagne, 46 Mont St. Geneviève. Taxi drivers know other places, as well as houses where you and your partner can join other couples in conversation, observation and sex in surroundings that range from flower prints on the walls to walls hung with towels and douche bags. The cost is less and so are the possibilities in arrangements of couples in cars searching for other amiables to take home from the Bois de Boulogne. The local word for this you will probably have learned from the girls around Les Halles (see page 99).

Not yet sick of too many cupcakes? Or already too broke? Pick up a copy of a magazine called *Flash* or *Spot, Naturiste, Naturisme* on the Boulevard Montmartre or Poissonnière where a rich vein of "art studies" awaits you on every newsstand.

⇜ *Des Belles Choses et des Curiosités*

One often hears that Paris, like Rome, is a "cat" city. Paris has nothing as beautifully strange as the jungle of fat cats that move through the tall white iris of the Largo Argentina, and pampered cats have been known to be abandoned in the prosperous *quartiers* when the family goes off to the country for the summer, but the cat is a cherished friend, for good, useful reasons, in poorer areas. One warm evening in the summer of 1966 a small cat lost her footing and slipped into a sewer on a corner of the Rue des Blancs Manteaux. Heads came out of the windows; pushcarts on their way home from market stopped. The neighborhood concierges met to discuss possibilities of rescue and to tell stories of mishaps to other cats. It was decided to call the fire department which arrived promptly, asked searching questions, expressed doubts, then reassurance. Ultimately, one of the four young firemen put on his crash helmet, a heavy set of gloves and with a lantern descended an adjacent section of sewer. The crowd stood still, hardly breathing, as if it were witnessing major surgery. The fireman emerged, catless, and explained that the cat had run away at his approach. Several women returned to the opening, purring, meowing, calling the cat, while the firemen explained again that there were many places from which the cat could emerge, no one was to worry. Everyone, including firemen, stood around worrying until they were all too tired, and went off to troubled beds.

A light changes at the corner. An open sports car rolls to a stop, driven by a good-looking girl whose blonde hair is pulled into a sleek, virginal chignon. Her companion is a cherubic tousled girl. Both wear raincoats and dashing scarves. While the light holds its red face toward them, they neck warmly. In the crossing crowd only an American stares.

Surrounded by Les Halles, the Marais, the Louvre, in fact, set among some of the most significant of Paris places, sits the bulging old Samaritaine department store. You might want to do some shopping or mingle with who buys and see what is bought, but the place of primary interest for the visitor lies high above the counters and aisles. From a simple roof café and a circular walk above it, Paris spreads its fan of famous old beauties in felicitous groupings, and not so distant that they lose their distinct qualities.

Below, the Seine and the rhythm of its bridges, some darting efficiently across the river, the slower-paced Pont Neuf held back by the pauses of semicircle that once were shops and the spur of the Square du Vert-Galant under it. Across the river, the dour towers and walls of the Conciergerie (Palais de Justice) backed by the squat unfinished towers of Notre Dame, the heavy group lifted by the flight of the delicate spear of Sainte Chapelle. Farther off, the big dome of the Panthéon, echoed by the Invalides dome and, as the eye moves closer to the river again, the full, large restatement in the dome of the French Institute (Académie Française). To the right, the ubiquitous Eiffel Tower and the Arc de Triomphe at the end of a straight trench which turns out to be the Champs Elysées. As you turn, the tower of St. Germain l'Auxerrois, the parish church of French kings when the Louvre was the royal house and the burial place of many French artists of the 17th to the 19th centuries. Beyond it, the plump glass in iron corsets of the Grand Palais and farther on, the chalky puffs of Sacré Coeur. The eye returns over the gray waves of mansard and spume of chimney pots, past the soot and white streaks of the old church of St. Eustace (so much and traditionally a part of Les Halles that the trucks treat it with intimate contempt, parking in its sleepy portals), over the glass and metal vaults of Les Halles and into a garden of yellow and red banners that shout "Samar," "Samaritaine," and closer still to a tile circle that marks the distance from Moscow, New York, Berlin and St. Petersburg—which gives some notion of the age of the store and its blinkered view of events in the non-French world.

From the Passage de la Petite Boucherie (6th) looking at the tipsy buildings of the Rue Cardinale leaning and swaying as they swoop around a curve, dancing to the dulled hammers of iron workers, the slap and clang of small print shops and the hiss of pressing machines that come from the ateliers below.

To get away from Left Bank mannerisms, go into any side-street café in an obscure neighborhood at about 6:00 P.M. when the local men are having an aperitif between Métro and home. Ask anyone at the bar what the nearest and best Métro stop might be for point X. Your one informant becomes three or four many-armed, strong-voiced authorities. One holds out, with detailed knowledge, which encompasses most of the Métro system, for station A because it leads to Châtelet which has a choice of many *correspondance* lines. An opponent says that to walk through the mazes of Châtelet takes as long as to walk home altogether. (He is right.) Number three insists that a one-ticket bus ride to Station B, on a direct line, is the best way to do it. Number four shouts, "What? Waste a bus ticket?" The argument grows and amplifies, almost as if it were a dispute over a *boules* score, until one of the contenders turns to you and asks where you're from. Then, the cousin in Chicago, the nephew who spent a summer as an exchange student in a *banlieue* of New York; does it really take more than a day of driving to go through the wheat country; are all Texans seven feet tall; how do you say *bonjour* and *merci* in English and you're launched on a convivial hour or two, Métro and home forgotten.

Three friends wander through the dark dawn of Les Halles, at about 11 o'clock. The full-throated ensemble is just beginning to gather: a truck grinding to a halt, men conversing quietly as they arrange a formal garden of watercress in a box, the thud of crate on crate of fruit, the duller thud of sacks of potatoes piling up to a wall. The streets and most of the market are in faint light. The strollers stand in front of a small fortress of peaches, sniffing their scent through the slats of the boxes. As they turn to go, a hand comes out of the dark, proffering three large peaches, then disappears into a crate-lined alley before it can be thanked.

A rainy day—count on them, they exist and commonly—is good, clearly, for museums, for shopping, for seeing a string of classic movies at one of the *cinémathèques*, but better still for walking.

Walk down to the river to watch the ripple of its gray silk become deep folds as a *bateau-mouche* skims by, its open deck holding a few redoubtable tourists in the heroic, Viking posture the deck of a ship (even the plastic bubble of a new *bateau-mouche*) seems to require of its standees. The shapes of bridges and buildings, towers and domes soften and merge as in Whistler paintings. An orange awning someone has forgotten to pull back catches the eye and leads it to gloss over the gray of shutters, the wet green feathers of a willow tree, the dim light over the bar of a café. The old irregular streets on the Left Bank look more than ever like slices of cheese ready to fall and crumble on each other. The metal of a balcony and the sturdy colors of its flowers pin together the shredded grisaille of an old wall, about to slide into the street. Neighborhood cafés hum, sing, bang, and their cats lie coiled on the surface of the pinball machines, warming themselves on the tiny bulbs of triumph.

At dusk the lights of the Alexandre III bridge go on. The rain has tempered its aggressive optimism; the ladies, the lions and the horses are wrapped in the tact of rain. The pearls of light in the graceful clusters drop pearl-shadows into the river where they lengthen and shimmer as silver fish.

A final reminder. Wherever you are in Paris at twilight in the early summer, return to the Seine and watch the evening sky close slowly on a last strand of daylight fading quietly, like a sigh.

Index